INTELLIGENT
LOVE

INTELLIGENT LOVE

THE STORY OF
CLARA PARK,
HER AUTISTIC
DAUGHTER,
AND THE
MYTH OF THE
REFRIGERATOR
MOTHER

MARGA VICEDO

BEACON PRESS
BOSTON

BEACON PRESS
Boston, Massachusetts
www.beacon.org

Beacon Press books
are published under the auspices of
the Unitarian Universalist Association of Congregations.

24 23 22 21   8 7 6 5 4 3 2 1

This book is printed on acid-free paper that meets the uncoated paper
ANSI/NISO specifications for permanence as revised in 1992.

Text design and composition by Kim Arney

Library of Congress Cataloging-in-Publication Data

Names: Vicedo, Marga, author.
Title: Intelligent love : the story of Clara Park, her autistic daughter,
    and the myth of the refrigerator mother / Marga Vicedo.
Description: Boston : Beacon Press, [2020] | Includes bibliographical
    references and index.
Identifiers: LCCN 2020030878 (print) | LCCN 2020030879 (ebook) |
    ISBN 9780807025628 (hardcover ; alk. paper) | ISBN 9780807025635 (ebook)
Subjects: LCSH: Park, Clara Claiborne. | Park, Jessy, 1958- | Mothers of
    autistic children—United States.—Biography. | Autistic children—United
    States—Biography. | Motherhood—United States. | Autism—United States—
    History—20th century.
Classification: LCC RJ506.A9 P32135 2020 (print) | LCC RJ506.A9 (ebook) |
    DDC 618.92/858820092 [B]—dc23
LC record available at https://lccn.loc.gov/2020030878
LC ebook record available at https://lccn.loc.gov/2020030879

To Margarita Castelló Martinez, my mother,
and to Mark Solovey,
for helping me navigate the world.

And to the youngest in our family:
Marta, Aitana, Judit, Aitor, Valeria, and Naia.
I hope they will thrive in their own unique
ways and help construct a better world
that values diverse ways of being.

CONTENTS

INTELLIGENT
LOVE

INTRODUCTION

AT TWELVE YEARS OF AGE, a girl named Jessy invents the following system:

Sun with clear sky: four doors

Sun with one cloud: three doors

Sun with two clouds: two doors

Sun with three clouds: one door

Sun with four clouds: zero doors

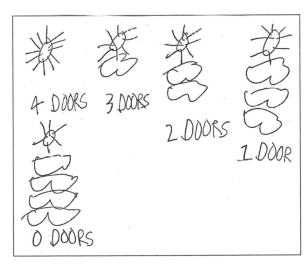

Jessica Park, Clouds and Doors (1970).

The girl also classifies days into twenty-nine different types, depending on the presence or absence of clouds and the sun's position in the sky. She names each day: In summer, *dayhigh* is a day with high sun and no clouds. In winter, *daynothing* refers to a clear sky. The state of the sky also has affective consequences: the sun brings her happiness, while any cloud will ruin her mood. When she gets up in the morning, Jessy rushes to look at the sky. Terrifying surprises are always possible. It could be a *dayhighdarkcloud* day. Despondency, sadness, and despair will follow.

Over the years, Jessy establishes diverse relationships within her system. The different types of days correlate with numbers, flavors, and gum wrappers. The number 3 is "rainbow-colored 'when cloud has color outside looks like rainbow and white inside,'" her mother tells us.[1] The system also helps Jessy organize and evaluate other experiences in her life. She assigns four doors and no clouds to hard rock music. Why? Because it brings her such intense pleasure that she needs to put four doors in between her and the sound to make it bearable. She allocates two clouds and two doors to classical music. For her evening meal, she measures the green juice she pours into her favorite green cup. The amount she'll drink depends on the clouds in the sky that day. The idiosyncratic character of this system reveals the unique mind of its creator, Jessica Park.

Born on July 20, 1958, Jessica Park was delivered by the local doctor, Edmund Larkin, in North Adams, Massachusetts. Her parents, Clara and David Park, took her home to a comfortable house with many books, a piano, and a garden in nearby Williamstown. Her father was a physicist at a prestigious college. Her mother was a homemaker who wanted to teach literature and write poems and essays. Her sisters Katy and Rachel and her brother Paul welcomed their new baby sister. They were eager to play with her and teach her what they knew. But Jessy, as her family called her, did not seem interested in learning from them. She did not seem to need any of them.

Jessy's mother, Clara, described her at one and a half years of age:

> We start with an image—a tiny, golden child on hands and knees,
> circling round and round a spot on the floor in mysterious, self-

absorbed delight. She does not look up, though she is smiling and laughing; she does not call our attention to the mysterious object of her pleasure. She does not see us at all. She and the spot are all there is, and though she is eighteen months old, an age for touching, tasting, pointing, pushing, exploring, she is doing none of these. She does not walk, or crawl up stairs, or pull herself to her feet to reach for objects. She doesn't *want* any objects. . . . One speaks to her, loudly or softly. There is no response. She is deaf, perhaps.[2]

Having watched her daughter intensively over the previous months, Clara noticed certain things she never saw in her other children. Jessy seemed happy, but her mother started to feel uneasy about the solitary nature of her happiness. Clara spent much time playing with Jessy, but also observing her carefully and taking detailed, precise notes about her behavior. One of Clara's closest friends was a psychologist. She had suggested Clara record some observations about Jessy's behavior. If the Parks needed to bring Jessy to a doctor one day, it would be good to have reliable written information about her. Later she would, in fact, show those notes to many doctors. They would not always appreciate her efforts.

Clara's journey to understand Jessy's unusual character started in earnest on May 15, 1961, when Jessy's pediatrician told her parents that she seemed to be autistic.

In the early 1960s, the Parks took Jessy to a psychoanalytic clinic, hoping for suggestions about how to support her. Instead, the doctors blamed Clara for being the source of Jessy's self-isolation. According to the experts in childhood emotional development, Clara was the prototype of a cold, refrigerator mother: an intellectual mother who starved her children of the natural affection they needed to develop properly. These experts saw Clara's diligent efforts to study Jessy's behaviors in order to figure out why she behaved so differently from her siblings as evidence of Clara's intellectual and, therefore, misguided approach to motherhood. Additionally, the experts told her that there was very little they could do to help Jessy.

This book tells the story of Clara and Jessy Park, focusing on their struggles to find their place in the world as they fought against narrow visions of motherhood and autism. Clara was called "an intellectual mother." Jessy was categorized as "autistic." For a long time, both labels made them suffer deeply and restricted what they could become. But in their remarkable journey together, Clara and Jessy broke through the straitjackets of those labels, learning from each other and eventually helping each other to construct a life on their own terms. Exemplifying different ways of combining intelligence and love, Clara and Jessy also helped transform our understanding of what mothers and autistic people can do.

But what was autism? Autism, we read in textbooks, was discovered by Hans Asperger and Leo Kanner in the early 1940s. We will see that the story is more complicated, because what we consider autism to be is the result of various views and practices that were put forth, tried out, argued over, and modified from the 1910s to the present. During that period, ideas about autism changed in striking ways. Autism was first considered a symptom of a mental illness, then a psychopathy, later a developmental condition, and now a disability or form of neurodiversity.

Those changes were driven by a combination of research and changing social perspectives about how we should value people's different neurological makeups (what is now referred to as neurodiversity). Scientific attention to autism as an independent condition has developed mainly since World War II through research and therapeutic work in several fields: psychiatry, psychoanalysis, psychology, and, more recently, genetics and neurology. The changing views about the nature and causes of autism also entailed new ideas about the treatments and social supports for autistic people. Just as importantly, this period witnessed profound changes in views about disability.[3]

In the 1970s, disability rights activists and scholars in Britain and the United States criticized what they called the "medical model of disability." According to its critics, this model privileges the role of medical experts who define disability as an individual's deficit or pathology. Assuming that disability has no value to the person or society, these experts call for a cure or treatment. Critics have powerfully illustrated how the medical model of disability leads to the stigmatization and disempowering of disabled people. Furthermore, the belief that people with disabilities need to be "fixed" or cannot function as full members of a community encourages what is known as "ableism" or discrimination in favor of more able-bodied or non-disabled people.[4]

As an alternative to the medical model, disability rights advocates presented a "social model of disability." According to this model, a person's impairment is not in itself disabling. Rather, the individual's disability results from the environment, that is, from society's failure to provide adequate accommodation and resources. Therefore, instead of focusing on the perceived failings of a person's body or mind, the goal should be to contest the social and cultural forces that define a difference as a disability with the aim of eliminating the social conditions and discrimination that produce it.[5]

Activists and scholars in the disability rights and justice movement have achieved crucial changes in the social, political, and scholarly realms. Their work has increased social awareness about the pervasive prejudice, inequities, and genocide of disabled people in different societies through history and the ubiquitous lack of accommodations and services for them to this day. Disability activists have also played a key role in the passage of laws that protect the rights of disabled people in all areas of society. And scholars in this area have demonstrated the need to center the voices of disabled people and study the historical construction of disability in different societies. In doing so, activists and students of disability have raised profound questions about how medicine and society have constructed what counts as normal in body and mind over the years, showing how the medicalization of behavior has often turned differences into pathologies.[6] The significance of all this work that has led to greater acceptance of the diversity of human bodies, minds, and behaviors cannot be underestimated and should not be underappreciated.[7]

Building upon the ideas and strategies of the disability rights movement and adopting the social model of disability, in the late 1990s autistic advocates launched the neurodiversity movement to promote justice and pride. This movement stresses the existence of different and valuable ways of thinking, feeling, and being in the world. It has also raised important questions about ableist scientific and social perspectives that assume sociality and spoken language are fundamental to all human relations.[8]

For many autistic people and advocates working in the neuro-diversity movement, full acceptance of autism implies rejecting the medical model of autism, including research on the biological basis of autism or the use of treatments or therapies to ameliorate certain autistic behaviors. Favoring a social model of disability, these advocates argue that autism is turned into a disability only because of society's emphasis on conformity and uniformity.

Yet, neither the medical model nor the social model of disability is monolithic and static. In a recent review of criticisms to the medical model, historian Andrew J. Hogan has pointed out that "the medical model has often been made to appear uniform, ahistorical, and uncontested within medicine."[9] Some disability scholars and activists have also argued that extreme versions of the social model completely erase the real aches and pains of people with certain disabilities. In a number of writings, British social scientist and disability activist Tom Shakespeare has called for acknowledging the role of both impairment effects and disability in the lives of disabled people.[10]

The history of the neurodiversity movement and the social model of disability underlying it are beyond the scope of this book, which follows the story of Clara and Jessica Park during events that took place mainly from the 1940s through the 1980s. My account thus focuses on the views held by child psychiatrists, psychoanalysts, and psychologists working on autism during that period. To assess the legacy of those views and the legacy of parents such as Clara Park, though, it is important to be aware of the profound challenges to the medical model of autism that came later. Being aware of these different lenses about disability is crucial as we consider the varied lessons we can learn from this history.

Autism, motherhood, and disability are capacious terms, and our views about autism, parenting, and disability have changed throughout history and differ among communities. Since autism was first introduced as a stand-alone diagnosis in psychiatry in the early 1940s, there have been many mothers who have raised many autistic children. They lived and worked and raised their children while confronting different medical and social views about autism, about disability, and about mothers. This book pays careful attention to the shifts in understanding autism, mothering, and disability, and shows the value in examining history in order to build a path forward. I hope to show that, in contesting the experts' views about autism and about motherhood, Clara Park and other mothers who became activists challenged many aspects of the medical model that autistic people have found oppressive.

We are still far from having a fully comprehensive picture of the history of autism. This book does not aim to provide that. It is neither a full history of autism nor a full biography of Clara Park. But through a close account of one particular story, and building on what other scholars have already done, it invites us to look at history to better reflect on questions that are still central today.[11]

Through Clara and Jessy's compelling story, we learn about major developments and controversies in the history of autism: the identification of childhood autism as a unique condition; changing scientific views about diagnosis and causation; the rise and fall of different therapies; and the establishment of the autism spectrum paradigm, which became the dominant approach and remains widely influential. Clara and Jessy were affected by the ways in which experts on the human mind and behavior, from psychiatrists to psychoanalysts to psychologists to therapists, conceived of autism. But Clara and Jessy also contested some of their views. In the process, they actively helped shape the history of autism.

Their story illustrates how science affects people and how people contribute to transforming science. Thus, this book weaves together the story of several searches: the scientists' search to understand the origin and treatment of autism; a woman's search to find her voice as a mother in order to help her daughter and other children like her; and an autistic child's search to find an enjoyable way of being in a strange and unpredictable world.

A NOTE ON LANGUAGE

Language is a powerful tool that shapes how we think and act. It can also be deeply harmful, leading to social stigmatization, discrimination, and violence. In writing this historical account, I have often used the terms that the people in my study—the historical actors themselves—used. This is necessary not only for historical accuracy, but because altering language can sanitize history and conceal important distinctions about the meaning people ascribed to some terms at different points in time. Whenever it is reasonable, I have eliminated language that is offensive altogether. In some cases, however, using that language can serve a valuable purpose. When Jessy was a child, sometimes other kids on the school bus shouted at her: "Retard!" Episodes like that were painful to her, her family, and her friends. But the pain they felt would be erased from these pages if I simply wrote, for example, that some children bullied Jessy because of her disability. To grasp that pain we cannot eliminate words that hurt our sensibilities. Some labels are offensive, and we should aim to eliminate them from current use; but if we erase them from our historical accounts, we also eliminate the very experience of those who were so labeled. That would not be fair to them. And it would compromise one of the greatest benefits that historical studies can provide—enlarging and deepening our understanding of human experience in different times and places.

Autism has been considered many things, including a mental illness, a personality type, a developmental disorder, a disability, a neurological variation, to name a few. My goal is to examine the different factors that played a role in bringing about these changing labels and their consequences, whether their legacy is positive or negative. To do so, and to show how different ideas had an impact on autistic people, I often need to use the language that the people in my study used, even if we now do not agree with the terms they used or their conception of autism. When I am not summarizing the views of historical actors in their own words, I will typically refer to autism as a condition while underscoring that no term is neutral.

Mental conditions are complex entities because of their hybrid nature. Though a mental condition may have a biological substratum, how a given community conceives of it and deals with it is always shaped by its culture, by its views regarding which human characteristics should be valued. In some instances, mental conditions were merely social constructs. In 1980, "female hysteria" was finally removed from the American Psychiatric Association Diagnostic and Statistical Manual of Mental Disorders. This category was used widely in the early twentieth century to diagnose many women whose behavior and desires did not fit traditional, often male social expectations for females at the time. In other cases, scientists have discovered neurological, biochemical, or genetic underpinnings for mental conditions that deeply affect some people's lives. Even in these cases, however, the way society evaluates the significance of these conditions and relates to the people diagnosed with them constitutes an intrinsic part of the conditions themselves.

Historian of medicine Charles Rosenberg writes that "in some ways disease does not exist until we have agreed that it does, by perceiving, naming, and responding to it."[12] That is even more so in the case of mental conditions, because their existence depends on scientific and social decisions about what is "normal." And what a given society considers normal has changed over time, sometimes dramatically so. All of these aspects make mental conditions—such as autism—very unstable entities, which is one reason why studying them historically is essential to understanding contemporary views.

Looking at the history of autism might help us in confronting fundamental questions we face: What type of science do we want? What type of society do we want to live in? Clara Park grappled with those questions. We don't have to agree with her answers, but paying attention to her search for them is worth our while. We can also learn much from Jessy's journey and her creativity. We read history not to validate our present, but to understand how we got here. We don't have to agree with the views presented by any of the psychiatrists or therapists either. But unearthing their history is important not only for grasping how things came to be the way they are, but also to see how to move forward.

CHAPTER I

BECOMING CLARA PARK

"**I** WAS BORN IN 1923, but I grew up in the 19th century," Clara Park wrote on a small yellow Post-it note, which she tucked away in a folder.[1] In her adult years, Clara put her thoughts and recollections on Post-it notes that she left here and there around her house, inside a cookbook, a novel, or a drawer. Clara felt she had grown up between two very different worlds. Both of them influenced her profoundly. Both shaped her outlook on life and motherhood.

Clara Justine Claiborne was born in Tarrytown, a suburb just north of New York City, on August 19, 1923. The second child of Robert Watson Claiborne and Virginia McKenney Claiborne from Petersburg, Virginia, Clara descended from upper-class, white Southern families. Her father was the son of a prominent doctor and medical administrator who had been in charge of Petersburg's military hospitals after the Civil War. Clara's mother was the daughter of William Robertson McKenney, a lawyer and onetime member of the US Congress for the Democratic Party. Yet neither of Clara's parents followed the conventional expectations for people of their social background.

A tall and elegant man who cultivated an aristocratic posture, Robert Claiborne considered himself a creative genius. Following his graduation from the University of Virginia in 1909, he taught at several boys' schools on the East Coast, including Groton School in Massachusetts, where he was head of the English department from 1910 to 1911. He later obtained a law degree from Columbia University and started practicing law in Richmond in 1918. During World War I he served as a captain in the Marine Corps.[2] His academic credentials and social status could have assured him a successful law career. However, Robert aspired to be a celebrated musician and did not feel bound by social conventions.

Virginia McKenney was not a conventional Southern belle either. Tall and stately, Virginia did not comply with many of the expectations—or the stereotypes—of an upper-class Southern lady. A woman one would not call pretty but handsome, her long braids and simple dress spoke of a practical person not interested in frills. Virginia received a college degree from Bryn Mawr in 1908, when less than 2 percent of American women did. Upon graduation, she returned to live with her family in Petersburg. Virginia idolized her father, by then a distinguished judge presiding over what someone at the time referred to as perhaps the only court in the South where a Black man could expect a fair trial. Inspired by him, Virginia became involved in educational reforms and other causes to advance women's rights. After her father's untimely death in 1916, marriage must have been expected of her. Virginia's age, education, and class left her with few prospects. At the time, the average age for a woman to marry was twenty-one.[3] She was a decade older than that when, in 1918, she wed Robert, a childhood acquaintance one year younger than she was.

In 1919, the Claibornes welcomed their first son, Robert Jr., and went through a taxing period. Robert was court-martialed at Quantico for alleged sexual advances toward another marine while he was on active duty on board the USS *Cincinnati*. Virginia supported her husband throughout the trial. In the end, Robert was acquitted, and their marriage stood. But her fortune was gone, spent on his legal defense. And Robert was not fully exonerated in the minds of some family members.[4]

Looking for a fresh start, the Claibornes headed north to Tarrytown, New York. Here, in 1923, they welcomed their daughter, Clara. Still, in work and family life, Clara's father struggled to find himself. He taught music at several schools in the New York City area. In 1927, he published *The Way Man Learned Music*, a method to teach music that combined storytelling, music history, and instructions for students to build their own instruments.[5] Through the book he also advertised private and group lessons. But Robert simply spent more money than he earned. He wanted to live in a big house, carrying on the wealthy lifestyle that he felt was befitting of his status. Virginia understood early on that she would need to support the whole family.

When Virginia found work at a vocational advisory service run by a non-profit organization, two-year-old Clara was sent away to Petersburg to live with her maternal grandmother, the woman she had been named after. Her brother, Bob, stayed with their parents. Over the next five years, except for the summers, Clara lived with her grandmother in Petersburg. She was left most of the time in the charge of an uncaring nanny. Clara's earliest years were spent very much in isolation.[6]

Yet her grandmother left an indelible mark: she awakened in Clara a strong sense of justice. Grandma Clara herself had made it through a difficult childhood. She lost her father as a child. When her mother died in a Civil War prison, she and her five siblings were scattered among relatives. At age seven, she was sent from her native New Orleans to her father's family in Georgetown. Mostly ignored by her relatives, she found a bit of kindness in her own old and bedridden grandmother, who gave her a gold watch. But an aunt then took the watch away and gave it to her own daughter. This was a story Grandma told Clara often, the memories of a displaced child passed on to another. Over thirty years later, when Clara wrote a column for a local newspaper, she recounted how "the child's feeling of outrage and injustice" was, after seventy years, still alive in her grandmother and was "conveyed to another lonely child, far from home."[7]

From her grandmother, Clara also learned to reach out for the comfort of words in the midst of difficult circumstances. Using poetry "for her own purposes," Grandma resorted to quotations as an emotional salve, which, Clara said, "was much of the time, for she was orphaned at seven and lived to bury her husband and all but one of her five children." On those frequent occasions, Grandma would quote Dickens's Mrs. Gummidge: "I'm a poor, lone, lorn critter, and everything goes contrary with me."[8]

After five years in Petersburg, seven-year-old Clara returned to her family, who had moved to Rye, not far from Tarrytown. Perhaps *family* is too grand a name for their living arrangement. "The family group," as Clara herself later called it, resided in a large house. By this time, her father was involved in a small music school. He, Clara's brother, and two boys from the school lived on the top floor of the house. Clara and her mother shared a room on the bottom floor. "And that's the picture of that marriage," she once remarked with sadness.[9]

Clara attended Rye Country Day School until 1932, when, at the age of nine, she left in the middle of the school year. Her last transcript reads: "Clara is a splendid pupil. She has a fine sense of fairness, co-operates nicely, does excellent creative work, and shows a good spirit. We are very sorry to lose her."[10] It is not clear why her family needed to move right then, in the middle of the school year, but it is another instance of Clara's unstable childhood.

The "family group" then changed residence to a duplex on Lexington Avenue in New York City. Here, Clara shared the first floor with her mother and two boarders, so they could afford their expensive Manhattan apartment. On the second floor, her father lived with her brother Bob and the two music students who had been living with them. Robert Claiborne now hosted a classical music radio program and gave private music lessons.

But soon the family disintegrated for good when, in 1934, Robert left for the Virgin Islands, with his son and one of the students.

There, he practiced law sporadically and persisted in his efforts to make it big—if not as a musician, then as an entrepreneur. In 1936, Robert moved again, this time to Puerto Rico, where he ran a farm. Over the years, his many projects included selling "expensive kumquat jellies," and having "Nubian goats delivered to the mainland by submarine during the Second World War."[11] To support his extravagant ventures, Robert sent his wife weekly letters with all sorts of requests. As Clara saw it later, her father just "soaked up money" while her mother paid "for his self-respect, for his dreams, for his nonsense."[12]

Clara and her mother reorganized their lives in New York. They rented a small flat and kept busy. "Bal," as Clara addressed her mother, worked as an organizational secretary for an educational foundation. For Clara, school became the center that held her life together.

In 1934, eleven-year-old Clara, tall and lithe, with wavy brown hair styled in a trendy bob, entered Dalton, a private day school in Manhattan that she later credited with saving her intellectually and socially. The school encouraged students to develop creative independence and a sense of responsibility toward others. Clara remembered it as a wonderful, progressive environment. The apartment she shared with her mother was just a two-minute walk from the school. Often Clara ran all the way there, up to the classroom on the fourth floor while humming the school song. In class she paid careful attention while fidgeting in her seat and constantly twisting her silver bracelet or her necklace. During the school year, Dalton was her world.

In the summers, Clara went back to Petersburg with her grandmother. She did not do it happily. "The disconnect was total," she remembered, "radicalism at school—school trips to NY slums, Jacob Riis's *How the Other Half Lives*—our social studies teacher . . . a Boston Brahmin and a Communist—and in the summers, the Confederacy, Ancestors, black servants."[13] Family was all her grandma talked about, and Clara found her house "airless." Clara also felt ashamed of her Southern white upper-class roots. Before the Civil

War, Petersburg had the highest percentage of free African Americans of any city in the Confederacy and the largest number in the mid-Atlantic region. But by the early twentieth century, conservative legislatures had instituted Jim Crow laws and racial segregation. Clara's interactions with Black people there were few and never in conditions of equality. In Petersburg, Clara encountered her "nineteenth century." She did not fit in. She did not want to fit in.

But Clara wasn't sure she fit well in New York City either. At the time, she was "a bespectacled girl convinced of her own inadequacy." While Clara and her mother rented a tiny railroad apartment, the girls she knew from school "lived on Park Avenue in rooms and rooms and rooms."[14] She felt miles away from her glamorous friend Jill, the editor of the school newspaper, who introduced her to editing, radical leftist political ideas, and many other things she had never heard of before. Clara was also unathletic, always among the last to be chosen for sporting events in school.[15] Clara loved Dalton, but while there she was very conscious of her own limitations—or what she perceived as such.

Her classmates and teachers, however, appreciated Clara's sharp mind and her vitality. Upon graduating from Dalton in 1940, her forty-four classmates named her, in the yearbook, "the walking braintrust," while noting that this well-deserved title didn't tell the whole story, because Clara had also been one of the school's most vibrant individuals.[16] Clara's graduation picture shows a young woman with full, thick hair down to her shoulders, and long, round eyebrows slightly over her glasses. Her shiny eyes look straight ahead, not in arrogance, but neither in shyness. Her lips remain closed. Not a giggling kind of girl. But there was also much more to Clara than a good brain. "Do you remember when we went skidding down a Maine Road with Waltie in the Midnight Moon?," wrote one of her friends in Clara's yearbook.

During those formative, adolescent years, then, Clara went back and forth between the decaying world of her aristocratic Southern family and the forward-facing world of her intellectual friends in New York City. These experiences ignited her sense of justice and responsibility, especially her interest in civil rights, and molded her powerful intellect alongside a strong conformist desire to belong. Above all, her experiences during those years filled her with a deep curiosity about people and ideas.

COLLEGE AND LOVE

In 1940, seventeen-year-old Clara entered Radcliffe College in Cambridge, Massachusetts, on a scholarship. A women's college, one-fourth the size of its all-male counterpart, Harvard, it did not have a faculty of its own. Harvard professors, who themselves were all male until 1948, repeated their lectures at Radcliffe. Not all the Harvard instructors taught at Radcliffe because some of them did not want to teach women. Joint instruction started in 1943, but as biologist Ruth Hubbard, a Radcliffe graduate from this period and the first female Harvard faculty member to receive tenure in the sciences, recollects, Radcliffe students in the sciences felt a bit like "second-class, or indeed nth-class citizens from day one." Perhaps this was less so for humanities students like Clara—perhaps.[17]

Clara's first main interest was in philosophy, but during her second year she changed her major to literature. She hoped that besides affording her the opportunity to "read the great works," she would be able to teach English upon graduation. Clara also dreamt of becoming a writer and wrote poems in her spare time.

In Cambridge, Clara lived in a small student co-op house, sharing the cleaning and cooking with other residents. Her friend Janet offered a revealing glimpse of Clara's practical character: "In need of funds," she remembered, Clara "dreamed up the idea of attaching a large trailer-basket behind her bike. Early every weekday morning for perhaps two years, Clara would wheel around the residential quad, all the 7 or 8 dorms, collecting reserved books from the college library, held overnight and due first thing. Sleepy students were glad to pay well for the service."[18] This was typical Clara: creative, practical, and hardworking. She had to be, as her scholarship did not cover all living expenses.

In New York City, her mother, Bal, barely made enough money to support herself and Clara while sending some funds to her husband in the Caribbean. In 1942, Bal returned to Virginia and became the director of Richmond's Valentine Museum. But finances were still tight: the following fall, she had to request an extension from Harvard to pay part of Clara's tuition.

Clara wrote long letters to her mother, her closest confidant, not only about school and social issues, but also about her feelings. On November 17, 1943, Clara told her how cautious she was socially for fear of being hurt. She recognized that her attitude came with a price: she could miss out on interesting or joyful experiences, just to avoid the risk of being disappointed. Yet she was open to change: "I'll be waiting for the time when I pull down all the defenses and fall in love. I hope it will come soon, since people have told me that it is a Good Thing."[19]

The Good Thing arrived soon enough, when Clara fell in love with David, a Harvard man and native New Yorker she had met earlier. From a family that traced its origins back to seventeenth-century British settlers, David Allen Park was the only son of Edwin Avery Park and Frances Paine. Born in 1919, David's parents divorced when he was five years old. His father taught architecture at Princeton and Yale, while his mother fancied a more bohemian lifestyle in New York City's Greenwich Village.

David had entered Harvard in 1937 to pursue a degree in physics. Toward the end of his studies, he heard about a remarkable Radcliffe girl from his friend Howard Nemerov. A poet, Nemerov was struck by Clara, but their shared passion for literature was not enough to win her over. A different kind of mind dazzled her. In 1941, David graduated. He began work as a research associate at the Radio Research Laboratory in Cambridge, an important secret wartime research center; soon he was hired as an instructor of physics at Williams College, a private liberal arts institution in Williamstown, Massachusetts. After his departure from Cambridge, Clara and David corresponded often.

Clara's letters from the period in which they were still only friends betray the nervousness of a hesitant young woman, albeit a self-reflective one. For example, on May 3, 1943, sensible Clara confessed to David: "You have the doubtful honor of being the only person to whom I ever start letters + then tear them up. You bring out all the not quite-bright elements in me."[20] At summer's end Clara wrote again: "I'm twenty now, which is quite a change, I suppose, from being 19, but I'm still no surer of what I think. You are sure about a great many things, and sure also of the possibility of sureness. Working with science, which is for me still magic, may do it."[21]

David impressed Clara with the confidence that a Harvard degree in physics inspired in a man still too young to doubt his own abilities. David became a physicist during a period of great faith in science. He knew physics was his calling. As Clara had put it, David was sure of himself and certain of the possibility of sureness. She, on the other hand, was immersed in the world of literature, where certainties are rare. Clara wrote to David about Russian literature, politics, and other matters, but with numerous caveats and hesitations, as if submitting her views for his approval. The adulation worked. David missed her. Within a month, he told her that he was feeling down in Williamstown. He was ill, lonely, and depressed. He was human after all. If his secure demeanor attracted her, his vulnerability won her over. Slowly, the flirtation turned into passion, and David went from dear to darling.

In June of 1944, Clara graduated from Radcliffe and took a job as an editorial assistant at the Metropolitan Museum of Art in New York City. She also got engaged to David. During 1944–1945, he went to England as a scientific consultant attached to the Eighth Air Force. Clara wrote him short, caring letters. Growing more confident, she dared to send him her poems and drawings. She became more playful, more assertive, with no more talk about his being so perfect.

On August 18, 1945, just days after Japan surrendered, Clara and David got married. Only their immediate families attended the ceremony at St. Mark's Church in New York. Clara's brother, Bob, gave her away in marriage. Frugal Clara splurged on a wedding dress with a scoop neck and a soft pleated skirt that came to the knee. Many years later, she still remembered her "beautiful, expensive, pebbly crepe" dress, in "turquoise blue with rosy white clouds drifting across it."[22]

For a white, upper-class young woman in mid-century America, things were going as expected. She had acquired a good education and held a respectable job for a while. Now, she was marrying a man a few years older and with a few more experiences than she had. She loved him and admired him. In the era of "togetherness," cherished by millions of Americans after the economic and social upheavals of the Great Depression and World War II, neither Clara nor David had any doubts about what was to come next. Clara Claiborne, now Clara Park, accompanied David in his pursuits, first to Washington, DC, where he had a job, and then a year later to Ann Arbor, where he began a PhD program in physics at the University of Michigan.

In Michigan, the Parks settled into a small flat in Willow Run Village, between Ann Arbor and Detroit. Back in 1941, the Ford Motor Company had built the Willow Run Bomber Plant for the construction of B-24 bombers. It added dormitories to house the thousands of workers employed there. After the war, when the plant was used for car production, housing at Willow Run Village was made available to veterans and others coming to the area. The Parks' residence was basic: a one-story plywood structure with a kitchen–living room, a bedroom, and a bath for $27 per month. Buses ran from the Village to the university campus in Ann Arbor.[23]

At first, Clara assumed a quiet domestic routine. In Washington, she had spent much of her time reading, writing, walking, and meeting friends. In Michigan, she took care of the cooking and sewing, in order to maintain a comfortable household but also to save money. She gardened, which she loved. She read in diverse fields. She did a bit of writing too, but was not satisfied with it.

While happily following this conventional path, Clara was aware of the limited experiences it afforded women. Sending a new poem to her father, she noted: "It is over-literary, but as yet all my images, like most of my experiences, come from books." For Clara, women's limited lives explained why there had been few great female artists. Women had simply not had "enough opportunities to experience life to enable them to reflect it in art." Clara asked her father to consider "the subject matter of Dickens, or Dostoyevsky, or Tolstoy. Respectable women do not frequent low dives or prisons, are not competent to speak on religion as it appears to men, or war, or politics (increasingly this is less true, but it is still mainly so) or law—etc."[24]

Clara lamented her own restricted engagement with the world as well. "My own experience," she wrote to her father, "is limited to books and university people." In contrast, a man her own age, "whatever his temperament, has been in the army and known all sorts of conditions, been in men's clubs, heard them discussing important things, hitch-hiked alone across country with truck drivers," and had other experiences that she had not had and could "only learn about vicariously." Clara told her father about a boy she knew from college who had already written a novel, *The Naked and the Dead*, which took in "the whole war, and through it, all mankind." With sadness, she added: "Regardless of whether or not I am temperamentally fitted to write such a book, I could never do it, because as things stand now, no woman can experience enough of life to write an ambitious book." Clara recognized that there were certain "experiences—children, etc., other women from a woman's point of view" that only a woman could write about, but these experiences seemed "tangential to the main business of the world, to war, politics, religion, economics, destruction, death. They are the material only of minor art."[25]

Indeed, as a woman Clara could not have had the experience of participating in the US campaign in the Philippines that Norman Mailer—that Harvard boy—drew upon to write *The Naked and the Dead*, which was published in 1948 and turned him into an overnight success at age twenty-five. The novel dealt with the lives of seventeen men during World War II, a man's affair. Clara realized that society saw women's life experiences and knowledge as "tangential to the main business of the world."

Before her marriage, Clara had considered going to graduate school, but she decided not to because she found the social and academic climate too discouraging to women. In Ann Arbor, she first got a job filing X-rays at the university health center. She often went to David's office to share soup and conversation with him and his physicist office mates. She also met some graduate students from the English department. When a teaching fellow broke his leg, she summoned the courage to meet the chairman to offer her expertise. She left with a teaching job and an invitation to join their graduate program. Thus, almost by chance, she returned to academic life and found an intellectual community where her curious mind reveled in discussions with well-educated and worldly friends.

One of those friends was Freeman Dyson, a young English physicist who had recently arrived in the United States and was participating in a 1948 summer physics seminar taught by renowned theoretical physicist Julian Schwinger. Dyson had worked at the British Bomber Command when David Park served in the US Eighth Air Force Operations Research Service at High Wycombe. Freeman and David did not meet there, but later they bonded over their common war experience. In Michigan they found much else to talk about, including exciting developments in theoretical physics. David and Clara also shared with Dyson a love of literature and concern about social justice, which would help to nourish a lifelong friendship.[26]

Clara had always been interested in social causes, but now she believed the political situation demanded action. Regarding the upcoming 1948 US presidential election, she informed her mother that her "mild efforts in collecting signatures (only twenty-five) for [Henry] Wallace on the ballot have been miraculously rewarded with an invitation to attend the Third Party Convention in Philadelphia" in July.[27] Clara put her hopes on the Progressive Party for a combination of idealistic and pragmatic reasons. She pointed out that liberals like herself, who could "see the seamy side of every question," could never have "the party of their dreams."[28] But a democracy needed to provide voters with real choices. She believed the two mainstream parties, the Republicans and Democrats, did not offer such choices at the moment.

Furthermore, Clara could not see how another world war could be avoided if the same two parties continued on as they had been. Under the threat of a nuclear escalation, a new war would be more terrible than any the world had suffered through before. She ended this four-page, single-spaced letter to her mother with a pragmatic reflection: "The lesson all of us must learn I think is this: One does not choose between what one wants and what one disapproves of— one chooses between what there is available. A critical mind will find fault with every course of action, justifiably. But until he can suggest *another* alternative, a possible one, not an ideal one, he must choose among those available."[29]

Pragmatism over idealism was Clara's philosophy for life. In this case, though she did not fully agree with all the positions taken by the Progressive Party, she thought it was her duty to help a party that could provide a healthy liberal alternative.

As for a career, among the options open to her at that point, Clara chose teaching. Still in her early twenties, Clara was teaching English literature to classes of mostly thirty-year-old male students who had returned from World War II and, thanks to the GI Bill, which provided veterans with funding for education, were now attending college. With a pinch of resignation, she told her mother that she was teaching Thoreau's *Walden* to men who "had not fought a war and come back to read some prick from Harvard who tells them that a house is just a burden and that they can live on beans and so forth."[30] Clara found these men to be wonderful students. Teaching was hard for her, however. She could not sleep. She could not eat anything. She taught a class at 8 a.m. and another at 4 p.m. In between, she agonized. She felt terrified, except for the two hours when she was in the classroom. She loved debating ideas with her students. Then and there she had found her calling.

Writing, another central part of Clara's life, came hard to her as well. An obsessive perfectionist, she was never satisfied with what she wrote. Nevertheless, others recognized early her literary abilities. In one of her courses at the University of Michigan's English department, she wrote a paper about modern poetry. Impressed, her professor was going to contact *The Atlantic* about publishing it. Clara wasn't quite sure whether she wanted to write poetry, novels, essays, literary criticism, or all of them. She simply had a passion for ideas and for chiseling a good sentence that expressed her thoughts in the right words.

Politics, on the other hand, turned out to be disappointing. Discouraged by the defeat of Wallace and Harry S. Truman's reelection in the 1948 presidential race, she decided to give up active involvement. Clara thought Wallace had lost votes due to his own mistakes, the worst being to "echo the Communist apologetics on Russia."[31] Thus, while her husband, David, continued to work on his physics thesis, she wrote to her mother that she planned to focus on teaching classes and occupy herself with the many household matters that many people, herself included, often took as an excuse to avoid political action.

But Clara remained interested in social issues, especially inequality. She lamented her lack of opportunity to meet Black people in conditions of equality. In her opinion, she told her mother, the best way to eliminate prejudice was through "personal contact." In her case, the social environment at Dalton, which had many Jewish faculty and students, had "destroyed forever any chance for antisemitism." All the rest, however, was "empty theory," which could only reach those few like herself "whose feelings are conditioned by what they read." She continued: "We will never learn to respect the rights of people whom we hold at arm's length because respect is founded on understanding and sympathy."[32]

During these years, Clara remained profoundly concerned about the grave problems in the United States and international relations. Looking at newspaper pictures of a Southern law school class where white students sat at the front and behind them, separated by a barrier, sat a single Black student, she wondered whether at least "*some* if not all of those white students will wake up to realize that they are witnessing pathological behavior, an incredible collective insanity." If the insidious discrimination against Black people remained appalling, the international political situation was also grim. As the Cold War conflict deepened, both the possibility of political repression and nuclear war loomed ever larger.

Yet, amidst the fear of impending catastrophe, the Parks continued with their daily routines—teaching, studying, and reading books together in the evenings. In 1948, Clara completed her master's degree in English literature. The next summer, after David put his half-done thesis in a bank safe, he and Clara embarked on a much-anticipated trip to Europe. With the help of some money inherited from David's grandmother, the young couple sailed for France on a converted troopship. Following a couple of weeks in

Paris, they rented bikes and traveled around. In Siena, they started trying for a baby.

They returned to Ann Arbor in the fall, and Clara found out that she was pregnant.

A FAMILY OF ONE'S OWN

Preparation for motherhood brought out Clara's practical side. Writing in April of 1950, she thanked her mother for a pair of smocks, which she also planned to wear after the pregnancy. She herself was making a shawl for the baby. After reading the "current Bible" in child rearing, Benjamin Spock's *The Pocket Book of Baby and Child Care*, Clara followed the pediatrician's exact advice to get three to six nightgowns, three to six sheets, two dozen large-size diapers, and some big sweaters. In the same letter, she presented a lucid analysis of the case of Karl Fuchs, the German theoretical physicist who worked on the Manhattan Project and was found guilty of nuclear espionage on behalf of the Soviet Union. In her unique way of combining intellectual discussion with the mundane, Clara concluded: "If the Russians, as they claim, got nothing from Fuchs, that was nobody's fault but their own." And, in the next line: "Pillow cases are fine. We are pretty well supplied now. Love and thanks for the indefatigable sewing."[33]

David's and Clara's first daughter, Katy, was born in Ann Arbor on June 24, 1950, on the eve of the Korean War. Clara's mother arrived the next day and stayed for a month with them. As a young and inexperienced mother, Clara welcomed her mother's advice and help.

Clara's life now centered on Katy and their plans to move to New Jersey. David had just received his PhD and was awarded a yearlong postdoctoral fellowship from his department. They decided to spend a year at the world-famous Institute for Advanced Study (IAS) in Princeton. Their friend Freeman Dyson was also there as a member of the School of Natural Sciences. David attended lectures by the eminent physicist and IAS director Robert Oppenheimer, conducted his own research, and saw Albert Einstein strolling to his IAS office every day, though hardly ever discussing physics with anyone.[34]

That same year the physics department of Williams College, where David had taught after graduating from Harvard, offered him a job. He accepted. David felt more attracted to being a big fish in a small pond than a small fish in a big pond, which likely would have been his fate if he were to pursue research in the highly competitive field of postwar theoretical physics. Of his neighbors in IAS housing, three would later travel to Stockholm to receive Nobel Prizes. David chose a quieter route.

In 1951, the Parks moved to Williamstown, Massachusetts, in the midst of the majestic Berkshire Mountains. They lived at 4 Chapin Court, in a big, two-family stucco house with sloped roofs to handle the heavy snow in the winters and surrounded by a large front lawn with trees. Set on an enclosed block and removed from traffic, this was an ideal environment for children. The street was full of rambunctious kids from young families of other junior faculty members.

Established in 1793, Williams was still an all-male college when the Parks arrived. The professors were all male as well. Their wives, many of them college graduates, devoted themselves to raising the children. Although the Great Depression and World War II had made having children difficult, the postwar peace and rapid economic expansion had enabled a baby boom across the country. For Clara, having a secure home filled with happy children was a luxury neither she nor David had known while growing up.

On March 29, 1951, Clara told her mother that she was expecting again. While preparing for her second baby, Clara's letters to Bal overflowed with details of Katy's antics: "I wish you could see Katy now. All of a sudden she learned to crawl, to pull herself to her feet (she still can't sit down again), and her first 2 words 'bye-bye' and 'dada' (sometimes really 'daddy')." Clara gushed about her "wonderfully sturdy" daughter, with her "rosy cheeks." Katy had gone through periods of colic crying and the expected difficulties for infants, but her mother delighted in her character: "She is, except for occasional teething spells, a joy to know."[35]

Still, having little time for herself took a toll on Clara. Exhaustion set in when her second child, Rachel, arrived on September 23,

1951. Bal came up from Virginia to help with household chores and the babies. After her departure, Clara had no time for herself. This was a new experience, as she explained to her father: "I had never before gone for 6 weeks with never an hour to myself—every moment preempted by feeding 4 people, all of whom eat different things at different times, and 2 of whom need to be fed it. Not to mention keeping them clean, and comforting them when they cry, which, in Rachel's first few weeks of life, was a good proportion of the time."[36]

Clara still managed to juggle household duties with some intellectual pursuits. For three dollars she hired a local high school student to mind Katy and Rachel two days a week, from 11 a.m. to 2 p.m. During those hours, she began a long-term project: studying the English novel. She thought that this would keep her happily occupied and be useful when she returned to teaching. She also hoped it would lead to some publications. She started an essay on Victorian English novelist Anthony Trollope as well. That did not distract her from paying close attention to her daughters. Now she had to minimize sibling jealousy, so she made sure that Rachel had the same toys as Katy, even the same dress.[37]

The juggling persisted as the years passed. Clara's letters to her mother continued to combine minutiae about domestic matters with reflections on world affairs: the dishwasher and threats to first amendment rights from anti-Communist pressures; suggestions for the hemlines of children's dresses mixed with commentary on the nuclear espionage trial of Julius and Ethel Rosenberg. Her long letters were jam-packed, with no empty space, even on the sides, as if the pages could not contain all she wanted to say. Clara longed to discuss social and intellectual issues, but most of her time centered on her two children, their needs, and their activities around the house. Soon, the balance would shift further in this direction.

On October 1, 1954, the Parks welcomed their third baby, this one a boy: Paul. Grandmother Bal once again came to Williamstown for a month. Her assistance was much appreciated, though by now there were few surprises. Clara already knew about diapers and rashes, crying at night, and little games to keep Paul entertained.

Rachel and Katy welcomed him as their new toy. Since he was born shortly after Rachel's birthday, she considered him to be her birthday present. The household was busier than ever. The project on the English novel would have to wait. Given her limited time for writing, Clara found it easier to compose short pieces on contemporary topics.

In the late 1950s, Clara started publishing brief articles on a wide variety of issues in a local newspaper, the *Berkshire Eagle*. Some of the first ones reflected on their time in Colombo, Ceylon (now Sri Lanka), where the Parks lived from June 1956 until the summer of the following year. David had received a Fulbright lectureship in physics at the University of Ceylon. The Parks rented a bungalow with a walled garden, where Katy and Rachel enjoyed the carefree lifestyle of walking barefoot and Paul got around on all fours. Covered with terracotta dust, the kids played in the courtyard while their father impressed them by climbing the palm tree growing in the center.

With Katy and Rachel studying in a nearby school run by nuns, and with a sitter to care for baby Paul, Clara now had plenty of time to herself. She took long walks. An enthusiastic swimmer, she went alone or with the kids to a beach filled with coconut trees and swam in the warm water of the Indian Ocean. She also spent long periods sketching outside the house. She was a talented draftswoman, and passersby gathered around to admire her portraits of local people. She had time to observe, reflect, and write about life around them.[38]

In "The High Cost of Human Machines in Ceylon," Clara commented on family life in Ceylon, an experience that involved cultural adjustment and awareness of social inequalities. Reflecting on their privileged position, she wrote: "We had an ayah (children's nanny), a cook, a 'boy' (waiter and houseworker) and a gardener. Their combined wages, *after* I had given the thirty percent raise expected of Americans, were 40 dollars a month. A dream to brighten a Berkshire winter—bananas and African daisies in the garden, and at the shouted word 'boy!' someone bringing lemonade on silent bare feet." But she added: "it isn't everybody who can bring herself to shout 'boy!'"[39] Back home, she found ways to promote equality.

In 1960, Clara started teaching English at the newly formed Berkshire Community College in Pittsfield, near their home in Williamstown. It was the first publicly supported junior college in Massachusetts. Clara carpooled with other faculty wives who had also been hired there. Like Clara, they were educated women who had left aside their intellectual aspirations to raise their children. They were happy to find a community to engage their minds educating adults. Clara rejoiced at the opportunity to be part of this new project. She loved teaching, and she felt a sense of mission in teaching local students for whom a community college presented the only opportunity to gain a college education. It was very different from the elite schools she had attended. She loved it because she could make a difference in the life of her students.[40]

Then, to her surprise, Clara learned she was pregnant again. Her wavy hair became straight, as had happened during all her pregnancies. With three children already, she had not planned on another. She had only recently started teaching and writing again. After a brief period of depression, sensible and practical Clara accepted the unexpected news.

The pregnancy was uneventful, except for a case of the measles during the sixth month. All of her kids got the measles; a vaccine would not be developed until 1963. Clara, who had not had it before, became worried because measles can lead to complications during pregnancy. But her doctor reassured her, telling her everything was fine. She had a mild case that only lasted a week before everything went back to normal.

Jessica Hillary Park was born July 20, 1958. Just weeks before the release of a movie based on the novel Clara thought only a man could write, *The Naked and the Dead*, she became a mother for the fourth time.

Clara enjoyed raising her children. Having always felt that she wasn't pretty, she now basked in her children's good looks. Her kids were alert, and she put a lot of thought and energy into teaching them through games and various activities. She was proud that her family enjoyed the amenities of a middle-class home: a garden, a piano, books, and home-cooked dinners together.

Clara worked hard to build the kind of family life she never had. She believed in the power of negative example. She never forgave her father, whose lifestyle forced her to be separated from her mother and brother during long periods in her childhood and, eventually, led to the family's permanent breakup. Still angry many years later, she said: "I knew what I didn't want to be. I knew what my family should not be."[41] Her mother, however, continued to be a trusted source of guidance.

For Clara, motherhood was tremendously important, enjoyable, and worthwhile. She wrote about her children to her mother. She kept journals with snippets of her kids' funny stories. She invented activities for them and played with them often. She read child-rearing literature and children's books. Sometimes, she discussed them in her newspaper columns. In other columns, she reflected on how to help children develop a love for poetry and grow up happy.

But Clara did not think women were well served by society's efforts to romanticize motherhood. In one of her columns in the *Berkshire Eagle*, titled "The Home and Mother Boom," she critiqued the superficial glorification of mothers in celebrations such as Mother's Day. In another, she noted in her typically ironic fashion: "I am hoping my girls will decide to be spinsters—archaeologists, perhaps mathematicians, members of the breed of unmarried lady scholars who used to grace our women's colleges. They are all dying off now." Today, she ruefully noted, many people would look with pity at women such as the writers Jane Austen and Virginia Woolf or the nurse Florence Nightingale because they did not have children. Without denying the many positive aspects of motherhood, she left writing about its "sunny side" to others.[42]

Clara's writings rarely dealt with the sunny side of either personal experiences or social events because she wanted to improve things. That required a critical eye, especially when it came to the cultural mores of one's own place and time. In a 1960 article, she wrote about Black people's right to vote, which, she noted, was "unequivocally established 90 years ago in the 15th Amendment to the US Constitution."[43] The following year, Clara wrote about people who had been imprisoned in Southern jails because they demanded racial equality.

For her, "this new crowd of witnesses" was going to "light such a candle in our country as (I trust) shall never be put out."[44]

Clara's life continued along these grooves. She used her gift for language to ask her readers to reflect on social injustices. And she raised her children with love and care, even knowing that many others did not consider mothering as "essential to the main business of the world." She wrote in one of her *Eagle* columns: "One of a woman's minor crosses is that what she does for the most part goes unrecognized in the world of Things that Count."[45]

But Clara would soon discover that the world believed mothers were important in at least one crucial respect: they were essential for their children's healthy psychological development.

Sitting in a rocking chair, Clara relished her peaceful time while nursing Jessy. A high-strung person, Clara had found nursing her babies a calming experience. Jessy also seemed to love their time rocking together. As she grew, Jessy laughed often, bouncing and rocking back and forth in her crib. She was very attached to her stuffed teddy bear. Later, on the floor, Clara and Jessy scribbled with colored crayons and played with blocks. For a few months, Jessy busied herself building block towers, then arranging the blocks in perfect parallel rows. Pictures of Jessy show her, by turns, smiling in her mother's arms, sitting, and playing peacefully. Jessy was a delicate toddler, rosy-cheeked and graceful in her movements. She enjoyed her time with her siblings. Katy, Rachel, and Paul loved their baby sister, and frequently initiated games on the floor with her.

As babies grow, they change and learn new things constantly. When they are about a year old, most of them take their first steps, begin pointing at things and reaching for objects, and engage more with their surroundings and with people. Yet there is much diversity. By the time Clara was raising Jessy, child psychologists had devised scales of normative development. In 1926, Yale psychologist Arnold Gesell published his influential book *The Mental Growth of the Pre-School Child: A Psychological Outline of Normal Development from Birth to the Sixth Year, Including a System of Developmental Diagnosis.* Historian Ellen Herman has argued that by 1947 the Gesell scales were the most widely used developmental tests in the

United States.[46] Clinicians and educators used these scales. In addition, widely read child-rearing books popularized these findings and conveyed to mothers rigid timelines by which their children should reach specific milestones. These normative scales shaped mothers' expectations and set prescriptions for what mothers should do. In doing so, they determined not only what a "normal" child was, but what a "normal" mother should be as well. A good mother was a mother whose child developed according to a schedule established by scientists.

For Clara, Jessy was developing exactly as her siblings. Jessy cried incessantly for around six weeks when she was born, but Katy and Rachel had gone through colicky periods. Jessy did not attempt to walk early; neither had Clara's other children. Katy, Rachel, and Paul had been slow to develop many skills in comparison to the expected norms of the time. So, Clara did not worry that Jessy seemed to follow their path.

But slowly Clara started to wonder if her beautiful, quiet girl was a bit too content alone. When left on the floor to play, Jessy did not try to leave the spot where she was left. She did not point to or reach for any object. She was extremely cautious, never coming close to the stairs or putting herself in any potentially dangerous situation. If friends came with another young child, Jessy did not pay them any attention. As far as her family could tell, Jessy did not seem to need much from the world or from those around her.

When Jessy was about twenty months old, the Parks were truly concerned. Jessy remained uninterested in people outside her immediate family. Her language usage was unexpected and inconsistent. Jessy would utter a word and then never use it again. Clara tried to engage Jessy in games and activities. Jessy was happy to play with her. She was also happy to be left alone—happier, even.

In May of 1960, Clara started taking notes on Jessy, following a friend's suggestion. The friend, a psychologist, thought keeping a record might be useful later, if Jessy's peculiarities required further observation and analysis.[47] As Jessy's behavior became more and more reclusive over the following year, the Parks decided to see a pediatrician.

On May 12, 1961, David and Clara took Jessy, almost three years old, to Dr. Sydney S. Gellis, director of pediatrics at Boston City Hospital and a professor at Boston University School of Medicine. Three days later, Gellis wrote to Jessy's physician, Dr. Larkin, with his medical opinion. To him, the picture was not clear. In many ways, Jessy seemed "to be an autistic child." Gellis noted the aspects of Jessy's behavior that, in his view, supported that conclusion: she related poorly to other children; her development seemed to have reached a plateau; she had an unusually strong interest in small objects and their orderly arrangement; and her speech was underdeveloped. But other behaviors did not support the diagnosis of autism as it was understood at the time: Jessy enjoyed "being played with physically," and she liked "to have her parents enter into" her games. Gellis added that although he did not notice any congenital problems, he recommended admitting Jessy to Children's Hospital for tests.[48]

Gellis then informed Clara that he had arranged a hospital visit for June 7. "You will be asked all about her food preferences, sleeping habits, etc.," he noted, and encouraged her to bring along Jessy's favorite toys and blankets.[49] On the given date, David and Clara took Jessy, her toys, and her beloved teddy bear to the hospital.

On June 19, 1961, Dr. Gellis wrote to David letting him know that the test results were all negative—the analysis of Jessy's skull, brain, urine, and blood did not show any abnormalities. Thus, he could not find any physical explanation for Jessy's development. He concluded: "I think that all that can be said at present is that she has an autistic type of behavior, although she is certainly not a typically autistic child. There would seem to be nothing further to be done except to wait patiently and give her the usual love and affection."[50]

Nothing should be done but to love her? And what exactly was autism? As Clara and David would soon find out, there was no clear answer at the time, though the term had been introduced in the psychiatric literature fifty years earlier.

√

CHAPTER 2

AUTISTIC CHILDREN . . .
AND THEIR MOTHERS

HE TERMS "AUTISM" AND "AUTISTIC" were first introduced
in psychiatry to refer to behaviors related to extreme self-
isolation, which was considered one of the characteristic symptoms
of adult schizophrenia. In the late 1930s, Hans Asperger in Austria
and Leo Kanner in the United States put forward two different types
of autism as independent conditions: autistic psychopathy and infantile autism. Kanner was a leading child psychiatrist in the United
States, and his views would become the main reference point for
scientific debates about autism in postwar America. At the hands of
psychoanalyst Bruno Bettelheim's gifted storytelling, autism became
a topic of widespread popular interest in the 1960s. Both Kanner
and Bettelheim ended up saying that cold mothers pushed their infants into autism.

Autistic behavior started receiving considerable attention during
the rise of child psychiatry in the 1920s. Though hundreds of children were admitted to and cared for in asylums and hospitals in
many countries, the first forty-five volumes of the *American Journal*

of Insanity (1844–1889) did not include a single article on children.[1]
However, in the 1880s, physiologist Wilhelm Preyer in Germany and
psychologist G. Stanley Hall in the United States published accounts
of children's psychological development. "How soon can a child go
mad?" asked the well-known British psychiatrist Henry Maudsley in
1895. His 1867 textbook *Physiology and Pathology of Mind* was the
first to include a chapter on "the insanity of early life." British physician John Langdon Down pioneered the study of cognitive disability
in childhood in his 1887 work *On Some of the Mental Affections of
Childhood and Youth*. In 1899, the term "child psychiatry" was first
used as a subtitle in the Frenchman Marcel Manheimer's monograph
Les Troubles Mentaux de l'Enfance: Précis de Psychiátrie Infantile.[2]

Scientific interest in this area followed the development of institutions for children and youth during the nineteenth century: juvenile
courts, schools for mandatory education, and custodial residential
centers. During this period, children whose behavior departed from established norms were considered either "insane" or "feebleminded."
Those capacious categories had already been used to identify adults
who deviated from what was considered normal behavior. These cases
fell into two categories. One was mental illness (variously referred
to as insanity, madness, and lunacy). Mental illnesses often appeared
after adolescence, could be transitory, and were treated by alienists
or psychiatrists. The other category was cognitive disability (commonly named "feeblemindedness"). In general, feeblemindedness was
thought to be hereditary and untreatable.[3] Further differentiation of
childhood ailments started when clinicians who dealt with adult conditions began to wonder how early an individual could develop the
first symptoms, as it happened with one of the most discussed mental
conditions of the early twentieth century: schizophrenia.

In his influential 1911 book *Dementia praecox oder Gruppe der
Schizophrenien* (*Dementia Praecox or Group of the Schizophrenias*), Swiss psychiatrist Eugen Bleuler talked about "the schizophrenias," a group of conditions where patients suffered from diverse
symptoms that could include hallucinations, delusions, disorga-
nized thinking, lack of motivation, social withdrawal, and a tendency to disconnect from reality.[4] Bleuler, who had coined the term

schizophrenia, introduced the concept of autism as well. The word *autism* comes from αὐτός (autós), the Greek term for "self." Bleuler adopted the term to refer to the tendency of schizophrenic individuals to self-isolate. He also wrote about "autistic thinking," which he defined in opposition to logical thinking and as being disconnected from reality. According to Bleuler, all people engaged in autistic thinking sometimes, but schizophrenics did so more often and in a more extreme form.

After Bleuler, the terms *autism* and *autistic* were quickly adopted in several fields to refer to a person's limited engagement with the surroundings or with other people. Sometimes, the words were used simply to describe specific behaviors or tendencies in an individual. More often, the terms were used in discussions of adult schizophrenia. As symptoms of a mental illness, autistic behaviors were considered pathological. The fascination of psychiatric science and society with schizophrenia led to an increasing number of studies about this condition, many of which discussed autism as well.

These discussions took place amid the rise of the eugenics movement that originated in the late nineteenth century.[5] Eugenics supporters promoted diverse measures, including educational programs and legislation, to encourage those people they considered to have superior physical, mental, and moral abilities to have more children. Many also backed measures to discourage or prevent the reproduction of those they considered to be inferior. In many countries, eugenics led to coercive policies such as the involuntary sterilization of people not deemed worthy of passing on their allegedly bad hereditary traits. Eugenics rested on false assumptions about the hereditary basis of mental abilities and moral characteristics, on racist beliefs about the superiority of certain groups, and on widespread social devaluation of people with cognitive and physical disabilities. Numerous politicians, social reformers, educators, and scientists in different fields in Europe and North America supported eugenic measures during this period.[6]

Psychiatrists did as well. For example, though Bleuler called for social reforms to improve the lives of individuals in asylums and introduced many changes to help schizophrenic patients, he also advocated

what was then called "racial hygiene," the Central European version of eugenics. Specifically, Bleuler supported the sterilization of
schizophrenics; in its absence, he claimed, "our race must rapidly
deteriorate."[7] Bleuler's eugenic beliefs were shared by many of his
colleagues in different countries. The concern about the hereditary
basis of mental conditions and its eugenic consequences fueled an
increasing interest in schizophrenia.

One central question in those debates was how early schizophrenia manifested itself. Bleuler believed that schizophrenia was rare in
children; he had seen very few cases. However, some psychiatrists revealed that more children than previously assumed displayed the early
signs of schizophrenia or, at least, showed autistic withdrawal. Now
that Bleuler had given a name to behaviors related to self-isolation,
some psychiatrists who reviewed the diagnostic files of schizophrenic
patients found earlier notes of such behaviors that had not been labeled or recognized as possible early symptoms. Then, psychiatrists
working with children started identifying autistic behaviors in children in various countries.

In a 1926 paper, Russian child psychiatrist Grunya Sukhareva
discussed autism in the context of her work on "schizoid psychopathy." The adjective "schizoid" was applied to people who showed
some but not all signs of schizophrenia. "Psychopathy" referred in
the psychiatric literature to a "personality type" comprising individuals who were troublesome in social settings as a result of their
difficulties in establishing interpersonal relations. Sukhareva described one child as shunning the company of other children, repeating questions over and over, and displaying obsessive and repetitive
behaviors. His personality, she claimed, made social relations very
difficult. On the other hand, this child had very good musical skills.
Sukhareva argued that there was a type of psychopathy that had
many similarities with schizophrenia, but children with this condition were different in other ways. The children she described often
improved over time, which was not typical in schizophrenia.

Later, in a 1932 paper, Sukhareva asked: "What is schizophrenia
really?" In an effort to examine the development of the condition,
she analyzed 107 cases, which she separated into two groups: those

who had shown peculiar characteristics in infancy, and those who only showed them much later, around puberty. In the first category of chronic rather than acute schizophrenia, there were fourteen boys and six girls who did not engage in common children's activities, didn't have "affective contact" with people, displayed "a certain autism," and developed very specific and strong interests such as in numbers, calendars, and astronomical phenomena.[8] Regarding the cause of their behavior, she believed that all signs pointed to an endogenous condition.

Endogenous was a term used to mean that the condition had a biological cause, as was the word *organic*. Today these terms may still be used, though we usually refer to the genetic, biochemical, or neurological factors underlying a condition, if it has a biological origin. *Endogenous* or *organic* were used in opposition to *exogenous* or *psychogenic*, which meant that a condition was due to some environmental factor, such as poor childrearing.

Many of the children Sukhareva described would likely be diagnosed as autistic today. But the point of presenting her work is not to claim that she was the "discoverer" of autism. Today, numerous articles are written with the aim of pinpointing who used the terms *autism* or *autistic* first or who described children we now would consider autistic first. While it is important not to overlook the contributions of past scientists, it would be simplistic to say that any one person discovered "autism" at a specific point in time.

What "autism" has been considered to be and, therefore, the people who have been described as "autistic," have changed over time in profound ways. The child psychiatrists who started to describe children with autistic behaviors interpreted those behaviors within the medical framework of their period. Though they may have used the same terms as we do today, their meanings were different. Within the prevalent medical model of psychiatry the children's "social withdrawal" and "lack of contact" were considered pathological because they were seen as early symptoms of schizophrenia.

Sukhareva's work was important, not because she "discovered" autism, but because she started to point out some problems with the basic categories used at the time. She called attention to children who departed from standard conceptions of normality but did not really fit the psychiatric categories available. She asked: what was schizophrenia, really? If autism was a sign of schizophrenia but the children she saw did not become schizophrenic, then there was some problem with the category. Or with the way psychiatrists perceived those children. Sukhareva, as other child psychiatrists around this time, started to realize that if one paid careful attention to children, behaviors that so far had been interpreted as early symptoms of adult psychiatric illnesses might be something completely different.

In the 1930s, the growth of the field of child psychiatry—marked by its first international congress held in Paris in 1937 along with the founding of specialized journals—enabled psychiatrists in many different countries to read about the work of others and to discuss children who displayed similar behaviors. The Americans Howard Potter and Lauretta Bender, the German F. W. Künkel, the Russian Eva Grebelskaja-Albatz, the Briton Mildred Creak, the Swiss Jakob Lutz, and the French American Juliette Louise Despert all described numerous children as autistic, meaning that they tended to self-isolate and seemed uninterested in people.[9] Child psychiatrists in several countries, including Germany, Switzerland, Italy, the United States, Spain, and the Netherlands, cited those publications in their own studies of children with similar characteristics. Many of these psychiatrists continued to diagnose these children as suffering from childhood schizophrenia. They did not use "autism" as an independent diagnostic category. But psychiatrists were not the only ones seeing children who defied previous categorizations.

During this time, generally only young children who had serious behavioral difficulties at home would be taken to a psychiatric clinic. Children who might have been seen at home as being somewhat odd did not become cases for analysis and treatment until they went to school. Schools have norms for intellectual performance and for social behavior. Those who depart from them stand out. At the turn of the twentieth century, the child guidance movement in the United States and the field of therapeutic pedagogy in central Europe arose precisely to deal with children who were not doing well socially, which often became apparent when they entered school.

At the University of Vienna's therapeutic pedagogy ward, Erwin Lazar, the ward's head, set out to identify different "types" of children so that teaching methods could be adjusted to their personalities. He encouraged his staff to pay attention to the children's abilities to establish "emotional contact" with others. The significance of this aspect of a child's personality became quite explicit in publications by members of his unit. In a 1934 article, Georg Frankl, a young Austrian pediatrician originally from Czechoslovakia, tried to figure out why some children did not follow orders. In some cases, he attributed this to a "disturbance of emotional contact." As Frankl saw it, those children could understand words, but they could not grasp the "emotional content" of communication as expressed in gestures, facial expressions, and the various emphases that accompany words.[10] In two other publications focusing on some children's "disturbances" of "affective speech," Frankl proposed that the children suffered from an "interruption of affective contact" with other people and an "extreme autism." Frankl believed these disturbances arose from the children's "inability" to respond to other people's emotions in the standard "instinctive way."[11]

Children who did not grasp what the group called the "emotional" aspects of language did not perform well in standard intelligent tests from the time, as another member of Lazar's group had shown a couple of years earlier. Anni Weiss, a German social worker with some training in psychology and pedagogy, argued that standard intelligence tests could not effectively measure the abilities of some "psychopathic children." Though these children performed above average on some questions, they were unable to understand many social situations "with any fine shade of feeling." Weiss also claimed that these children suffered from "a disorder within the deeper regions of mental life," a disorder of the instincts. Yet, she also noted that some of them possessed a special talent, "which, although limited as to extent, often surpasses the capacity of average men. Calendar experts, jugglers of figures, artists of mnemonics often belong to this type."[12]

Like Sukhareva, Frankl and Weiss were identifying children whose social behavior was not typical. When they encountered difficulties in school, they were perceived as troublesome or as having cognitive deficits. But Weiss realized that the standard instruments used to assess the abilities of these children were inadequate. Like Sukhareva, too, they used the term "psychopathy" to refer to this type of children. The term referred to behavior that society found problematic but that could not be considered the result of a mental illness. For Frankl and Weiss, these children were born with what they saw as a disturbance of the social instincts. Political events, however, put a stop to their work in this area.

In the mid-1930s, their unit underwent profound changes. Lazar died in 1932. Shortly afterwards, Viennese pediatrician Hans Asperger was hired. The situation for Jewish academics such as Frankl and Weiss deteriorated under the growing influence of Nazi anti-Semitism in Vienna. In 1934, one year after the Nazis came to power in Germany, Weiss was let go, and she left for New York. Asperger was promoted to director over the more senior Frankl. In 1937, Frankl escaped to New York as well, right before the Germans annexed Austria the following year. Asperger started publishing on the children they had seen at the unit for many years, drawing heavily on the insights of Weiss and Frankl.

Asperger introduced the concept of "autistic psychopathy" in a 1938 lecture given to the Viennese Medical Society and subsequently published in their weekly journal. He began by referring to the Third Reich's recommendation to consider the population as more important than the individual. In the medical arena that goal was linked to Austria's possible implementation of the 1933 German Law for the Prevention of Genetically Diseased Offspring, which approved the forced sterilization of persons thought to have heritable diseases. While nodding to the importance of that goal, Asperger wanted, however, to discuss the value of the individual, including those with mental conditions. To begin, he said that not everything "abnormal" should be considered "inferior." He then described two boys as representative of children whose "abnormalities" were the price to be paid for other superior aspects of their intellect.[13]

In his unit, Asperger noted, they referred to those children as "autistic psychopaths," because their self-absorption had led to a limitation of their interactions with the environment. These children didn't have the "instinctive understanding" needed to grasp those essential aspects of communication such as gestures and tone of voice. Therefore, these children were uninterested in doing things with others. Asperger then proposed that autistic psychopathy could be differentiated into two subtypes. He claimed one included children with limitations in the social realm but a high intelligence. They had scientific and technical interests, sometimes of an esoteric nature. As adults, this group included many scientists who might be awkward in social settings but made important contributions to their fields. The children in the other group displayed what he called eccentric and useless interests. These children, he claimed, sometimes ended up developing schizophrenia. Asperger said "autistic psychopathy" was innate. To provide evidence for this, he said that the mother of the child he described in his paper was "very similar" to her son. She was "completely unfeminine, intellectual, peculiar in her nature" and did not engage emotionally with her child. She lacked "warm motherliness." Asperger proposed that she had "transmitted her psychopathic disposition to her son."[14]

Asperger called for educating these children rather than seeing them as individuals with a "damaged constitution" and without "social value."[15] With appropriate educational methods properly fitted to their personalities, these "abnormal" children could grow up and do well personally and socially. At least, some of them could. In his better known 1944 paper, "Autistic Psychopathy in Childhood," Asperger presented the same ideas about the nature of the condition, but now described only children with "high intelligence," the ones capable of exceptional achievements. As he did in 1938, Asperger ended this paper with a section about "the social value of autistic psychopaths," because they could make important contributions to society.[16]

Under the Nazi regime, whether an individual was considered to be of value to society was a matter of life or death, as became clear in the Law for the Prevention of Diseased Offspring, enacted in Austria on January 1, 1940. Despite Asperger's defense of the social value of autistic psychopaths, recently some scholars have argued that he was influenced by Nazi ideology. In his 1944 paper, Asperger only defended the value of autistic children who had high cognitive abilities. Was that because he wanted to shield these children from the depredations of the Nazi regime? Or was that because he had become convinced that children with cognitive disabilities were a burden on society? Did Asperger collaborate with the Austrian institutions in which many of these children were killed? These matters are of extreme historical and ethical importance but remain controversial among students of Asperger's life and work.[17]

This brief summary of some early work in the history of autism shows two central developments. First, in attempting to find the earliest signs of adult schizophrenia, some child psychiatrists, such as Sukhareva, noticed children who displayed "autistic withdrawal" but did not show other signs of schizophrenia. Second, several pediatricians in Lazar's unit who dealt with schoolchildren deemed troublesome also noticed that many of them did not attempt to establish social relations and showed autistic withdrawal but did not later develop schizophrenia.

These psychiatrists, pediatricians, and social workers had begun to notice many children who did not fit the established categories used to diagnose behavioral difficulties in childhood, namely, "insanity" or "feeblemindedness." In Europe, their work thus marked the beginning of the effort to construct a new category for these children. Although Asperger proposed a category and a name, autistic psychopathy, his views were not discussed widely, as the start of World War II disrupted the exchange of publications and ideas that the first international conference on child psychiatry in Paris had fostered less than a decade earlier.

On the other side of the Atlantic, however, children who appeared to be socially withdrawn had also been noticed. As in Europe, many of them were considered to suffer from childhood schizophrenia. But, around the same time as Asperger, child psychiatrist Leo Kanner developed his views about infantile autism at Johns Hopkins University in Baltimore.

KANNER: INFANTILE AUTISM

Born in 1894, Chaskel Leib Kanner, the son of a rabbi, grew up in Brody, current-day Ukraine. *Leib* is Yiddish for "lion." In his youth,

Kanner changed his name to Leo. In 1913, Kanner entered the University of Berlin to pursue a medical degree. After serving in the military during World War I, he completed that degree and received his medical license in 1920. He then married Dziunia Lewin and practiced general medicine in Berlin. Four years later, the young couple, concerned about the uncertain economic climate due to rampant inflation, migrated with their one-year-old daughter to the United States, where a friend helped Kanner obtain a position at the State Psychiatric Hospital in Yankton, South Dakota. There, Kanner learned about psychiatry on the job.[18]

In 1928, Kanner moved to Baltimore to take up a fellowship at the Henry Phipps Psychiatric Clinic of the Johns Hopkins University Medical School. At the Phipps, Kanner initially worked under its director Adolf Meyer, a Swiss émigré who became a towering figure in American psychiatry. For Meyer, mental disorders resulted from inadequate thinking and behavioral habits a person would develop as defenses against environmental stress. Hence, psychiatrists needed a detailed record of a patient's history, including childhood events.[19] Meyer collaborated with Edwards A. Park, who directed the JHU pediatric clinic, to open a children's psychiatric unit in 1930. They asked Kanner to head it. There, Kanner learned that understanding children's minds required combining knowledge from psychiatry and pediatrics, as he emphasized in his highly influential *Child Psychiatry* (1935), the first textbook on child psychiatry in English.[20] Each case has a particular story, Kanner pointed out. Following one of them closely, he encountered a child like no other he had seen before.

At a Phipps staff conference held in 1938, Eugenia Cameron, a psychiatrist at the Maryland Nursery and Child Study Home, introduced a five-year-old boy named Donald. A year earlier, Donald's father had sent Kanner a thirty-three-page-long typewritten letter describing his son. On Kanner's recommendation, Donald was admitted to the Maryland nursery home, where Cameron and Georg Frankl—the recently arrived émigré from Vienna who had worked with Asperger—observed him for two weeks. Now, Cameron was ready to present Donald's case to a group of about thirty physicians. Donald appeared oblivious to all of them. Playing with his toys on the floor, he only looked up when Cameron took them away. She then led him out of the room.[21]

Cameron told her colleagues that Donald did not use the pronoun "I" to refer to himself and that his language appeared without "emotional tone." He did not interact much with other people, except his mother. By age three, Donald could count and recite the alphabet forwards and backwards. He had a great memory and demanded that sentences and stories "be repeated in precisely the same way every time." Donald spent most of his time spinning objects, tracing numbers and letters in the air, grimacing, smiling, and shaking his head from side to side. Cameron highlighted the contrast between Donald's cognitive abilities and his apparent lack of interest in people and the world around him. She asked her audience: "What is the difficulty?"

None of the attending experts could figure it out. Starting the discussion, Meyer wondered whether "kindred observations" were available. But no one offered any. Regarding diagnosis, Kanner mentioned that he had considered the possibility of *dementia infantilis*. However, Donald did not show the quickly degenerating trajectory typical of that condition. Without much conviction, others suggested various possibilities, from word deafness to brain injury. None brought up childhood schizophrenia, though Swiss psychiatrist Jakob Lutz had presented a review of this condition at a recent Phipps staff conference. Neither did they mention Asperger's ideas, which were only published that very year for the first time in a local Viennese medical journal.[22]

Donald's case was puzzling to these physicians because he did not fit into either of the two categories used to understand children's conditions: mental illness and mental "retardation." Kanner did not think that Donald suffered from childhood schizophrenia because his development showed improvement, the opposite of the progressive deterioration characteristic of schizophrenia. But Donald did not seem to have a cognitive disability either.

Which category a child was put into was not a mere academic matter in the United States either. During this period, the Nazi regimes in Germany and Austria were using eugenic ideas to justify the genocide of millions of people, including disabled children. But in the United States some medical doctors had proposed the elimination of "feebleminded" children as well. In a 1942 paper published in the *American Journal of Psychiatry*, Kanner criticized those proposals, pointing out that there had not been "one single instance" in history when "feebleminded" people had brought about suffering to others. In contrast, he stressed the immense suffering that "one man, Schicklgruber, whose IQ is probably not below normal," had brought to the world. Kanner accused Hitler (whose grandmother's name was Schicklgruber) of inhumanity, remarked that the value of a particular ability or skill depended on the context, and emphasized that an individual's worth was not tied to a measure of specific cognitive capacities.[23]

In the late 1930s, Kanner was frantically writing to European colleagues to ask for help in learning the whereabouts of his mother and other family members. He was also helping European Jews, including many physicians and medical researchers, to escape and settle in the United States.[24]

In the midst of these difficult political and personal circumstances, Kanner continued his work on children similar to Donald in collaboration with Frankl, who had fled Vienna in the fall of 1937. Frankl had gone first to New York City and married his former colleague Anni Weiss. In the summer of 1938 Frankl moved to Baltimore to work with Kanner on a volunteer basis. A year later, Kanner helped him obtain a paid psychiatrist position at the Maryland Nursery and Child Study Home, after Cameron left that post.

In Vienna, Frankl had worked in Lazar's clinic and written about children who didn't communicate well because they weren't grasping the emotional aspects of language and gestures. Frankl had used the term autism only once in one of his papers. In Baltimore, Frankl continued his studies about the affective "contact" of children, a project Kanner found "highly meritorious."[25] Several authors have argued that Kanner stole his ideas about autism from Frankl (or Asperger via Frankl), and Frankl did not say anything because Kanner had saved him from the Nazis. Kanner, however, did not help Frankl flee Vienna, and there is no evidence that he knew about Asperger's

1938 paper. Kanner did not steal Frankl's ideas, which were already published when he arrived in Baltimore.[26] However, there can be little doubt that Frankl influenced Kanner's focus on what they called "disturbances of affective contact." During these years, Kanner and Frankl characterized children with similar characteristics as Donald's as "autistic."[27] As we saw earlier, by the late 1930s, using this term to refer to the self-isolation tendencies of some children was common practice in the psychiatric community.

In 1941, at another Phipps staff conference, Kanner presented a paper, entitled "Autistic Disturbances of Affective Contact in Small Children," in which he said that he had identified "a small number of children displaying profound disturbances of behavior of a unique and remarkably similar character," referring to two boys and two girls in addition to Donald. He described one of these two boys. At age five, the boy had been sent to Kanner's clinic for testing because he seemed to have a "severe intellectual defect." He engaged in repetitive behavior, never used the first-person pronoun when referring to himself, and had "no affective tie to people." Kanner wrote that when he "had any dealings with persons at all, he treated them, or rather parts of them, as if they were objects." He concluded that the "salient feature" of these children was "the peculiar *lack of any sort of affective relationship to persons.*"[28]

From this time on, Kanner continued to study these children without Frankl. As a result of an external negative report of the Maryland Study Home that criticized the institution's apparent focus on research rather than on helping children, Frankl was asked to resign and left Baltimore by the end of the spring of 1941. Kanner kept in touch through correspondence with him and also his wife.

Two years later, Kanner presented a revised and extended version of the paper he offered at the 1941 staff conference with the title "Autistic Disturbances of Affective Contact in Small Children." Kanner painted a vivid picture of eleven children, including Donald. Though most had been diagnosed as "feebleminded" before coming to Kanner's clinic, he noted that many of them had good potential cognitive abilities and often had extraordinary musical skills. While many of them had problems with language and did not use speech to communicate with others, most displayed good motor coordination and manual dexterity. Kanner pointed to the children's perceived low level of emotional engagement with other people and their "*extreme autistic aloneness.*" Despite their diverse language abilities and intelligence, Kanner identified several "essential common characteristics" in these children: not using language for communicative purposes, a strong insistence on the "maintenance of sameness," and a tendency to relate to people as objects. In his view, these features formed a "rare" and "unique 'syndrome,' not heretofore reported," characterized by "the children's *inability to relate themselves* in the ordinary way to people and situations from the beginning of life."[29]

According to Kanner, the condition he described differed "in many respects from all other known instances of childhood schizophrenia." Childhood schizophrenia appeared after a period of typical development, but these particular children had displayed these features "from the very beginning of life." Schizophrenic children usually became increasingly disconnected from the world. In contrast, Kanner noted, "our children gradually *compromise* by extending cautious feelers into a world in which they have been total strangers from the beginning."[30]

Kanner argued that parental influence could not be the cause of this distinct syndrome because the children had many of the symptoms from birth. Thus, he asserted: "We must, then, assume that these children have come into the world with innate inability to form the usual, biologically provided affective contact with people, just as other children come into the world with innate physical or intellectual handicaps." Kanner presented these children as "pure-culture examples of *inborn autistic disturbances of affective contact.*"[31]

His colleagues disagreed. Hilde Bruch, a pediatrician who was studying psychiatry at Johns Hopkins, challenged Kanner's "assumption of some innate inability." The other discussants sided with Bruch. John Whitehorn, Meyer's successor as head of the Phipps psychiatric clinic, was also "skeptical about the 'innate inability'" thesis, wondering: "when the parents of a child are obsessed with intelligence and its development—what happens to the child? The child may be distorted in its emotional development." Yet Kanner stood his ground.[32] Shortly thereafter, he published the paper, with a slightly revised title, but without changes from the version presented to his colleagues.

Kanner's 1943 paper, "Autistic Disturbances of Affective Contact," appeared in a special issue of the *Nervous Child* on "Affective Contact Disturbances in Children." Kanner coedited this issue, and following a suggestion by the editor, he included a paper that Frankl had submitted to the journal. In "Language and Affective Contact," Frankl provided a summary of ideas that he had first developed in the 1930s about how some children were unable to understand the emotional tone of communication both in spoken language and gestures and how this inability affected their social relations. Discussing different groups of children with speech difficulties, Frankl noted that one of them suffered from the "predominance of the disruption of the affective contact over the intellectual disorder." This group included cases that varied "in intelligence from idiocy to the astonishing and peculiar performances of a certain type of child prodigy."[33]

In their papers, both Kanner and Frankl discussed what today we would identify as autistic children (though Frankl did not use the terms autistic or autism), but each had a different focus. Frankl emphasized the importance of understanding language to form social relations. Kanner saw the children's self-isolation as the root of their inability to develop affective relationships. Some of these children also had intellectual disabilities, but neither Kanner nor Frankl believed the children's emotional difficulties resulted from them. The relationship between social isolation, use of language, and cognitive abilities in autistic children would become a central question in the following decades.

In 1944, Kanner published another paper based on studies with a total of twenty children, where he gave a name to their condition: "infantile autism."[34] He again presented infantile autism as a child's innate inability to form affective relationships with others. Kanner said that infantile autism was a very rare condition. Though he had searched for autistic children for several years, he had found only about twenty of them.

At first, only a handful of experts in child psychiatry paid attention to Kanner's papers on this rare condition. In the following decade, however, two major changes occurred: Kanner shifted his position and started blaming mothers for their children's autism. And child psychiatrists, psychologists, and psychoanalysts began writing extensively on autism.

REFRIGERATOR MOTHERS

Though Kanner believed infantile autism had a biological origin, he also thought that parents could influence a child's psychological development. His 1935 book *Child Psychiatry* noted that behavioral disorders could result from parental overindulgence, overprotection, indifference, hostility, rejection, and excessive ambitions for a child.[35]

Still, at the time, Kanner was one of the few prominent psychiatrists who opposed blaming mothers for anything that went wrong with their children. In a 1941 book addressed to a general audience, *In Defense of Mothers: How to Bring Up Children in Spite of the More Zealous Psychologists*, Kanner pointed out that psychoanalysts and psychologists from different schools had ensnared parents in a mesh of conflicting advice. In addition, they blamed mothers if their children departed from some artificial standard of childhood perfection. As Kanner put it: "If your child does not accommodate you by being perfect, then you have either not studied enough or failed to apply the rules to the letter. Then a chorus of experts will point accusing fingers at you and say with devastating contempt: Cherchez la mère [search for the mother]."[36] A review of Kanner's book in the *Journal of Pediatrics* welcomed his call for common sense.[37]

Kanner's defense of mothers took place in the early 1940s, right when he was developing his views on autism. His appreciation of mothers is evident in his positive opinion of Donald's mother. For example, at the staff conference of April 1941, Kanner told his audience that, after the family's visit to Baltimore back in October of 1938, Donald's mother had kept the clinic "informed about further developments in letters showing excellent observation and judgment." In addition, to describe the children in his 1943 paper,

Kanner quoted extensively from two reports from fathers and five from mothers.[38] At this point, Kanner did not think mothers were to blame for their children's autistic behavior and he trusted their observations about them.

But the parents of autistic children intrigued Kanner from the beginning. In his 1943 paper, he called attention to a "very interesting common denominator" among the parents: they seemed "persons strongly preoccupied with abstractions of a scientific, literary, or artistic nature, and limited in genuine interest in people." In his 1944 paper, Kanner paid special attention to mothers and noted that several of them had worked professionally before marrying. Many were college graduates, including a physician, a clinical psychologist, and a businesswoman. These data probably piqued Kanner's curiosity because at the time only about 10 percent of mothers of children under the age of six worked outside the home. Kanner also suggested that one mother's extensive notes "indicated obsessive preoccupation with details and a tendency to read all sorts of peculiar interpretations into the child's performances."[39]

Kanner's comments might seem at odds with his call to stop blaming mothers, but his defense of mothers proved to be a double-edged sword. In several articles written for a popular audience during the early 1940s and in his 1941 book *In Defense of Mothers*, Kanner criticized "child rearing by the book" and rejected the "mechanization of parenthood." He defended the value of "genuine parental affection," something that could not be "learned from books or lectures."[40]

Kanner's emphasis on "genuine" affection illustrated the rising concern in American society and science about the role of the emotions in an increasingly technological world. However, instead of stopping mother blame, this focus on emotions, and specifically maternal affection, intensified psychologists' emphasis on the crucial role of mothers in child-rearing. That, in turn, led to the notion that ultimately mothers were responsible for anything that society found wrong with their children.

In the United States emotions became central to scholarly discussions about personality and social order during and after World

War II.[41] Struck by the fact that scientific and technological advances had done little to prevent two horrendous world wars, many psychologists and psychiatrists warned that society needed to pay more attention to human relations. A true democracy could not work by "grace of technocracy alone," warned Edward A. Strecker, chair of psychiatry at the University of Pennsylvania, in his 1944 presidential address to the American Psychiatric Association.[42] Worried about the overblown emphasis on technological advances in contemporary society, Harvard psychologist Gordon Allport also called, in 1947, for more attention to "problems of human affection and the conditions for its development."[43]

This concern inspired widespread interest in the field that placed the most emphasis on the role of emotions during childhood: psychoanalysis. According to Sigmund Freud, the child's relationship with his mother served as "the prototype of all later love-relations— for both sexes."[44] Many of his followers emphasized that mothers were responsible for their children's emotional development. As American psychoanalysts Karl and Jeanetta Menninger expressed it, "the patterns of emotional behavior" were determined "not by 'the parents' but by *the mother*."[45] Even when studies referred to "the parents," the research and conclusions were almost exclusively about mothers. Mothers allegedly caused emotional disturbances in their children by loving them too much or too little, by paying them too much or too little attention.

During the early 1940s, scholarly and popular publications most commonly alerted readers to the danger of mothers who loved too much. In his 1942 best-selling book *A Generation of Vipers*, popular author Philip Wylie warned against "mom," the overly doting mother who emasculated her sons. Influential scholars also cautioned against too much maternal love. David M. Levy, respected psychoanalyst, chief of staff at the New York Institute for Child Guidance, and professor of psychiatry at Columbia University, explored the devastating effects of "maternal overprotection" in his widely cited 1943 book of that title.[46] Shortly after his presidential address calling for more attention to the emotions, Strecker published *Their Mothers' Sons* (1946), a work directed to the general public. In it,

Strecker adopted Wylie's term and divided bad mothers into several categories, including the "pseudointellectual" mom, the "Pollyanna" mom, and the "self-sacrificing" mom. The popular press was quick to warn that moms could endanger their children and the whole nation, as seen in articles such as "Are American Moms a Menace?" in the *Ladies' Home Journal*, "Mama's Boys" in *Time*, and "Momism" in the *Washington Post*.[47] Though mainly focused on white families and what many at the time perceived as a crisis of masculinity, some literature also covered the perceived pathological effects of Black mothers on their families and the country.[48]

As the decade wore on, and in response to social concerns about the increasing number of mothers entering the work force, scholarly attention shifted toward the dangers of children receiving too little mother love. The early 1950s saw a surge in mothers of young children in the paid labor force, rising from 12 percent at the end of the 1940s to 20 percent by 1955.[49] Studies that had earlier explored the consequences of too little mother love for children were now widely discussed and cited. For example, in his 1937 paper "Primary Affect Hunger," in the *American Journal of Psychiatry*, Levy had argued that children had "an emotional hunger for maternal love and those other feelings of protection and care implicit in the mother–child relationship."[50] In her 1943 book *The Rights of Infants*, Margaret Ribble, another New York psychoanalyst, also claimed that infants have an "innate need for love, which is a necessary stimulus for psychological development," and that "emotional hunger is an urge as definite and compelling as the need for food."[51] In the postwar era, this metaphor of mother love as food or essential nutrient for an infant's mind became prevalent among psychiatrists, especially those with a psychoanalytic bent. The work of René Spitz became especially influential even among those who did not like psychoanalysis.

Spitz, an Austro-Hungarian psychoanalyst who immigrated to the United States, had observed infants in the nursery of a women's prison in New York and in a foundling home in Latin America (he never disclosed the exact locations). In the prison nursery, the inmate mothers took care of their babies, who developed well. In the foundling home, although nurses fulfilled the children's material and physical needs, the infants developed a range of physical and psychological problems, from eczema to weight loss and withdrawal. According to Spitz, these children literally withered away because they did not receive maternal care and love. Spitz's publications and his films, such as his 1947 black-and-white documentary called *Grief: A Peril in Infancy* that depicted the progressive deterioration of infants suffering from what he called "hospitalism," became widely known in the United States.[52]

Swayed by these studies, Kanner altered his views about autism's origins, as can be appreciated in the 1948 revised edition of his textbook *Child Psychiatry*. Here, Kanner called attention to the works by Levy, Ribble, and Spitz.[53] Kanner even adopted the common metaphor of mother love as a psychological nutrient, writing: "psychological deprivation results in affect hunger and emotional shallowness."[54] In Kanner's view, infants needed a "sustained atmosphere of warmth, equally removed from refrigerator and oven" for their "wholesome personality development."[55]

In the 1948 edition of *Child Psychiatry*, Kanner included early infantile autism in the chapter on schizophrenia, a move that also raised concern about mothers. Previously, Kanner had asserted that infantile autism was different from schizophrenia. But other psychiatrists working in the area, such as Lauretta Bender and Louise Despert, disagreed. In a 1943 letter to Kanner, Despert strongly objected to "the coining of new terminology for entities which, while perhaps not so carefully described, have been previously reported."[56] In her view, Kanner had basically given a good description of childhood schizophrenia. Kanner replied that he had been stunned by the "distinctive phenomenology" in autistic children since they seemed unable to form adequate affective contact from the beginning of life, rather than withdrawing "from adequate or near-adequate contact already established."[57] Bender and Despert remained convinced that autism was just a variation in the onset of childhood schizophrenia.[58]

At this time, many psychiatrists blamed schizophrenia on mothers. In 1948, the same year Kanner's revised textbook appeared, the German-born psychiatrist and psychoanalyst Frieda Fromm-Reichmann, working at the Chestnut Lodge mental hospital in

Maryland, argued that the reactions of distrust and rejection shown by the schizophrenic individual toward other people were due "to the severe early warp and rejection he encountered in important people of his infancy and childhood, as a rule, mainly in a schizophreno-genic mother." In schizophrenia, Fromm-Reichmann claimed, the re-treat to "an autistic private world" was due to maternal rejection.[59] Shortly after, a deluge of studies about this new type of pathogenic mother appeared. Psychiatrist Trude Tietze, Kanner's colleague at the Phipps, published one of the earliest and most widely cited works. Ti-etze studied the mothers of twenty-five adult schizophrenic patients. She described them as "fundamentally insecure people," character-ized by "emotional emptiness" and "lack of genuine warmth." Ti-etze concluded that these mothers lacked the "intuition or empathy with the child" that psychoanalysts had identified as the basis of the proper mother–child relationship.[60]

Kanner tried to find a compromise position on the relation of autism to childhood schizophrenia. His 1948 textbook gave infan-tile autism its own section and highlighted the point that schizo-phrenia was only a useful category, not a "unitary disease," a fact that Eugen Bleuler had, back in 1911, recognized by talking about "the group of the schizophrenias."[61] In a 1948 conference presenta-tion, Kanner explained that, having by this point seen fifty-five chil-dren with infantile autism and having knowledge of many others, he felt confident that the syndrome was well established. But, after being prompted by Despert, he had reconsidered its classification. He had reflected on the strong similarities between his cases and those reported by Despert, Sukhareva, and Grebelskaja-Albatz.[62] He now believed that early infantile autism could be understood as "the earliest possible manifestation of childhood schizophrenia."[63] However, Kanner remained ambivalent about this point. He always maintained that autistic children did not show the same prognosis as children with later onset of schizophrenia.

Regarding the cause of autism, Kanner now claimed that mothers led their children to retreat into autism. In his revised textbook, he commented that the parents of autistic children included "very few really warmhearted fathers and mothers."[64] Most autistic children, he argued in his 1948 talk, "were exposed from the beginning to parental coldness, obsessiveness, and a mechanical type of attention to material needs only." Despite the reference to parental care, the blame was directed mainly at the mothers. Kanner described fathers as hardly knowing their children, and being entirely focused on their work. Regarding the mothers, he noted: "Maternal lack of genuine warmth is often conspicuous in the first visit to the clinic." As Kanner now saw it, autistic children "were kept neatly in refrigerators which did not defrost. Their withdrawal seems to be an act of turning away from such a situation to seek comfort in solitude."[65] So, whereas Kanner had earlier claimed that children were born autistic, here he said that they withdrew into autism as a way to escape their cold mothers.

Kanner noted some facts in conflict with his interpretation: some cases did not fit the picture, some of the parents had reared other children without autism, and some parents who were cold had reared children who reacted with aggression, not withdrawal. These exceptions, although few, were "puzzling." Clarifying the issues, he said, would require "much further thought and study."[66]

However, before there was time for any further thought and study, indeed just one week after Kanner's talk and before his conference paper made it into print, a 1948 piece on autistic children in *Time* magazine announced Kanner's change of heart: "Psychiatrist Leo Kanner used to stand up for parents. He championed them against the experts, said that it was unfair to blame the mother or father every time something went wrong with the child." But now, the report continued, Kanner was taking "a hard look" at the parents, finding them to be "Cold Perfectionists." The reporter did mention Kanner's ambivalence: "Were the cold parents freezing their children into schizophrenia? Dr. Kanner did not say yes or no." But the article's title suggested a clear verdict: "Frosted Children."[67]

When Kanner started blaming mothers, autism gained considerable prominence. Kanner had always emphasized that infantile autism affected only very few children. And his early 1943 and 1944 papers had—as he himself noted—hardly received any attention beyond some psychiatrists working on childhood schizophrenia.

However, in the early 1950s, Kanner noticed a surge of interest in his views on autistic children and their mothers.[68] Kanner could not explain the reason for this. But the striking rise in social and scientific concern derived to a great extent from the tendency to see mothers as determining their children's psyche, a tendency highlighted in the works of two influential psychoanalysts.

One of the most influential texts came from the German-born psychoanalyst Erik Erikson, who had worked with Anna Freud in Vienna and then moved to the United States. In his 1950 book *Childhood and Society*, Erikson argued that the establishment of a sense of basic trust in childhood was the foundation for healthy emotional development.[69] In his view, this healthy development did not depend on the amount of parental care or other environmental factors, but in Erikson's words, "on the quality of the maternal relationship."[70]

The very next year, 1951, the World Health Organization (WHO) published a report by John Bowlby revealingly entitled *Maternal Care and Mental Health*. A British psychoanalyst, Bowlby was the head of the children's department of the Tavistock Clinic in London.[71] According to Bowlby's report, "if mental development is to proceed smoothly, it would appear to be necessary for the undifferentiated psyche to be exposed during certain critical periods to the influence of the psychic organizer—the mother."[72] Backed by the authority of the WHO, Bowlby's ideas reached a large audience and had an immediate impact on research and policy.[73]

With major psychoanalysts sounding the alarm bells, those working with autistic children showed no restraint in blaming mothers, as seen in other 1951 publications by three influential authors. Louise Despert emphasized the "lack of spontaneity and emotional response in the mother" and the "robotlike mechanical" nature of her relationship with her autistic child.[74] Building on those ideas, Margaret Ribble maintained that mothers come in two varieties: the positive, good mother who loves her baby "without hesitation, without feeling of duty . . . and without a feeling of sacrifice," and the "negative mother" who does so "without warmth." In Ribble's view, "the mother of the child who develops autistic behavior is an extreme case of this negative woman, and unfortunately the infant is the first to sense her unconscious hostility."[75] Margaret Mahler, yet another influential psychoanalyst working in New York, argued in a similar vein that "autistic infantile psychosis" (Kanner's syndrome) resulted from the basic defensive attitude of infants for whom the beacon of emotional orientation in the outer world—the mother as primary love object—is nonexistent."[76] In sum, children became autistic as a defense against their bad mothers.

Kanner was not enthralled by psychoanalysis and always believed biological factors played some role in the genesis of autism, but during the fifties, two factors led him to blame mothers. One was his belief that mothers of autistic children showed a "maternal lack of genuine warmth" which led to an "impersonal, mechanized relation with their children."[77] The other was his collaboration with Leon Eisenberg, who joined the Johns Hopkins Hospital as a fellow in child psychiatry in 1952. Eisenberg knew the literature on maternal deprivation well. In their joint publications one finds a growing emphasis on the significance of maternal emotions in the child's development and specifically in the genesis of autism, supported by references to authors such as Bowlby.[78] Even then, however, Kanner and Eisenberg noted that autism had to be seen as "a total psychobiological disorder," which required "a comprehensive study of the dysfunction at each level of integration: biological, psychological, and social."[79]

In the 1950s, new studies also emphasized the significance of sensory deprivation, but many of them put the mother at the center.[80] The child's needs in terms of stimulation from the environment were often conflated with emotional contact with the mother. In a thorough review of the literature, Eisenberg and Kurt Glaser, professor of pediatrics at the University of Maryland School of Medicine, tried to separate these two aspects. They pointed out that a mother is important for two main reasons: one, she "transmits to the child emotional warmth and cultivates within him responsiveness and attachment to other human beings, and (2) she provides an endless source . . . of stimulation for intellectual growth." Despite their nuanced review of the literature, they ended up concluding that

infantile autism was "the prototype of maternal emotional deprivation without intellectual deprivation."[81]

Thus, the trend of blaming mothers continued in psychiatry and
psychology during the 1950s, with the purported consensus in one
area influencing the other. Kanner, the leading scholar on autism,
placed increased emphasis on the role of parents, though he continued to reject the notion that autism was entirely due to environmental causes and maternal care and emotions the only factor to be
considered. Yet other prominent figures argued that psychological
causation was, in fact, the whole story. Foremost among them was
Bruno Bettelheim.

BETTELHEIM'S MECHANICAL BOY

Bruno Bettelheim was born in 1903 into a middle-class, Jewish family in Vienna. After his father's death, in 1926, Bettelheim dropped
his studies of art history and commerce at the University of Vienna
in order to take charge of the family lumber business. Marriage and
unfulfilling years as a businessman followed. In 1936, he returned to
the university and took courses in aesthetics and psychology. When
Nazi Germany annexed Austria in 1938, Bettelheim was sent to the
Dachau concentration camp, and later to Buchenwald. Thanks to
the intervention of family and friends, he was released a year later
and he moved to the United States, where he took a job teaching art
at Rockford College in Illinois.[82]

Bettelheim attracted widespread attention with his 1943 article
"Individual and Mass Behavior in Extreme Situations."[83] According to Bettelheim, concentration camp prisoners reacted in different ways to the brutal treatment they received. Some inmates broke
down and behaved in ways reminiscent of schizophrenic behavior.
Others adopted childlike attitudes. Still others underwent such profound changes of personality that they ended up accepting Nazi values as their own. Bettelheim's claims about the behavior of Jewish
people in the camps became quite controversial. Regardless of the
validity of his assertions, there is no doubt that his camp experiences
affected him profoundly. Having witnessed deep personality changes

in many people, he became convinced that environmental factors powerfully shaped an individual's behavior. This belief influenced his understanding and treatment of children.

In 1944, Bettelheim was offered the directorship of the Sonia Shankman Orthogenic School, a center associated with the University of Chicago and devoted to the treatment of children with severe emotional issues. The offer was made on the basis of the impeccable academic credentials that Bettelheim presented, including psychoanalytic training in Vienna and a degree in psychology. Richard Pollak, a journalist and brother of a child treated by Bettelheim, would discover that many of these claims were fabricated. In addition, allegations of plagiarism and mistreatment of children under his care have deeply tainted Bettelheim's reputation. But these revelations came much later, most of them after Bettelheim's death in 1990. During his lifetime, Bettelheim enjoyed a successful career as a respected psychotherapist, public intellectual, and author of best-selling books for a general audience. In addition, his tragic experiences in concentration camps lent moral weight to his views about the devastating consequences of psychological anxiety.[84]

After a few years at the Orthogenic School, Bettelheim published *Love Is Not Enough: The Treatment of Emotionally Disturbed Children*, in 1950. For Bettelheim, "while the frequent admonition to 'love one's child' is well-meant, it falls short of its purpose when the parent applies it without the appropriate or genuine emotions." Later, he drilled the point home: "it is not even enough to do the right thing at the right moment, it must also be done with emotions that belong to the act."[85]

In the summer of 1955, Bettelheim applied to the Ford Foundation, the richest philanthropic organization in the world at the time, for $673,200 (the equivalent of over $6 million in 2020), to study autism and the dynamics of early personality development. He was awarded about half that amount to be used over five years. Substantial funding for his project is just one indicator of the considerable prestige enjoyed by child psychoanalysis and the rising interest in autism during this period. Bettelheim, however, had already reached his main conclusions about autism before his funding—and his research project—began in 1956.

That year, Bettelheim published a paper, "Schizophrenia as a Reaction to Extreme Situations," in the *American Journal of Orthopsychiatry*. He said his conclusions were "derived from observations made in 24-hour-a-day living" with a number of schizophrenic children at the Orthogenic School "over a period of years." In the paper and his other writings, Bettelheim used the terms childhood schizophrenia and autism interchangeably, as many others did at the time. Bettelheim did not see them as separate diagnoses, though he never clarified why he saw them as the same condition. Many other psychoanalysts at the time did not differentiate between childhood psychosis, childhood schizophrenia, and childhood autism. At the start, Bettelheim referred mainly to childhood schizophrenia; later he would more often use the term *autism*.

Bettelheim noted that psychoanalysts working on childhood schizophrenia had focused so much on mothers that studies of the mother seemed "to have taken the place of the study of the disease itself." Not only was this misguided, but, in his view, it also led to the wrong therapeutic approach. By viewing the schizophrenic child as "not much more than a negligible appendage of maternal pathology," scientific efforts to help the child were somehow expected to work "through the very person who, it is assumed, destroyed his humanity in the first place—his mother."[86]

Furthermore, Bettelheim saw the focus on the mother–infant dyad as a symptom of the current pathological situation in the modern world. For him, the perfect mother–child dyad was a myth, "the consequence of an unrealistic ideal—that of the perfect infant–mother symbiosis, where both form a completely happy psychological monad." The intense focus on this "monad" reflected the anxieties of modern society, where so many people felt lonely and isolated. In a desperate effort "to escape the isolation of man in modern society, to do away with the anomy from which we suffer in reality," people had "created the wish-fulfilling image of the perfect twosome, mother and infant."[87]

Accordingly, Bettelheim thought the literature should focus more on children, but that did not mean he was about to let mothers off the hook. Quite the contrary, as Bettelheim argued that the condition he indistinctly referred to both as childhood schizophrenia and autism was an emotional withdrawal in response to an overwhelming reality: an individual's feeling of being "totally overpowered." As support for his views, Bettelheim provided his firsthand experience in concentration camps. There, he witnessed how living in a situation of extreme powerlessness led some prisoners to exhibit behaviors that "would be tantamount to a catalogue of schizophrenic reactions." Some people developed suicidal tendencies, catatonia, went into melancholic depression, or responded with illusions and delusions. By analogy, Bettelheim concluded that "to develop childhood schizophrenia it is sufficient that the infant is convinced that his life is run by insensitive, irrational, and overwhelming powers who, moreover, have total control over his life and death."[88]

Seeing autism as the result of a child feeling "deprived of any interpersonal, need-satisfying relationship" would surely lead to suspicions about the mother. Although Bettelheim believed that the key factor in autism was the child's subjective perception, the "child's subjective feeling of living permanently in an extreme situation," the children in those situations had, presumably, developed that perception on the basis of real experiences. Much as different individuals reacted in different ways in the concentration camps, different children would have different subjective perceptions of their family situation. But, as in the camps, the inhumane and dehumanizing treatment was an objective reality. Why would a healthy child with a good mother develop subjective feelings of living in an extreme situation? So, Bettelheim did blame mothers after all, as became clear in his account of Joey, a boy he referred to as autistic at the end of his 1956 paper, and whose story Bettelheim presented in detail in a 1959 paper published in *Scientific American*.[89]

Nine-year-old Joey represented himself as a machine in his drawings. He also behaved as if he were attached to a concoction of light bulbs and radio tubes that were his life support system, which he adjusted in different ways to breathe, eat, and excrete. At night, he connected imaginary wires to his body in order to digest his food and be kept alive while he slept. "How had Joey become a human machine?" asked Bettelheim.

Joey retreated into autism because his existence "never registered with his mother," Bettelheim claimed. From "intensive interviews" with the parents, Bettelheim concluded that Joey had "been completely ignored." He quoted Joey's mother as saying that she was indifferent to her child. She left Joey, a colicky baby, in the crib or playpen during the day. He was fed on a strict schedule and toilet-trained with rigidity. After a year and a half, Joey became "remote and inaccessible." As Bettelheim saw it, "Joey had created these machines to run his body and mind because it was too painful to be human." Joey, whom he identified as an example of classic infantile autism, had chosen to behave like a machine because his mother had not acknowledged his existence as a human being.[90]

Relying on widely accepted psychoanalytic ideas about child development, Bettelheim argued that in order to feel loved and worthy, a child needed care that was given with pleasure. Echoing Erik Erikson's views about how a child develops a sense of trust, Bettelheim said that the child felt the mother's pleasure, and this led to the child's ability to trust. Out of that trust, the child then learned to form close and stable relationships.[91] Joey, though, had none of that. Having never experienced nurturing maternal care given unconditionally and with pleasure, the young boy retreated into a world of machines.

Bettelheim added that autism resulted from the mechanization of social relations in the modern world. As he put it: "It is unlikely that Joey's calamity could befall a child in any time and culture but our own. He suffered no physical deprivation; he was starved for human contact." Joey's story was thus not an isolated one, but one that spoke to the maladies of his time and place: "His story has a general relevance to the understanding of emotional development in a machine age."[92] With this grand pronouncement, Bettelheim had diagnosed not only Joey, but also modern society, whose focus on machines and technological development created a dehumanized atmosphere in which even a mother could treat her own child as an object.

A master storyteller, Bettelheim finished his piece with a happy ending: Joey escaped from his prison. At age twelve, he made a float for the Memorial Day parade featuring the slogan "Feelings are more important than anything under the sun." Bettelheim thus concluded this dystopian tale with a note about his own remarkable therapeutic powers and a moral: "Feelings, Joey had learned, are what make for humanity; their absence, for a mechanical existence. With this knowledge Joey entered the human condition."[93]

In this way, Bettelheim turned the mechanical boy into a metaphor for a mid-twentieth-century fear of mechanization and dehumanization. As Susan Sontag has shown in her powerful analysis of illness as metaphor, diseases whose causation is not well understood are likely to be turned into "metaphors for what is felt to be socially or morally wrong."[94] In "Joey: A 'Mechanical Boy,'" Bettelheim used the story of an autistic boy to convey a powerful moral: a child cannot become fully human without mother love.

The conception of childhood autism that developed from the 1930s to the 1960s framed the condition as a mental illness. Though many of the pediatricians and psychiatrists who worked with autistic children noticed their capability for personal growth, the conflation with childhood schizophrenia emphasized the need for finding the causes of the condition in order to provide a cure. Within this medical model, autistic behaviors were seen as pathological. Influenced by numerous studies about the essential role of maternal love for a child's psychological development, the focus on finding the cause of the pathology led not only to seeing autistic children as ill but to pathologizing their mothers as well.

In the United States, infantile autism, which had been virtually ignored outside insular academic communities until the early 1950s, began to attract significant public and scientific interest, just when social worries about maternal deprivation peaked and writings by Kanner and Bettelheim presented mothers as the culprits. The rise of child psychoanalysis, widespread concerns about working mothers, and pervasive mother blame went hand in hand as the decade unfolded. The confluence of those factors encouraged the view that dire consequences occurred when women, especially those with intellectual aspirations or professional ambitions, failed to provide a nurturing and loving environment for their infants.

Infantile autism became known as a condition of the emotions caused fully or at least partially by the lack of maternal affection. Entering the 1960s, any mother of an autistic child would need to contend with a pretrial verdict: guilty until proven innocent.

CHAPTER 3

ON TRIAL

I N THE SUMMER of 1961, Jessy was three years old. She played often with her siblings and her mother. In the winter, Katy, Rachel, and Paul took Jessy sledding on the low sloping hills near their house. Jessy did not speak, and she wasn't toilet trained. Dr. Gellis, her pediatrician, could not find any physical problems that explained her developmental delays. He thought she engaged in autistic behaviors, but was not a "typical" autistic child. Thus, on November 30, 1961, he wrote to Clara: "I think it will be best to have Jessie [sic] seen by a Psychiatrist."[1] The Parks followed his advice.

By the end of the 1950s child psychoanalysts and many child psychiatrists working on autism had reached a consensus: mothers played a key role in causing, eliciting, or exacerbating their children's autism. And yet, as Leo Kanner noted, there were exceptions. When Clara took her daughter to the experts, would they give her the benefit of the doubt?

Clara and David took Jessy to the James Jackson Putnam Children's Center in Roxbury, Massachusetts, in early 1962 for an examination. There, they diagnosed her as an atypical child, the center's way of characterizing autistic children.

Dr. Marian Cabot Putnam and Beata Rank had founded the James Jackson Putnam Children's Center in 1946. Active clinicians with connections to the American and European psychoanalytic communities, they turned it into a well-known center for child psychotherapy in the United States.

Marian Putnam belonged to Boston's elite, the powerful and influential social network based on intermarriages between old colonial upper-class families. She named the center after her father, James Jackson Putnam—a pioneer American neurologist, founder of the American Psychoanalytic Association, and Sigmund Freud's host on his first and only visit to the United States in 1909. Unlike others attracted to Freud's theories, James Putnam focused on Freud's contribution to treatment and therapies.

Marian Putnam shared her father's interest in psychoanalysis with a therapeutic bent and had worked with children at leading institutions. She was part of the second wave of women medical doctors in the US, having received an MD from Johns Hopkins University School of Medicine in 1921, four years after graduating from Radcliffe College. She then worked at Children's Hospital in Boston from 1923 to 1925 and another two years at the Henry Phipps Psychiatric Clinic at Johns Hopkins. Subsequently, she became a research associate at Yale's Clinic of Child Development and assistant professor at the Yale School of Medicine. She also trained in psychoanalysis in Vienna. In 1940 she joined the Judge Baker Guidance Center, a Boston clinic for the psychiatric treatment of children, where she opened a small unit for infants and preschool children in 1943.[2] Three years later, this unit became independent and Marian Putnam changed its name in honor of her father.

Her codirector, Beata Rank, was a Polish émigrée who had been introduced to psychoanalytic circles when she married Austrian psychoanalyst Otto Rank, one of Freud's major disciples, in 1918. Beata Rank did not have formal psychoanalytic training, but she had translated Freud's *The Interpretation of Dreams* into Polish. In 1923, she was admitted into the Vienna Psychoanalytic Society with a talk on the role of women in the evolution of human society, and became one of the first lay analysts (an analyst without a medical degree). Sigmund Freud considered her like a daughter. But jealous rivalries among Freud's star students and Freud's own zeal to maintain the purity of psychoanalysis threatened their relationship when her husband, Otto, defied some of the master's views in his 1929 book *The Trauma of Birth*. Years later Beata divorced Otto. She moved to Boston because of her friendship with Polish psychoanalyst Helene Deutsch, a doyenne of female psychoanalysis who had established a professional practice there. Deutsch introduced her to Marian Putnam, whom she had analyzed earlier in Vienna.[3]

The Putnam Center admitted children with various emotional difficulties, including many autistic children, usually referred to as "children with atypical development." By using this diagnostic concept, they did not commit themselves to the views of the researchers who used the diagnosis of "autism." Beata Rank's influential 1949 paper described atypical children as displaying lack of contact with reality, no need for communication with others, and repetitive behavior. Their play was repetitious and compulsive. It often included rocking, swinging, and spinning. Rank also noted that these children often had a special talent for music, acrobatics, or a great skill in another area.[4]

For Putnam and Rank atypical children had suffered "emotional deprivation" as a result of the "emotional climate" created by their mothers.[5] Rank divided the mothers of children with atypical development into two groups: psychotic (manic-depressive and schizophrenics) on one side, and emotionally immature on the other.[6] The second group was predominant. Rank claimed that these mothers could give "the impression of being well-adjusted" and "not too rarely" they were "highly intellectual," but the majority were narcissistic and fit a particular type.

According to Rank, emotionally immature mothers had "a very definite picture of what a good mother should be." They saw motherhood as a path to experiencing true emotions. But "barren of spontaneous manifestation of maternal feelings," they had to study methods of childrearing. Using those methods they created "an orderly, scientific atmosphere where routine and dietary prescriptions" prevailed. As a result, their children missed out on "the sunshine" that a "spontaneous, tenderly devoted mother" radiated. For Rank, this type of mother was simply "a fraud."[7]

"The child becomes the real victim," Rank wrote. In her view, the child of such a fraudulent mother could only survive by withdrawing, "not only from the dangerous mother but from the whole world as well." That explained why the most significant characteristic of atypical children was that they were "out of contact with reality and apparently without need for communication with others."[8] These children retreated from the world—or rather, were forced to retreat by their mothers.

By the early 1960s, Putnam and Rank were still listed among the center's psychoanalysts, but the center had a new director: David E. Reiser, recently arrived from the Utah Child Guidance Center. Reiser calculated that the center had diagnosed 240 of the 2,800 children of pre-school age they had seen between 1943 and 1963 as having "atypical development." He replaced that term with "infantile psychosis," which, he wrote, referred to what Kanner had named "infantile autism."[9]

Like his predecessors at the center, Reiser also saw the "emotional climate" of the infant as determinant for a child's adequate psychological development.[10] And, like them, he saw the parents, especially the mother, as playing a key role in that climate. In his papers, he often cited the recent work of John Bowlby, René Spitz, and other psychoanalysts who had argued that deprivation of warm maternal care and love had grave consequences for a child's mind. Therefore, under Reiser, the center's therapeutic efforts to restore a good emotional climate included close work with a child's mother, just as it did earlier.

Clara and David brought Jessy to the Putnam Center in January of 1962. Clara took her notebooks about Jessy's behavior with her, thinking the doctors would find them useful. Phillip H. Gates, a child analyst, welcomed the Parks. Gates also used the term childhood psychosis to refer to the "atypical development" of children that others called autistic. His views relied extensively on Putnam and Rank. He had good knowledge of this area. Only a couple of years earlier he had presented his views on a panel at a 1960 international scientific conference in Portland, Oregon, alongside leading figures, including Lauretta Bender and Hans Asperger.[11]

At the time, diagnostic evaluations included a couple of individual play sessions with a psychiatrist, a couple of nursery school sessions, psychological and neurological tests, and interviews with the parents. The center's team then discussed their opinions in a staff conference.[12]

Jessy was evaluated with the center's standard procedures. She was given an intelligence test, and was also seen by a neurologist and observed in a nursery school setting. Dr. Gates saw Jessy three times, during which "she progressed from almost complete withdrawal to a grave acceptance of lollypops and bits of clay at his hands," in her mother's account. Clara found his approach passive, but not ineffective, since, at the end of the third session, Jessy allowed Dr. Gates to carry her. Nevertheless, Clara lamented that his meetings with Jessy did not include playful interactions with her parents. Thus Dr. Gates did not see Jessy "smile or be gay" as she often was at home.[13]

During their interviews, Clara felt that she and David were "on trial."[14] To begin with, she was unhappily surprised that her husband met with the doctor while she was interviewed by a social worker. Dr. Gates met with David; the chief social worker, Mildred McCarthy, met with Clara. In addition, she found the meetings rather unfriendly. In a letter to friends, Clara described the interviews as "steady, virtually unguided talking to an almost totally passive listener, studiously careful to betray no reaction and volunteer no comment beyond an occasional question."[15] Neither Gates nor McCarthy gave them any explanation or indication of their thoughts.

About six weeks later, on March 20, David and Clara returned for a joint meeting with Dr. Gates and Ms. McCarthy. Jessy needed psychotherapy because she had "many fears," they were told. Despite their efforts to obtain more information or advice, the Parks went home empty-handed. Dr. Gates mentioned that Jessy "would obviously be a case for the Center."[16] However, the family was planning to go soon to England, where David would spend a year on research leave from his university. So Gates recommended taking Jessy to Anna Freud's Hampstead Clinic in London.

For Clara, the whole affair at the Putnam Center "was Kafka's Castle from beginning to end," a confusing encounter with the alleged experts in children's psychological development. She was deeply disappointed that they had seen only a very partial view of Jessy, as their tests put her in new situations where she naturally did not behave as she did at home. The center's diagnostic tools were clearly insufficient to get a full picture of Jessy. Given the restricted environment of their testing sites, a child like Jessy, who mainly expressed herself with her immediate family, would not show her more social side. They could have complemented their clinical observations with Clara's extensive notes about Jessy's behavior. Clara had expected to share these notes, but the center did not use them.

Thus, she was also discouraged by the way they treated her. Clara had developed different games to playfully engage Jessy and she had documented thoroughly her development in several areas. However, the center did not use Clara's notes because, as director Reiser wrote in one of his publications, "the parents' recollection of events of the first two years in the life of the psychotic infant is usually subjectively charged."[17] For these professionals who defended the objectivity of their own beliefs, it seemed that the parents could only contribute subjective opinions.

Although they did not tell the Parks during their visit, there was another reason why the center did not welcome Clara's notes. In their view, they provided evidence for Clara's "intellectual" approach to motherhood. Therefore, in the eyes of the Putnam staff, Clara was to blame for Jessy's condition. Not that they had clinically evaluated Clara. But that conclusion was unavoidable once they diagnosed Jessy with atypical development. Beata Rank had written, "The tenuous relationship with an emotionally disturbed mother we recognize as the chief source of this condition."[18] Jessy's diagnosis was all the evidence they needed to see Clara as a disturbed mother. Clara was never directly blamed at the Putnam Center, but she had read some of the publications by Putnam and Rank; she knew their views. She had read a couple of articles by Rank, including the one containing Rank's comments on the two kinds of mothers of autistic children.

She also read William Goldfarb's *Childhood Schizophrenia*. In her notebook, she wrote that they were "each worse than the other."[19]

Still, Clara went to the Putnam Center because what mattered was not what they thought about her, but what they could offer to help her child. However, she and David felt disappointed because they had not learned anything useful for Jessy there. They concluded that the experts might not know more than they did.[20] Given their mounting anxiety about Jessy, this thought was truly worrisome.

Clara did not hide her dismay with these professionals. She wrote to Dr. Gellis about it. Responding to her concerns, Dr. Gellis wrote: "You expected too much; you want an exact science, and psychiatry has a long way to go before it can deserve the name of a science."[21]

Exact science or not, these doctors used their professional authority to make a diagnosis, one that carried a label for Jessy and a condemnation of her mother. Clara had turned to the experts on children's minds for knowledge and support. She got neither.

Back home, Clara did not waver in her commitment to Jessy's development and soon saw some changes. Upon her return from the Putnam clinic in February 1962, Clara started a second notebook on Jessy, writing about her daily progress with excitement. Three and a half years old now, Jessy didn't use many words, usually only one or two. The words she used came and went. Jessy would utter a new word one day, but never again. She did not imitate, which was very unusual. Most children start to imitate earlier, and learn many skills imitating others. To engage her child, Clara tried a game involving a reciprocal approach to imitation. *She* started imitating Jessy. Clara imitated the sounds Jessy made. After a while, Jessy also started imitating the sounds Clara produced. Clara then dared "risking it all" by trying a word. She said "eye," which Jessy had once said but had not used since the previous summer. Success! Jessy repeated it "all very gay and amused."[22]

Jessy also engaged more by playing with a doll, pretending to drink from a cup or eat lunch with the doll. One day, Jessy faced the doll and embraced it, "putting her lips to its head & hugging it." Her mother noted: "Just as she now occasionally does with us."[23]

While Clara and Jessy played new games, Clara also began taking more precise and detailed notes. She recorded the number of
words Jessy used at any given time. She made lists of the sentences
Jessy used and whether she thought she had used them to communicate with others. She wrote about how Jessy learned skills such
as turning on a faucet or climbing the stairs, later abandoned them,
and then regained them once more. Why, she could not tell. On
March 29, 1962, when Jessy was three years and eight months old,
Clara recorded that before having a bath, Jessy now would take off
her pants, socks, and shoes by herself.

Clara continued with her daily routines as best she could, but
managing her job and home became overwhelming. In April, she
wrote to her mother that she really needed some rest. She was
teaching a literature class for sophomores at Berkshire Community
College, and she still had to cover Dostoevsky's *The Brothers Kara-
mazov*, Joyce's *Portrait of the Artist as a Young Man*, and modern
poetry. Her father had recently sent her and David several letters,
trying to influence their son Paul's education, but Clara emphasized
that she did not want to become involved again with her father's
desires. She kept herself "deliberately" distant as she did not "dare
dissipate any of the strength" she needed for Jessy.[24]

Exhausted but undeterred, Clara continued to work with Jessy.
Only a few months later, in June 1962, she wrote two single-spaced
pages describing how Jessy was doing. She noted that her daughter
continued "to be gay and happy," and now played "with a wider
range of children." She also wrote on Jessy's behavior: she was good
at playing with puzzles, enjoyed tickling and hide-and-seek games,
and mostly ignored dolls and similar toys after quickly mastering
them. Step by step, she had learned to operate faucets and light
switches. Jessy loved when her mother cut up old magazines into
strips, yet she was not interested in learning to use the scissors.

For Clara, it was as if Jessy did not want to do some things,
though she was sure Jessy knew how to do them. In general, Jessy
lost interest in many activities quickly. Venturing an explanation,
Clara remarked that Jessy behaved "as if she were too intelligent

to stay interested in so sterile an occupation (so simple a toy, so easy a puzzle), yet is wholly cut off from what effort of emotion or imagination is necessary to do something more interesting."[25] Clara wondered: Was Jessy's behavior due to lack of interest? To inability? To unwillingness? She did not know.

During the summer of 1962, the Parks planned for their year in England and Jessy's visit to the Hampstead Clinic. In June, Dr. Gellis wrote to Anna Freud asking if she would see one of his patients. He noted: "Jessica is four years old and in many ways appears to have autistic behavior." He added that no test had shown brain injury or other physical problems. On the same day, he asked Dr. Gates at the Putnam Center to send his findings and recommendations to Anna Freud.[26]

Gates's report noted Jessy's early diagnosis as "infantile autism." Gates pointed out that Clara's pregnancy was unplanned, and Clara had described the delivery as an unhappy and painful experience. He added that the Parks taught college courses, and that the mother wrote "an occasional weekly column for the Pittsfield newspaper on the subject of Child Development and Child Rearing." Actually, this was incorrect, as Clara had written on children's issues only on a few occasions. Further, Gates reported that both parents "had clearly read considerably on the subject of infantile autism, particularly the papers of Kanner and Eisenberg, leaving me with the impression that the relationship that each of them has had to this particular child has been quite a highly intellectual one, perhaps more so than to the earlier three siblings."[27] Yet, the Parks had read those papers on Gellis's recommendation.[28]

Up to this point, Clara had not received any expert advice to help Jessy, and had found the professional literature on autism of little use. The scientific literature in child psychiatry and child psychoanalysis focused on the nature and causes of children's conditions, but it rarely offered any advice on how to help the children or how to obtain services for them. In contrast, Clara found "They Said Our Child Was Hopeless," an article in the *Saturday Evening Post* by Rosalind Oppenheim, the mother of an autistic child, to be the "most helpful thing I've read, still—in fact the only helpful thing, though not a scientific study."[29] After many frustrating experiences with medical experts, Oppenheim, with the help of a supportive psychologist, had created a home training program and started teaching her son how to read, play, and communicate. Her account provided practical advice on how to do things that benefitted the children. So far, in raising Jessy, Clara's only help had come from another mother.

ANNA FREUD'S HAMPSTEAD CLINIC

By the end of the summer of 1962, the Parks were settled in England. David went there first in order to find a five-bedroom house for all of them. Clara wanted an old house, full of "unexpected cupboards and spacious Victorian wardrobes" where her children would "climb and be rapt into imaginary countries."[30] It was not to be. They moved to Girton, a village a couple of miles away from Cambridge, and had to make do with an ordinary house with no central heating to assuage the cold, wet English winter ahead of them. But Clara was happy that, thanks to her thriftiness, she had saved $2,500, which was enough money to bring along Jill Hays, a Williamstown student who had accepted a part-time job taking care of Jessy after she finished high school the previous year.[31]

At first, life in England was challenging for all of them. Jill, a young woman who had never lived away from home before, required guidance and support. At this time, Katy was twelve years old, Rachel was nearly eleven, and Paul was about to turn eight. They felt excited about exploring a new place. They all did very well academically but found it difficult to make new friends. Paul was bullied in school. However, he did not tell his parents because he did not want to add to their burden.[32]

Katy, Rachel, and Paul did not think much about what was going on, but they grew up feeling that they should not draw attention to their own wants or problems. As Katy recalls it now, "the household was very focused on Jessy's needs because they were urgent." Until Jessy arrived in their lives, the Parks had prided themselves on being sensible. No shouting. No scenes. No arguments. None of their children remember them ever fighting. But when Jessy got older, Clara felt overwhelmed sometimes. Jessy threw huge tantrums for no discernable reason. One day, still in Williamstown, she had a terrible outburst. Unable to soothe her, Clara herself burst into tears. David went into the living room to hold Jessy. Katy, about eleven years old at the time, watched the scene too scared to move.[33] Such situations were difficult for them. In general, though, the kids got along well. Jessy was not too interested in other children, but she was always happy to play with her siblings, who spent much time with her.

Jessy was four years old when they went to England and, like most autistic children, she found changes difficult. Some she did not notice. Others threw her into tantrums and even provoked regression in her growth. Clara focused on keeping her routines constant and having her favorite foods available. A few new foods became a problem, particularly the fizzy apple juice. A week after their arrival Jessy became quite sick; she vomited everything she took in. She refused most unfamiliar foods, quickly going "on strike against all the strange English food" and for a few days subsisted mostly on candy. Then, it was "dozens of eggs," a food she had not eaten for two years. Eventually, she started eating regularly again. Later, researchers would learn that many autistic children have gut or digestive difficulties that have a biological origin. At the time, though, Clara did not know what to make of Jessy's desire to eat only very specific foods.

Other aspects of Jessy's behavior also changed. She stopped rocking her crib. Back at home, her rocking was so strong that David had to nail the cot to the floor.[34] She lost interest in leaving the house and walking around the neighborhood. In Williamstown, she had enjoyed going outside alone or with her siblings and sometimes playing with some of the children who lived nearby.[35]

David was distant from domestic affairs because he immersed himself in physics research at Trinity College at the University of Cambridge. One of the oldest universities in the world and the former home of eminent scholars such as Isaac Newton and Charles Darwin whose brilliant insights about the nature of the universe and life changed the course of humanity, Cambridge remained one of the leading research and teaching institutions. For David, his time there was an intellectual treat.

For Clara, the adjustments to new surroundings were hard. Routines can be boring, but they also enable people to function with some efficiency and comfort. Away from home, everything took more time: from finding her way to the post office to organizing activities for the children. For a mother increasingly anxious about her little daughter and struggling to find a few hours for her own work, the situation could be overwhelming. And it was.

Clara slid into a depression. She spent much time in bed.[36] The whole affair at the Putnam Center had affected her more than she was willing to acknowledge. The trans-Atlantic trip added physical stress. Jessy's difficulties were also hard on her. Jill, David, and Jessy's siblings played with her often and helped with her care. But Clara felt the weight of maternal responsibility.

At least Clara had high hopes about Anna Freud. She had expected too much from psychiatry, Dr. Gellis had told her. But on a more hopeful note, he had added: "Anna Freud is DIFFERENT." Could she really expect the dutiful daughter of Sigmund Freud to be different from the other psychoanalysts she had encountered?

Born in Vienna in 1895, Anna Freud was the last child of Sigmund and Martha. Her mother, who had already borne five children in eight years, had not welcomed the pregnancy and never felt close to her. Anna was an unhappy child. Some biographers see in that experience the source of her empathy toward children.[37] But none has explained how, if a good relationship with the mother is essential for a child's adequate emotional development (as many psychoanalysts claimed at this time), Anna could have turned into a sensible adult capable of deep and lasting emotional relationships. Yet she did turn into one.

Starting during her adolescent years, Anna was a great help to her father, a role that intensified over time. She trained to be a schoolteacher and worked in several nurseries. Her father analyzed her, though he discouraged his followers from analyzing their family members. He also supported her membership as a lay analyst in the

Vienna Psychoanalytic Society. Involved in children's education and welfare projects, Anna Freud's work was interrupted when German Nazi troops annexed Austria in March of 1938. Being Jewish, the Freud family fled to England. Shortly after settling in London, Sigmund Freud died of jaw cancer. Although her father's death was a great intellectual and personal loss, impending war left her little time for mourning. Anna quickly put her previous experience in children's nurseries in Vienna to good use.

In 1941, with funding from the American Foster Parents' Plan for War Children, Anna helped to establish the Hampstead War Nurseries to care for children who had become homeless or whose families could not properly care for them during the war. One building in the London neighborhood of Hampstead housed children under three years of age. It was near a subway station, so mothers could visit their children easily. The other house for older children was in a rural area about sixty miles from London. All the children were moved to the country house when Nazi bombing became indiscriminate in the city. Six conscientious objectors and a group of mostly untrained young women took care of about one hundred infants. Led by Anna Freud, the nursery staff gathered in the common room to discuss their work, "sometimes against a background of distant anti-aircraft gunfire."[38]

The staff noticed that children became less afraid of the air raids when they were away from their anxious parents, but the separation affected them profoundly. Disconcerted by the changes in their lives, and often not knowing when they would return home or see their families again, the children became aggressive, withdrawn, and experienced developmental delays and regression. The negative effects were greatly diminished if the move to the nursery was done in stages because it allowed the children to adapt gradually. The separation became more traumatic for those kids who had to be removed abruptly from their homes and for the younger children between one and two years old.

Take the case of two-year-old Bobby. When he was admitted because his mother had become pregnant and could no longer take care of him properly, he "looked the picture of health," was a good sleeper and eater, and had completed his toilet training. When his mother's visits became less frequent, Bobby became aggressive, sucked on his fingers and wet his bed at night. After his mother stopped visiting and a nurse who was taking care of him left the nursery, Bobby nearly stopped talking and started soiling himself. He soon "gave the impression of a baby."[39]

Anna Freud concluded that the nurseries were fulfilling the physical needs of the children, but not their emotional ones. Here, it is important to be clear about what her work at the nurseries showed. Often, these results are presented as evidence to argue that maternal love is essential for a child's adequate emotional development. However, the young children who had been taken away from their homes to live in a strange place with strange people while bombs fell all around them had lost much more than their mothers. They had also been deprived of their fathers, siblings, other family members, friends, teachers as well as their routines in their homes and schools. Often, they had to move without even minimal preparation for the deep changes in their lives. Thus, not all the difficulties these children experienced later could be attributed to lack of mother's love.

Anna Freud's views about the significance of mothers for young children's psychological development evolved over time. In some of her early publications she emphasized that the infant's relationship with the mother provided the basis for the child's "ability to love." She also used the common metaphor of maternal love as a nutrient for a child's psyche.[40] However, in the 1950s, she began to caution against the idea that the child's healthy psychological development depended exclusively on the mother. She criticized John Bowlby's position that any separation from mother had devastating effects. She further warned specialists to "guard against the error of confusing the inevitably frustrating aspects of extrauterine life with the rejecting actions or attitudes of the individual mothers."[41] In other words: once you leave your mother's womb, life will be frustrating. But not all frustrations you experience will be your mother's fault.

Worried about the increasing trend of blaming mothers, especially those of autistic children, Anna Freud continued to call for caution in her teaching and writings. The Hampstead Nurseries were closed

at the end of World War II, but in 1952 she opened the Hampstead
Child-Therapy Course and Clinic, which combined treating children
with training and research in child psychotherapy. In the clinic's seminars, she emphasized that whether a mother was responsible for
her child's condition should be a matter for research and careful discrimination, not a presumption. She urged analysts "not to confuse
the effect of a child's abnormality on the mother with the mother's
pathogenic influence on the child," a confusion that happened "easily, especially with autistic children."[42] That is, a mother's emotional
problems could be caused by her child's difficulties, not the other way
around. A mother should be considered innocent until proven guilty.

Though the Hampstead Clinic appeared to be a carbon copy of
the Putnam, Clara noticed a dramatic contrast in the way they were
treated. The Parks visited the clinic twice, with Jessy on September
12, 1962, and a week later alone. The clinics were similar physically,
in the makeup of the examining team (psychiatrist, testing psychologist, and social worker), and in their theoretical approach. However,
here, the staff appeared warm and sensitive.

On their first visit, Doris Wills gave Jessy a Vineland Test, which
was used to measure a child's behavior in daily situations, social
skills, and communication ability. Wills, a psychologist with extensive experience with children, had been hired as the first testing
psychologist when the center opened a decade earlier, just after she
took the Hampstead course in child psychotherapy.[43] Respected for
her work and liked for her cheerful disposition, she was a leading
member of the Hampstead group devoted to studying and helping
blind children with emotional issues. Clara accompanied Jessy to
her testing and appreciated Ms. Wills's good humor and friendliness.

In order to understand Jessy's behavior, the staff also conducted
interviews with the Parks and Jessy. During their first visit, Dr. John
Bolland, a psychiatrist and one of the center's medical directors, saw
Clara and Jessy together, then David and Jessy together, and finally
Jessy alone. Thus, he saw Jessy singing tunes, absorbed in her own
play when she was alone with him but also engaged in little games
with her parents. Jessy and Clara made cakes together with clay. David and Jessy joyfully stacked little pieces of clay onto each other's

faces. Both parents talked about Jessy's behavior. David noted that Jessy did not seem to notice other people, only members of her own family. Clara and David expressed their worry about Jessy's lack of engagement with people, either through language, gestures, or actions. Bolland interviewed David alone a week later. "Miss Ini," as she was referred to at the center, interviewed David and Clara separately. Sylvia Ini had worked during a brief period at the Hampstead Nurseries during the war. In March of 1961 she joined the Hampstead Clinic as senior social worker. She was also a member of the center's Group for the Study of Borderline Cases.[44] The Parks never saw the reports Bolland and Ini wrote, but copies survived and offer a detailed account of their visit.

Though she did not meet with Jessy, Ini's report included the most complete description of Jessy's history and behavior at the time. Clara told her that Jessy had made much progress since they visited the Putnam clinic eight months earlier, but in many areas she lagged behind the typical developmental milestones expected of children at the time. For example, Jessy, who was now four years and two months old, had employed about thirty words in her whole life, and had not pronounced many of them in the last year. She regularly used about ten words; some days she did not utter more than one. As far as they could tell, Jessy did not use words to communicate. Another unusual thing was that Jessy had not imitated until very recently. Clara offered to share her diaries on Jessy as well as notes she had taken about her other children. To her delight, Ini was happy to review them to get a fuller picture.

The staff's kindness softened their gloomy news about Jessy's diagnosis and prognosis. David pressed Bolland for a diagnosis, though the doctor hesitated to commit before the center could have a staff conference including Anna Freud, who was away on a trip. Overcoming his reluctance, he said the diagnosis was "psychosis." The prognosis was pessimistic, Bolland told David, because so little was known about children like Jessy.

The use of many different terms for autistic children was confusing for parents. Jessy's pediatrician in Boston said Jessy engaged in autistic behavior, though he did not think she was a "typical" autistic child. The Putnam clinic did not give the Parks a diagnosis, but they thought she showed "atypical development," which for them was equivalent to Kanner's infantile autism. They also referred to it as "childhood psychosis." Now, the Hampstead team considered Jessy to be psychotic. Though they were reluctant to use the term *autism* as an official diagnostic category, they used it in their internal communications, and they included autistic children within the category of psychosis. For the Parks, as for many other parents, the lack of clear terminology was not only frustrating, but also led them to wonder if the medical experts really knew much about their children. Bolland admitted they did not.

The clinic appreciated Clara's previous work with Jessy and saw her as a partner in moving forward. Bolland told David that the clinic could tentatively think of working with Clara "in Jessie's [sic] management." In his report, Bolland wrote that David seemed pleased with the idea because he had been very annoyed that the Putnam clinic "had never given a word of encouragement to his wife, despite the enormous efforts she had put into looking after Jessie." Ini also reassured Clara that the best strategy would be to figure out with her "what methods seemed to work with Jessie." Clara felt elated to be seen as a partner. "At this point," the report reads, Clara "broke down . . . saying 'you don't know how I needed that' and spoke of her relief that she might be of some use and of her feelings of guilt that Jessie should be like this."

To Clara's surprise, they also prescribed therapy several times per week, for *her*. However, if Clara had seen Bolland's and Ini's reports, she would have understood the reasons for that prescription.

After his first meeting with Jessy and Clara, Bolland concluded that Clara's attitude towards Jessy was not that of a warm mother but "rather like that of a good, patient and fond teacher." Bolland reported that "Mrs. Park dominated the whole interview with her intense wish to demonstrate Jessie's accomplishments to me." Clara had brought a set of Jessy's drawings, "neatly dated and with descriptions on them." These were mostly simple shapes that Clara had been teaching Jessie. Bolland noted: "I got the impression from Mrs. Park, both from the drawings and her comments that her way of approaching Jessie is as if teaching the child is her main project in life, rather like a research project, with observations to be tabulated as clearly as possible."

On the basis of his "impression," Bolland characterized Clara as disturbed. He noted that although Clara had many pet names for her daughter, such as "pumpkin, birdie, button," she did not address her as Jessy. During the interview, Clara only used Jessy's name when talking to Bolland. He interpreted this as Clara's way of disguising "her own disturbance." Clara's note-taking—which had been encouraged by her pediatrician to help his team better understand Jessy's development—and Clara's complaints about the way the Putnam Center treated them were in Bolland's eyes sufficient proof of an underlying disorder.

In contrast, Bolland's report presented a very positive picture of David. Bolland interviewed him twice, during his first visit with Jessy and during his second one alone. He noted that David seemed pretty relaxed, as did Jessy. David said that Clara had devoted herself for years to Jessy and that the progress the child had made was largely due to her. As for his own role, he claimed to be too impatient to work with Jessy. Bolland thought David's attitude had "some of the distance implied in the 'project' attitude of Mrs. Park." Yet he concluded that "his relationship with the child was a much warmer one" than the relationship between Clara and Jessy. Bolland continued: "He confirmed the earlier impression he had made on me, viz., that he is an intelligent, warm person who has somehow managed to combine sympathy for Jessie and his wife with a certain degree of non-involvement." Thus, as this doctor saw it, David's lack of involvement made him "a good reporter and able to speak of future possibilities in a considered way."

Ini's ten-page single-spaced report also portrayed Clara and David very differently. Ini found David to be "a pleasant person, easy to interview and with a sense of humour." She also remarked that discussion of Jessy's condition "came over vividly and, in mother's case, with at times uncontrolled emotion." Perhaps that uncontrolled emotion colored Ini's perception of Clara, which was rather unflattering. Ini started her report by describing Clara's appearance:

"Mrs. Park is fairly tall, thin with thick spectacles, rather protruding eyes, a dry skin and some facial dermatitis; though tidily dressed and groomed, she does not seem the kind of person who would spend much time on her appearance." Then, she characterized Clara as "an anxious and disturbed person who spent most of this short interview talking about her negative reactions to the Putnam Center." Though the report did not provide any evidence that could be used to support this view, after meeting Clara twice, the first time for "about 10 minutes," Ini concluded that she was disturbed.

At the end, Clara and David never met Anna Freud, but their visit to her clinic helped them in many ways. Since Clara had not seen their reports, she found her reception at the Hampstead cordial and was delighted that they thought her work with Jessy was helping her. Though they found Clara to be "disturbed," neither Bolland nor Ini suggested that her disturbance caused Jessy's autism. Clara was willing to give their recommendations a try.

FROM PREJUDICE TO PRIDE

Since the Parks were not living in London, it would have been difficult for them to take Jessy to the Hampstead Clinic for regular therapy sessions. Therefore, on the clinic's advice, Clara started working with a child analyst who had trained and worked at the Hampstead and now lived in Cambridge: Marie Battle Singer.

One of the few psychotherapists in Cambridge at the time, Singer was also one of the few African Americans working in the profession in the United Kingdom. Born in 1910 in Mississippi, Marie Battle did her undergraduate studies at Boston University and obtained a master's in social work from Smith College. In 1948, she went to Germany, where she worked for a relief organization assisting people displaced by the war. After moving to England, she joined the child therapy course at Hampstead in 1950, and qualified as a psychoanalytic therapist four years later. She also received a PhD in psychology from the University of London.[45]

At the Hampstead Clinic, Marie Battle Singer was well regarded personally and professionally. Through their shared love for painting, she had become a friend of Dorothy Burlingham, Anna Freud's lifelong companion and collaborator. Singer was a member of the Group for the Study of Borderline Cases, of which Sylvia Ini was also part. For them, "borderline" referred to patients on the border between neurosis and psychosis. In 1960, Singer published "Fantasies of a Borderline Patient," an account of Albert, whom she first saw when he was ten years old. He had been referred to the clinic because of his dangerous habit of walking along the tracks in the Underground tunnels, and Singer treated him for almost eight years.[46]

During her time in London, Marie Battle found someone who not only shared her wide-ranging interests but also the experience of suffering racial prejudice. In the early 1950s, psychoanalyst Karin Stephen—who was married to Virginia Woolf's brother Adrian—invited Marie to live in their house, which was usually full of patients and lodgers.[47] Through Stephen, Marie met James Burns Singer, a Jewish marine biologist, poet, and literary critic. Marie, herself a scientist, painter, and writer, found a soul mate in Singer. They also shared a sense of humor in confronting life's adversities. Sometimes she teased her husband, saying: "I won't tell anyone you are Jewish if you don't tell anyone I am black."[48] After their wedding, the Singers moved to Cambridge in 1959.

Singer became a respected analyst and lecturer. She taught a course on psychoanalysis to psychology undergraduates at the University of Cambridge and wrote well-received articles for newspapers. Described as vivacious and charismatic, her friend David Astor, a British publisher, wrote of her: "She trusted her own intuition and had a capacity to express herself that resembled someone belonging to the arts rather than to science. She was also splendidly downright in her opinions and would call a pretentious humbug just that if she felt the need."[49]

In Singer, Clara found not only a therapist but also a friend. A straight talker was just the kind of person Clara liked and needed. She told her friend Emily, "I enormously prefer the kind candour here to the cryptic evasion at Putnam." She also found Singer "fascinating & intelligent."[50] Although it was not advisable for analyst and patient to become friends, Clara noted that they "had too much in common" and "could not inhibit" their friendship. Like Clara, Singer combined roots in the deep American South with a New England education. They were both left-leaning politically. They shared a passion for the arts and science. Singer also had close ties to the academic world, teaching and eventually becoming a fellow of Clare Hall at Cambridge.[51]

Singer and Clara were also women who had met prejudice with pride. Clara did not share Singer's experiences of racial discrimination, but the Putnam episode, still so fresh in her mind, predisposed her to empathize with someone who had suffered from entrenched biases. As she would later describe this experience: "We know now in our skins that the most threatening of all attacks is the attack on the sense of personal worth, that the harshest of all deprivations is the deprivation of respect."[52]

The start of their relationship had been rocky, however. Following the psychoanalytic approach, which often posited that a mother's own disorder caused or exacerbated her child's condition, Singer first focused on treating Clara. Thus, Clara went to therapy sessions with Singer three times a week, "stirring up a good deal of mud." Singer encouraged Clara to find time for herself and to feel talented and heroic. It was flattering. But Clara believed that this approach only led to self-absorption or self-pity. She had no use for either. She thought the sessions were eating up precious time that she needed for Jessy.[53] She enjoyed meeting Singer as a friend, but soon Clara began to feel unhappy.

Luckily, Singer was a pragmatist like Clara and, recognizing the importance of practice over theory, she shifted the focus from Clara to Jessy. Singer now visited Jessy at home and guided Clara in her work with her daughter. As Clara told her friend Emily at the end of 1962, Singer conveyed what she needed to know, "guiding, supporting, recommending, teaching me, in fact, to be a better version of what I have been for 2 ½ years, Jessie's psychotherapist."[54] Singer helped Clara to stop feeling "unappreciated (because nobody but her had ever said such fine things about what I was doing, or indeed many fine things at all)."[55] Besides boosting Clara's confidence, she also taught her much about how to engage with Jessy.

Singer taught by modeling. She had tea parties with Jessy, where she encouraged her to play with little cups and saucers. She played the piano for Jessy. She went on the floor with Jessy to paint, making simple drawings like her, so she would feel comfortable.[56] Clara learned a lot from Singer's creative ways of interacting with Jessy in a manner that Jessy found enjoyable.

Looking at Singer as a trained and trusted advisor helped Clara overcome her distrust of psychotherapy. Singer, who was "not bullying or bossy," urged Clara to remain confident in her relationship with Jessy even when Clara's approach came in conflict with her own assessment. For Clara, there was still a bit too much psychoanalytic jargon sometimes, but she was happy because she felt free to take it or leave it. Furthermore, at the end of the day, a lot of the psychoanalytic jargon often just translated into "let Jessie play with cooking & refrigerators [go back to oral stage] & let the bathtub & potty-toys go." Clara found this "perfectly usable stuff."[57]

Clara's practical approach enabled her to separate theories from applications that could help Jessy. Eager to see what worked, Clara would try a game or suggestion proposed by Singer. If it helped Jessy, she continued using it. If not, she discarded it. While Clara did not think the analyst's aid was leading to immediate changes in Jessy's behavior, she appreciated the professional support of "a trained adviser, wise in the ways of children."[58]

Singer was the first expert with whom Clara worked as an equal, each aiding the other to understand Jessy's behavior and more importantly stimulating Jessy to grow in her own way. Singer was more pragmatic than was the norm in psychoanalytical therapy circles. "Often," she wrote, "the therapist must act before she understands." She was also much more receptive to the mother's perspective. Singer asked Clara to continue keeping notebooks with exacting accounts of specific issues. On November 14, for instance, Clara started writing an account of Jessy's napping and sleeping habits. Three days later, she began a "Report on Toilet History—for Dr. Singer." Clara and David had recently returned from an eleven-day trip to Paris. Jessy had started withholding her bowel movements, a fact that Singer interpreted as a possible protest against her parents' absence.

The notebook started with some historical information on Clara's other children, followed by details about each and every minor incident in Jessy's adventures in toilet training. A few days later, a report titled "Running Away" chronicled Jessy's walking behavior.[59]

During their time working together, Singer also asked Clara to share the materials that she used with Jessy. In April 1963, Clara sent Singer some drawings she had designed to help Jessy visualize special situations and that way make it easier for her to respond to them. Since Jessy was afraid of taking a bath, Clara had made some basic paper cut-outs of a bathtub with Jessy inside, to help her overcome her fear of bathing. This way of interacting with Jessy is similar to what today is called "social story," a narrative with pictures preparing an autistic child for a given activity so the child can get ready for it. Clara and Jessy used these materials when they played together. Clara also sent Singer other paper drawings of her, Jessy, and the rocking chair they sat in back in Williamstown.[60]

As important as the therapy sessions and general reinforcement of Clara's childrearing abilities were, perhaps Singer's most effective act was putting Jessy into a regular nursery school with other children.

Initially, Jessy showed much reticence, crying and screaming upon approaching the school. However, after only a few days, it became clear that she looked forward to her time there. It did not take long for her to respond to her kind teachers. It was there that she started to paint. She also began playing with other children.

Although Jessy only spent little over an hour twice a week in this nursery school, Clara was deeply impressed by the dedication of her teachers. Jessy's schooling in Cambridge only lasted five months because the Parks had to leave Britain at the end of David's sabbatical. But the experience opened new vistas.

Following the Parks encounters with the experts opened a window into the theory and practice of child psychoanalysis in the 1960s and, specifically, on their treatment of autism. Clara's journey revealed much about then-common views on child development and, above all, on mothers. For child psychoanalysts who believed a child's mind was shaped by her mother's feelings, even unconscious ones, Clara did not deserve the benefit of the doubt. She was assumed to have caused Jessy's autism.

The sojourn to the Putnam Center in Boston and the Hampstead Clinic in England taught Clara important things about herself and about Jessy. A woman of incredible common sense and resilience, Clara experienced the frightening depths of depression when she did not find adequate support for herself or for Jessy. But, pulling herself out of the blues, Clara moved forward. Relying on her pragmatic approach to life, she looked past the labels psychoanalysts assigned to her and Jessy. She disregarded the psychoanalytical theoretical framework of ego development and "translated" the heavy jargon into practical exercises that she could use in teaching Jessy while playing with her. With the help of Marie Singer and the kind teachers at the nursery school, Clara also made an important discovery about her daughter: Jessy was learning, and she enjoyed learning with others.

Upon their return to Williamstown the Parks enrolled Jessy in a small private school. There was no turning back.

CHAPTER 4

IGNITING A REVOLT

U PON THEIR RETURN TO WILLIAMSTOWN, the Parks enrolled Jessy in Pine Cobble School, a local private school, in the fall of 1963. Thanks to the recommendation of James Toolan, a Vermont psychiatrist, Jessy was able to attend nursery school three times a week. In November, David wrote to Clara's mother that Jessy was doing very well. She had reached a milestone: "Yesterday she said her first complete sentence: Mama dig, which happened to be perfectly accurate: she *was* digging."[1]

Back home, Clara was happy in her familiar surroundings, but remained concerned about some aspects of Jessy's behavior. She told her friend Emily, "Jessy gets gayer and gayer, & friendlier & friendlier, & understands more & more but as her remoteness recedes, the enigma of why she doesn't learn becomes greater. She learns so fast—immediately, in fact—what she does learn, then she reaches a plateau & goes no further." Clara kept wondering to what extent Jessy preferred her isolation. She also wondered whether Jessy chose not to do some things even when she could do them. How else could one explain that Jessy, who was seemingly unable to remember a particular word, could nevertheless "sing a Christmas carol *for the first time* a month after she last heard it"?[2]

Clara continued teaching part-time at Berkshire Community College. She also read more about autism. One night in April of 1964, she devoured a new academic book by psychologist Bernard Rimland, *Infantile Autism: The Syndrome and Its Implications for a Neural Theory of Behavior*.[3] Rimland sought to establish the distinctiveness of infantile autism. In addition, he argued that blaming parents for their children's condition had no scientific basis.

The day after reading Rimland's book, Clara sent him a letter, telling him how much she liked it. She found it "exhaustive and intelligent" and, "more unusually," also "sensitive and humane."[4] Clara did not know it, but the humanity she noticed came from the author's profound firsthand knowledge and lived experience. Rimland did not mention it in his book, but he was the father of an autistic child, a son named Mark.

Rimland's book represented a turning point in the history of autism in the United States. Rimland's life was transformed by his son's autism. In turn, he would help transform the field of autism research and the landscape of autism advocacy, which had been nonexistent up to then.

The son of Russian Jewish immigrants, Bernard Rimland was born in Cleveland in 1928. When he was twelve, he moved with his family to San Diego. In 1950, he graduated in psychology from San Diego State University, where he also received a master's degree in the same field a year later. Then, he married Gloria Alf and they went to Pennsylvania for his graduate studies. In 1954, Rimland received a PhD in psychology from Pennsylvania State University. Immediately after graduating, he accepted a position at the US Navy Personnel and Training Research Laboratory, at the Point Loma Naval Station outside San Diego. The Rimlands moved into a small house in the area. Ready to start a family, they eagerly awaited the arrival of their first son in 1956.

Things did not go as expected. From day one at the hospital, Mark Rimland screamed his lungs out. At home, his crying continued, relentlessly. Gloria carried him all day, pacing back and forth in an attempt to soothe him. When she recorded the amount of time Mark cried each day, his pediatrician did not believe her.[5]

As a toddler, Mark's behavior became increasingly troubling to his parents. He erupted in terrible tantrums whenever his mother put on a new dress, washed her hair, or changed anything in her schedule, appearance, or their home. Mark had a fit if anyone visited them. Gloria worried about leaving the house and ordered the same dress from the Sears catalogue in different sizes—for herself, her mother, and her mother-in-law. That solved one concern for Mark. Gloria and Bernard did not know what to make of their son's extreme dislike of any change in his surroundings. More troublesome, Mark started banging his head against the walls.

One day, Gloria was stunned to see Mark—who was not speaking at that point—reciting radio commercials word by word. Suddenly, she remembered reading in one of Bernard's college psychology text books about children who had the same ability. Searching through boxes stored in their garage, the Rimlands found the book. It described children just like Mark and provided a name for their condition: "infantile autism." That discovery ignited Bernard Rimland's lifelong search to understand autism, and his son.[6]

To confirm whether they were right in their assessment, Rimland turned to the leading expert in the field, whom he knew by reputation. In a letter to Leo Kanner dated July 30, 1959, Rimland asked if he agreed with a diagnosis of infantile autism for his son. He also sent Kanner a copy of Mark's electroencephalogram (EEG), a test used to evaluate the brain's electric activity. Mark's EEG report did not show anything unusual. Rimland also made plans to have Kanner see Mark. However, the Rimlands first went to a local child psychiatrist. After he diagnosed Mark as autistic, visiting Kanner seemed unnecessary.[7]

However, in 1960, Rimland wrote to Kanner again saying that he was studying autism "at a very intensive rate." A year later, he sent Kanner a manuscript with several chapters.[8] They discussed it when Rimland went to Baltimore and met Kanner for the first time in June 1962.[9] The book received the "Century Psychology Series Award" as most distinguished psychology manuscript for 1962. The

award consisted of $1,500 plus a good contract from the publisher
Appleton-Century-Crofts, which sponsored the competition.[10] Rimland continued revising his manuscript for over a year. Finally, *Infantile Autism*, the book that Clara Park would devour in a single
evening, was published in 1964.

In this ambitious work, Rimland argued for the specificity of infantile autism, presented his own hypothesis about its nature and
causes, and explored its implications for a general theory of human
behavior. As befitting such an important undertaking and drawing
on his extensive training in psychology, Rimland positioned himself
as a scientist. The title page presented the author's professional credentials: "Director, Personnel Measurement Research Department.
U.S. Naval Personnel Research Laboratory. San Diego, California."[11]

Kanner penned the foreword. Now professor emeritus at Johns
Hopkins University and Hospital, Kanner introduced Rimland as
someone who had "carefully and critically" scanned the extensive
literature available and, adhering to Kanner's clinical criteria for
identifying infantile autism, set forth a number of ideas that deserved
"sober scrutiny." Kanner was not convinced by all of Rimland's
claims, but he called them the kind of "courageous speculation" that
invited "sympathetic appraisal."[12] Though not an unqualified en-
dorsement, Kanner provided what Rimland needed: the imprimatur
of a leading scientist in the field that established him as a legitimate
newcomer.

United in their common cause of defending the specificity of infantile autism, Kanner and Rimland looked past their differences.
Kanner agreed with Rimland's two main goals: to show that infantile autism was different from childhood schizophrenia, and to encourage the study of its biological origin. In the book's foreword,
Kanner argued that progress in autism research had been ham-
pered by two main factors: (1) infantile autism was being used as a
"pseudodiagnostic wastebasket" for a variety of conditions; and (2)
"nothing-but psychodynamic etiology was decreed by some as the
only valid explanation."[13] Rimland knew that Kanner had originally
introduced the pernicious concept of refrigerator mothers, but he
directed his criticisms of mother blame at the psychoanalysts.

Mother blame cut close to home. Yet only one sentence in Rimland's book gave a subtle indication of the deeply personal story behind it. In his preface, Rimland thanked just one person: "The one partner whom I cannot bear to leave unnamed is my gentle wife Gloria, whose constant helpfulness, patience, and understanding throughout this tiring endeavour I must acknowledge with wonder and gratitude."[14]

Gloria Rimland had suffered from insidious comments about her role in causing Mark's autism. Many years later, painful memories remained vivid in her mind. A soft-spoken, mild-mannered woman, she remembered a dinner with some friends, a couple, soon after Mark was diagnosed as autistic. Toward the end of the quiet, pleasant evening, the woman said to her: "It's hard to believe that you caused all those problems in your son's life." Gloria did not say anything. She thought doing so would just make things worse. Besides, she reflected: "What do you say to something like this?"[15]

Rimland had plenty to say, but he chose to say it as a scientist. Why didn't Rimland mention his autistic son in his book? In her letter to Rimland, Clara had called his book "sensitive and humane." Yet Rimland omitted his own human experience. This was not because he considered his personal life irrelevant. However, by leaving that out and emphasizing his expertise as a psychologist, he was able to cultivate a detached scientific identity. Displaying his very personal stake would have undermined his credibility as an objective researcher.

Objectivity is a hallmark of modern science, though what is considered objective has changed over time. Historians of science Peter Galison and Lorraine Daston have shown that the meaning of scientific objectivity has evolved in close relation to different views and concerns about the influence of subjectivity on science. As they tell us, for modern science, "to be objective is to aspire to knowledge that bears no trace of the knower." That is, in order to be objective, scientists must keep their subjectivity "at bay" and cultivate emotional detachment. Historians of psychology have illustrated how the rise of experimental psychology encouraged this stance after World War II, and historian Mark Solovey has also shown how in the post–World War II decades, the scientific recognition and social status of the psychological sciences was closely tied to their quest for objectivity.[16]

As a scientist, Rimland first aimed to establish clear criteria to diagnose infantile autism. Though Kanner had identified the condition two decades earlier, diagnosis was still difficult for several reasons. For one, we have seen that as late as the early 1960s, psychiatrists, pediatricians, psychologists, and psychoanalysts continued to use various terms to diagnose children with autistic behavior: infantile autism, psychosis, atypical development, childhood schizophrenia, and autistic psychopathy. In addition, since there was no biological marker for autism, diagnosis always relied on an assessment of a child's behaviors, which presented its own set of difficulties. First, some toddlers engage in autistic behaviors, such as hand-flapping, walking on tiptoe, or rocking, but stop when they get older. Such behaviors at an early age do not necessarily indicate that the child is autistic. Second, some of the characteristics displayed by autistic children, such as self-isolation, are also present in conditions such as childhood schizophrenia or some brain pathologies. Third, some autistic children also have cognitive disabilities, catatonia, or other conditions. Finally, since many autistic children have difficulties with language, standard tests used to assess the intellectual and social abilities of children in general did not work for them, a point that Anni Weiss and others had made as early as the mid-1930s.

To address the complex problem of accurate identification of children with infantile autism, Rimland developed a questionnaire, called "Form E-1," which modified a "Check List of Symptoms of Autism of Early Life" put forth in 1959 by neuropsychiatrist Charles G. Polan and clinical psychologist Betty Spencer. Polan and Spencer had made their list of symptoms by studying the literature and relying on their own work with five children, four boys whom they diagnosed as autistic and a non-autistic girl included for comparison. Their list comprised thirty items divided into five categories: language distortion, social withdrawal, lack of integration of behaviors, obsessiveness/nervousness, and characteristics of the family. Most behaviors considered characteristic of autism at the time were

included, such as an infant's lack of anticipatory posture when being picked up from the crib and feeling upset by slight changes in
the environment. Under family characteristics, they listed five items,
three of which were about parents: they asked whether they were
professional or highly intellectual, whether they were "often obses-
sively accurate and compulsive," and whether they were "objective
in observation about the autistic child." They did not explain how
these three questions about the parents were related to diagnosing
a child. However, most likely they included these questions because
they were related to common perceptions about the parents of autistic children. The checklist, explained Polan and Spencer, was "a
diagnostic aid to distinguish early infantile autism from other types
of autism, from chronic brain syndromes, and from mental deficiency."[17] Their goal reveals that researchers were thinking about
differentiating various types of autism.

Rimland's questionnaire had more than double the thirty items
in Polan and Spencer's checklist, and he included many more specific
examples. To use it, parents would not need to understand technical
words such as "echolalia" or be able to interpret psychiatric constructs such as "behavior is not integrated."[18] Rimland's E-1 questionnaire asked specific and simple questions such as: "Did (does) it
disturb the child if you change things such as furniture arrangement,
the order in which you do things, or the route you take going some-
where? . . . Will the child readily accept new sweaters, pajamas,
etc.?" Form E-1 also contained many questions about the timing of
behaviors. Parents could provide detailed information about their
children's behavior in order to facilitate accurate professional diagnosis. Specific information about the time when the child acted
in certain ways was also essential because Rimland hoped his questionnaire would clearly separate children with infantile autism from
children with childhood schizophrenia.

"Infantile Autism Is NOT Childhood Schizophrenia" was the
title of one of the chapters of Rimland's book, which was fully devoted to proving this claim. At that point, many authors still believed that autism was a type of schizophrenia with a very early
onset. Recall that some behaviors present in autism are also present

in childhood schizophrenia. Since Bleuler had talked about the "group" of the schizophrenias, some authors (including Kanner at one time) thought that autism could be considered just one type of schizophrenia. To disprove this, Rimland analyzed about fifteen differences between the two conditions. As Kanner had pointed out in his initial 1943 paper, one major difference was that autism was present from birth, but schizophrenia appeared later. Schizophrenic children also suffered from hallucinations, whereas autistic children didn't. Further, autistic children's desire for sameness was not present in schizophrenic children. Their use of language was different too, as echolalia, affirming things by repeating them, and not using the pronoun "I"—were characteristic only of autism. In addition, childhood schizophrenia often appeared in families with a history of mental disorder, unlike infantile autism.

Rimland's fervent desire to establish infantile autism as unique also led him to omit discussion of Asperger's notion of autistic psychopathy. Although it is commonly believed that Asperger's work was not known outside Austria until the 1980s, this was not the case. While revising his book manuscript, Rimland began corresponding with one of the most prominent European students of autism, Dutch scholar Dirk Arnold van Krevelen. Van Krevelen was a lecturer in child psychiatry at the medical school in Leiden and founding director of Curium, a pedagogical clinic located nearby. In the early 1950s, he published some of the first descriptions of children with infantile autism in Europe. He also published several discussions of Asperger's work. Rimland sent van Krevelen his yet unpublished manuscript. In January 1963, van Krevelen told Rimland that clearly "the European concept of autistic psychopathy (Asperger) escaped your attention." According to van Krevelen, Kanner had mistakenly lumped together children who developed speech and children who did not. In his view, those children belonged to "two groups," one being Asperger's "autistic psychopathy" and the other, "Kanner's syndrome." Van Krevelen believed that infantile autism involved a cognitive problem, probably due to brain injury, which caused the children's speech difficulties. But van Krevelen also thought that the two types of autism were connected. He had seen two families with a child he had diagnosed with infantile autism and a sibling he had diagnosed with autistic psychopathy. So, he concluded that there was a "hereditary factor" of "aloneness" and "unrelatedness to people" that manifested itself in different forms in both conditions.[19]

Rimland disagreed. Busy with his full-time day job with the Navy, family life, and book manuscript revisions, he left van Krevelen's letter unanswered for almost six months. When he replied, he expressed his doubts that the children in Kanner's group who could speak were "Asperger's cases." He also rejected van Krevelen's view that these children's emotional difficulties were primary. One's "affect toward objects," Rimland argued, is "a function of how one cognitively perceives" them. For Rimland, cognition shaped the emotions, not the other way around.

Rimland found van Krevelen's suggestion that "Kannerians and Aspergians may have a common heredity" intriguing. However, he hoped the idea would not hamper the acceptance of autism as "a unique syndrome." Rimland remarked that he had planned to include a section discussing Asperger's ideas, but he was advised to leave it out because his book was "already overloaded."[20] Rimland followed the advice.

Rimland's other major goals were to prove that mothers did not cause their children's autism and to encourage biological research. If autism had organic roots, he poignantly noted, there was "no need for the parents of these children to suffer the shame, guilt, inconvenience, financial expense and marital discord" that often resulted from blaming them.[21] Many authors still argued that lack of maternal love led children to retreat into autism. Rimland challenged their position.

Rimland argued that influential studies about the effects of maternal deprivation on children's emotional development—including the work of William Goldfarb, René Spitz, Margaret Ribble, and John Bowlby—had been discredited on both methodological and empirical grounds. All these authors had defended the claim that without constant maternal care and love, infants developed all sorts of emotional and psychological disorders. Their views on the pathogenic effects of "maternal deprivation" were often cited to support the psychogenic

causation of autism. But in the mid-1950s child psychologists Sam-
uel Pinneau at the University of California and Neil O'Connor at
Maudsley Hospital in London had published thorough critiques of
Spitz's and Ribble's work, demonstrating their unscientific basis. Citing other critical studies, Rimland concluded that "despite Bowlby's
assurance" that deprivation of maternal care had grave consequences
for a child, the studies used to support that view had been "subjected
to criticisms of the gravest nature." Furthermore, Rimland noted
that, regardless of the consequences of maternal deprivation, studies
of its effects were irrelevant because there was no evidence at all that
parents of autistic children had neglected them.[22]

Rimland believed that genetic explanations of autism had not
been examined so far because they seemed to encourage a fatalis-
tic attitude. Indeed, some autism researchers, including Bettelheim,
dismissed genetic explanations in part for that reason. For them, if
environmental factors (including parental attitudes) led to autism,
there was reason for hope; environmental factors could be changed.
For Rimland, however, it was wrong to assume that if a condition
was genetic, it was therefore unchangeable.[23]

Having made the case for separating infantile autism as a unique
syndrome with a biological origin, Rimland presented his own views
about its nature. He proposed that it resulted from the child's inability to relate sensations with previously stored memories.[24] Rimland
hypothesized that the brain stem's reticular formation, a network of
neurons affecting different aspects of behavior, could be the site of the
organic impairment leading to the autistic child's cognitive problems.
However, he emphasized the speculative character of this proposal.[25]

Rimland also suggested that autistic children "were genetically
vulnerable to autism as a consequence of an inborn capacity for high
intelligence." In part, Rimland came to this conclusion because he
also believed that the parents of autistic children were highly intelligent, as Kanner and others had asserted. Most studies about autism,
Rimland noted, painted a similar picture of the parents "as cold,
bookish, formal, introverted, disdainful of frivolity, humorless, detached, and highly—even excessively—rational and objective." As
Rimland put it: "'Unemotional objectivity' is frequently reported to

be an ideal important to the parents."[26] Usually, those characteristics were used to criticize the parents. Rimland turned this on its head and used those characteristics as evidence for the parents' high intelligence.

Rimland knew that some critics had accused Kanner of extrapolating from a biased sample of parents in his clinic, but he disagreed with them.[27] After reviewing the literature, Rimland concluded that the evidence "overwhelmingly" showed that the parents of autistic children were a unique group. They were characterized by high intelligence, "single minded dedication to purpose," "conscientiousness," and "obsessiveness."[28] For Rimland, the same genetic heritage that influenced those traits also made their offspring more susceptible to autism.

Rimland's *Infantile Autism* was well received. In a review for the *British Journal of Social and Clinical Psychology*, psychologist Peter Mittler called Rimland's book "the most significant contribution to work on infantile autism that has appeared so far." Mittler and other reviewers such as psychiatrists Valerie Cowie (in the *British Journal of Psychiatry*) and Michael Rutter (in the *Journal of Child Psychology and Psychiatry*) praised Rimland's case against the psychological origin of autism and his attempt to differentiate between infantile autism and childhood schizophrenia. Most reviewers found Rimland's theory about the role of the brain's reticular formation in autism speculative and untestable.[29] Indeed, it never panned out.

Child psychoanalysts, as could be expected, did not agree with Rimland. British psychoanalyst Donald Winnicott, for example, chastised Rimland for his "ignorance" of the "earliest stages of integration of the personality" and for producing a diagnostic checklist that "does not contain the question that could produce the significant answer."[30] He did not say what that question was but, presumably, it would have been a question about the personality and behavior of the mother. In several influential writings, Winnicott had supported the view that "the basis of the mental health of the personality is laid down in earliest infancy by the techniques which come naturally to a mother who is preoccupied with the care of her own infant."[31]

Regardless of the criticisms of particular points, Rimland's book sparked discussion among different researchers in many countries and thus fostered the exchange of ideas about autism. When he was working on his book, Rimland corresponded with researchers all over the world. He sent many of them early versions of his manuscript and asked for feedback. He also told them about the research being conducted by others. In that way, he aided in the development of a research community.

After the publication of his book, Rimland intensified his networking efforts. In 1964, he obtained a grant to spend a year at Stanford University's prestigious Center for Advanced Study in the Behavioral Sciences. When his book appeared in England the following year, Rimland traveled to London. He already had a good relationship with important researchers on autism at the Social Psychiatry Unit of Maudsley Hospital, such as John Wing and Lorna Wing (parents of an autistic daughter), and Victor Lotter. Soon after visiting England, Rimland submitted a summary of his views for discussion to the British Working Group on Diagnostic Criteria for the Childhood Psychoses. This group included the psychiatrist Eleanor Mildred Creak, who in 1961 had chaired a committee of British experts that established nine criteria for diagnosing autism, which they still called the "schizophrenic syndrome of childhood."[32] Rimland shared with them important information he had obtained through his book.

In *Infantile Autism*, Rimland had included his E-1 questionnaire to identify infantile autism as an insert and asked parents of autistic children to complete and return it to him. He also kept revising the questionnaire. In the second printing of his book he included a new version called the "E-2 form." Rimland wanted to collect at least two hundred responses before drawing any conclusions, but his exchanges with British experts led him to review the data before he reached that number. In his paper for the British Working group, Rimland analyzed the responses he had received from the E-2 forms. Rimland wrote to them: "I think it is important that this Working Group recognize the inadequacy of our present methods (I use the word 'methods' very loosely), and use its good offices to stimulate the steps needed to put the problem of diagnosis on a scientific basis."[33] Networking with other researchers and clinicians was key to establishing uniform diagnostic criteria and stimulating further work on autism. Collecting data from parents of autistic children was just as invaluable.

Beyond attracting considerable scholarly attention and stimulating international scientific discussion, Rimland's book received strong support and thoughtful reactions from parents of autistic children.

ADVOCATE FOR PARENTS

Despite being a complex scientific text, Rimland's book attracted the attention of parents not only because it exonerated them, but also because it encouraged their participation by inviting readers to send him feedback about his views and write to him about their experiences. And write they did.

The first letter Rimland received was Clara's. In a four-page, single-spaced typed letter, Clara informed Rimland that she had filled out the questionnaire, and the score for her daughter was 43 on the autism side. The E-1 had 76 questions that were marked either as a "+" (autism side) or a "-" (non-autism). The final score was the net score (the number of pluses minus the number of minuses). A net score of more than 20 meant a diagnosis of infantile autism. The revised E-2 questionnaire Rimland developed later had 79 questions. Among the 2,218 E-2 forms collected by Rimland as of March of 1971, the maximum score was +45. So Jessy scored on the high end of this questionnaire.[34] While a number of doctors had been puzzled because some of Jessy's behaviors, such as playing games with her mother and siblings, did not fit their vision of the autistic profile, Rimland's thorough questionnaire gave an unequivocal answer.

Clara also engaged with some of Rimland's ideas. She challenged Rimland's view that the parents of autistic children were all highly intelligent by offering an alternative explanation of why this seemed to be the case. "Imagine," she suggested, "a household without jigsaw puzzles, or blocks, or pencil and paper, or with parents who would make no particular effort to introduce these to a child who seemed satisfied without them. Such a household would very possibly never discover the odd abilities of the autistic child, who without stimulation would deteriorate into something resembling true feeblemindedness."[35] As a result, those children would not be diagnosed as autistic. In short, Clara suggested that the reason why so many parents of autistic children appeared to be intellectuals was that intellectual parents were, by training, the ones most likely to notice it early and to seek help from medical experts.

Clara told Rimland that she had acquired much more evidence about Jessy's autism than she could summarize. This, she claimed, should not surprise anybody: "Being a ringer for Kanner's parents," she said, a bit tongue-in-cheek, "I have, of course, pages of records, observations, interpretations, and hypotheses." At the end of her letter, Clara expressed her hope that researchers would no longer mistake parents' lack of demonstrative behavior for lack of concern, or even suffering: "We can be impersonal too; it is our natural refuge. But those who do not cry do not feel less pain."[36]

The pain of parents who struggled to find services and support for their autistic children would surface in other letters sent to Rimland after his book's publication. William Blanchard, a clinical psychologist, wrote about his daughter Mary and praised Rimland for his "balance and objectivity." Frances Eberhardy, a nurse, wrote about her son Dan and offered to share a paper she had written about him. She complained about all the criticism directed at parents of autistic children: "Intellectual and conscientious are not dirty words in my vocabulary." The parents of a boy named Terry talked about going from one specialist to another over the years, doing the rounds with their "'lengthy case history' in hand." A research scientist and a historian who had an autistic boy named Danny shared their struggles "in defiance of the entire community, without social life, friendly contact with neighbors, etc."[37] And so it went, on and on, as parents poured out their frustrations, their loneliness. But not for much longer.

By sharing their experiences, these parents began to develop a sense of community. Upon hearing from other parents that Rimland also had an autistic child, Becky's parents, from Iowa, confessed how "right then and there a bond was created that had in no way existed before. . . . I suddenly felt very proud that the person who had done such an unprecedented, eye-opening piece of work about autistic children was 'one of us'—a parent." They encouraged Rimland to continue writing, since they could feel "so much more 'at home' comparing notes, so to speak, with another parent, than in writing a report for a behavior scientist, if you will pardon me for saying so."[38]

Mark's father was one of them. And that mattered. It was Rimland the parent, more than Rimland the scientist, who truly gave these parents hope. The very bit of information he had not mentioned in his book was the one thing that brought him closer to all the parents who had felt alone for so many years.

Rimland responded generously to their cries for help and encouraged them to work together. In October, he sent parents who had filled out the questionnaire his first "Dear parent" letter, where he requested more specific information: snapshots of their children, answers to questions, and other "fresh observations." He also asked them to check his views against their own experiences raising autistic children, in order to evaluate whether his theory was adequate. Thus, he trusted parents to provide reliable observations and believed they were qualified to offer evidence for or against his ideas. Lastly, he gave them some news about scientific research in the field and recommended some readings. In a sense, he had sent them a newsletter, though it was simply a letter from one parent of an autistic child to another.[39]

A couple of months later, Rimland sent a second letter asking some parents for permission to show their letters to other parents and to scientists, particularly to some of his peers who were skeptical about his ideas—even of the very existence of autism as a specific syndrome. He thought that the parents' descriptions of their children could convince the skeptics of infantile autism's uniqueness. He also let parents know that he intended to write a book on "the mistreatment afforded us parents by child psychologists and psychiatrists." In addition, he was planning an edited anthology composed of the personal stories of different families touched by autism.[40]

Before going much further, Rimland brought Clara on board
as a coeditor of the anthology of family stories. By the summer of
1965, they were hard at work reading book chapters contributed by
several parents. In October, Rimland decided to move the parents'
voices into the spotlight. As a result, his original plan for two books
was reshaped into a single book entitled *Parents Speak*. As an account of the experience of living with autism, the project was missing the voices of the children themselves, who were still too young.[41]

Some of the book chapters were new, while others had already
appeared in various magazines, including Rosalind C. Oppenheim's
"They Said Our Child Was Hopeless." Published in 1961 in the *Saturday Evening Post*, this was one of the first public accounts of the
trials parents and their children faced when searching for services.
This was also the story that Clara, as mentioned before, had found
most helpful in her own work with Jessy. The story of the Oppenheims, who lived in Chicago, was fairly typical. Before the age of
two—and before he spoke—their son Ethan had learned to sing a
vast repertoire of melodies, from nursery songs to operatic arias.
They thought he might be musically gifted. But one day, when Rosalind returned home after spending some days in the hospital due to
a miscarriage, she and her husband noticed changes in Ethan's behavior. He began to ignore people, including them. He would learn
a new word, use it for a few days, and then never use it again. Their
pediatrician told the Oppenheims that they were just "overprotect-
ing" Ethan and that he had begun to regress as a result. But, increasingly worried about their son, the Oppenheims searched for other
expert opinions. And they found them, one after the other.

After hearing the Oppenheims's description of Ethan and observing him for a few minutes, a psychologist diagnosed Ethan as
autistic on the basis that he was withdrawn and did not speak. The
psychologist explained that Ethan's emotional disturbances were
halting his intellectual development. Next, an audiologist told them
that Ethan had probably suffered a prenatal brain injury and was severely "mentally deficient." Then, a famed neurologist told them that
Ethan was "seriously disturbed" and had "gone as far as he can go
intellectually."[42] Though exhausted and depressed, the Oppenheims

did not give up. They learned to live as frugally as possible in order to save money to pay for any help they could find.

"And so we boarded a medical merry-go-round that led us from psychiatrist to speech clinic to psychologist to child-guidance agency with a growing sense of futility," Rosalind explained. Their search all over Chicago left them empty-handed: schools for the "mentally retarded" rejected Ethan as "emotionally disturbed"; schools for the "emotionally disturbed" rejected him as "mentally retarded."

Finally, when Ethan was four and a half, they found a summer camp led by a professor of psychology at Purdue University—Newell C. Kephart—which focused on helping each child's individual and unique development. With Kephart's guidance, Rosalind created a home training program and started teaching Ethan how to read, play, and communicate on his own terms. Having at last been treated, as Rosalind put it, "as people," the Oppenheims had hope for Ethan and enjoyed "the satisfaction of playing a creative role" in his development.[43]

The parents of autistic children who wrote to Rimland had not been able to find any good advice on how to help their children. But now that they had found each other, they began working together to change that.

ADVOCATE FOR CHILDREN: NSAC

Rimland's involvement with parents led to another crucial development in the history of autism. One mother, Patricia Caruthers, notified Rimland of her attempts to put together a mailing list of parents in Southern California, and suggested creating a newsletter to keep the emerging community informed about news on autism. She asked: "Is there a Professional Society for Autism? I have never heard of one." On the same day that he answered Caruthers's letter, Rimland wrote to another researcher: "There is at present no autistic children's society (except, perhaps, me) but there is some talk of starting one."[44]

Rimland had valuable connections needed to establish such a society. Since the early 1960s he had been compiling a list of families with autistic children. Many of the parents were looking to other

parents for advice. For example, when Rosalind Oppenheim's 1961
article appeared in the *Saturday Evening Post*, the number of letters
she received from parents interested in her experience quickly overwhelmed her. She referred these parents to Rimland once he had
published his book. UCLA psychologist Ivar Lovaas did the same
after *LIFE* magazine published an article on his work with autistic
children in May 1965. And so did Louise Ames and Frances Ilg,
founders of the Gesell Institute of Child Development in New Haven, Connecticut, and authors of a syndicated daily newspaper column on child behavior entitled "Parents Ask."[45]

By 1965, just one year after his book's publication, Rimland's
office had become the central node of a growing network of parents.
Rimland provided them with information and put them in contact
with one another. In October he sent Clara's address to Ruth Sullivan, the mother of an autistic son.[46] Ruth and her husband, William
P. Sullivan, also fit the stereotype of parents with autistic children.
He was a professor of English at Marshall University in Hunting-
ton, West Virginia. Ruth had trained as a public health nurse, held
a master's from Columbia University, and now devoted herself to
raising their seven children, ranging in age from toddler to teenager.
Rimland had asked her to contribute a chapter about her autistic
son, Joseph, for his edited book. As many other mothers did, Clara
and Ruth started corresponding about their children's development;
they exchanged ideas about how to teach them and discussed new
scientific research.

Soon, these parents, who had struggled alone before, decided to
get together to share their knowledge, support each other, and fight
for public services for their children. Ruth Sullivan, who had honed
her considerable organizational skills in her volunteer work for the
League of Women Voters, joined forces with Rimland to launch a
new association.[47]

On November 14, 1965, about sixty people—most of them parents of autistic children—met one evening in Teaneck, New Jersey.
Hosted by Herbert and Rosalyn Kahn, who had an autistic son, the
event, as Sullivan later recalled, was "electrifying." Rimland participated, as did David Park. Clara could not attend because she stayed

home with Jessy. Some of these parents heard about many children similar to their own for the first time. At the end of the evening, they decided they needed a national organization, following in the footsteps of British parents and researchers who, three years earlier, had established the British National Society for Autistic Children.[48] Only a few days later, on November 17, the parents held a second meeting in Washington, DC, this time organized by Mooza Grant, a writer and producer for the US government news broadcast Voice of America. Grant, fluent in several languages and an expert on public relations and advertising, became the society's first president. She was the mother of two autistic daughters. Rimland gave a speech at both meetings.

In the coming months, Rimland focused on discussing the scope of the society and refining its name so it would give a good sense of their objectives. Rimland was torn between the British model, centered on autism, and that of another parent-organized group, the more inclusive American National Association for Retarded Children. He thought that focusing exclusively on infantile autism would limit the organization's potential membership and, as a result, its power to change things, since there were few diagnosed cases of autism at the time. Rimland, like Kanner, thought infantile autism was a rare syndrome, so he did not think a society for autistic children could ever grow substantially in size or influence. Rimland suggested one compromise: the name of the society would refer only to autism, but its motto could be more inclusive, with a reference to childhood schizophrenia, phenylketonuria, "and all other severe behavior disorders of childhood." Kanner adamantly opposed "such a conglomeration." Finally, in 1966 the organization was chartered in Washington as the National Society for Autistic Children. Its motto underscored its dedication "to the welfare of children with infantile autism, autistic like behavior, childhood schizophrenia, or other profound behavioral disorders."[49]

From the start, the society was a grassroots movement that relied on volunteer efforts and was run on a shoestring. Mooza's husband, a lawyer, drafted the charter. The society had no office, no staff, and no funds for operating expenses. The membership fee

($2.50 per person, later raised to $3, or $5 per family) helped defray the costs of copying and mailing a newsletter. That fall, the society published its inaugural newsletter, which included a message from Mooza Grant and information about events, publications on autism, and the founding of state chapters. Grant's first message as president listed three main objectives for NSAC: securing legislation to provide educational help for disabled children, organizing programs to train personnel to work with these children, and establishing adequate service facilities for diagnostic, therapeutic, educational, and recreational activities.[50] These were ambitious goals for a small fledgling society, but the association grew with the help of many parents.

Local mobilization was key to the new society's continuous growth. The newsletter encouraged the formation of new chapters, emphasizing that "if autistic children in your community are to be helped, it is essential that effort be mobilized for this purpose at the *local* level." Local chapters often had their headquarters in parents' homes. The newsletter kept the different chapters informed about activities undertaken at different locations and encouraged people to get involved. By 1967, the society had chapters in nine states and over five hundred members.[51]

In July 1968, Ruth Sullivan became the society's first elected president. Clara was elected to the board of directors.[52] The change of officers was an acrimonious affair, as many people had become unsatisfied about the society's financial accounting. Rimland had quit after several disagreements with Grant. When Sullivan took over, she reported that the organization's bank account had a mere $56.11. Rimland was invited back and he agreed to become a member of the board again.[53] NSAC's headquarters moved to Sullivan's home in Albany. As she explained in her first message as president, the society's "office" was a corner of her dining room. "Office hours" started at 10 p.m., after her children went to bed. From the corner of her dining room, as NSAC's president, Ruth Sullivan begged members from different chapters to become active because the alternative was "the back ward of a state mental institution for our children when we are gone."[54]

Clara also encouraged members' active participation in her role as newsletter editor, a position she took in 1968. The newsletter appeared irregularly at the start, then was published quarterly from 1968. There were also some occasional supplementary newsletters. Under Clara's editorship the newsletter became longer and included more information about events and more references to papers about autism, from academic journals to general audience magazines. Little happened in the field that escaped her eye. She reported on new scientific publications, often evaluating their merit. In this way, Clara encouraged other parents to become experts in their children's development and on autism in general.

Before coming together through NSAC, each mother was already an expert on her child, but now they also became experts on each other's children. The parents met at conferences, where they often brought their children. They also visited each other. Only a few months after Rimland put them in contact, in 1965, the Sullivans drove to Williamstown to spend an evening with the Parks. Ruth wrote to Rimland about the experience of meeting Jessy: "a fascinating little girl, so different from Joseph in so many ways, yet the same."[55] Because of their firsthand knowledge of autistic children, Clara and other parents felt competent to assess if scholarly studies had anything to offer to autistic people and their families.

NSAC promoted interactions of parents and professionals "on an equal footing, with the parents acting as coordinators and the professionals as resources."[56] It encouraged parents to present at professional conferences and meetings, and then report back to the other members. Ruth Sullivan and Clara, for example, attended the 1968 Joint Conference on Childhood Mental Illness held in New York. In her report on the conference, Clara emphasized that they attended the conference as "parent-experts."[57]

NSAC was a new type of advocacy organization—what sociologist Gil Eyal and his colleagues characterize as a *"network of expertise,"* as opposed to a lobbying group. This network connected researchers, parents, activists, therapists, social workers, educators, and others interested in autism. As they saw it, rather than a mere "teaming-up" of parents and practitioners, the parents' work involved a "hybridization of identities" that blurred the "boundaries between expert and layman." At NSAC, many of these parents created a new social role: "the parent-activist-therapist-researcher."[58]

Rimland was the most visible example of this hybrid expert, but not the only one. Although a psychologist by training and profession, he knew nothing about child psychology before the birth of his son Mark. Motivated by his personal experience, he *became* an expert in the field by contacting established researchers, reading the scientific literature, and taking parents' knowledge seriously. Parents such as Ruth Sullivan and Clara Park became hybrid experts as well.

Rimland also supported research on autism through a nonprofit organization, the Institute for Child Behavior Research (ICBR, later renamed the Autism Research Institute) that he created in 1967. One of Rimland's first public activities involving ICBR was the twenty-six-minute documentary *The Invisible Wall* (1968), one of the earliest documentaries on autism. According to psychologist Stephen M. Edelson, Rimland's longtime academic collaborator, the documentary was often shown in university psychology courses. The film combined Rimland's explanations about autism with scenes featuring four autistic children with their mothers. One of the mothers was Ruth Sullivan, filmed with her son Joseph. Poised and cogent, she rejected the view that blamed autism on mothers and explained why it had no scientific basis.[59]

Rimland played a crucial role in the early history of autism in the United States by criticizing the conflation of autism with childhood schizophrenia, establishing national and international networks among researchers, encouraging communication between researchers and parents, fighting against the insidious practice of blaming mothers, calling for the study of the biological basis of autism, and helping to launch the first advocacy group for autism. With his writings and activism, he ignited a revolt that led to important changes for autistic children and their families.

Later, Rimland's unflinching search for a cure and his support for some controversial therapies would make him a champion to some and a villain to others. During the 1960s, Rimland's desire to find a cure was connected to his conception of infantile autism as well as the historical moment in which he was working. Using very strict criteria for diagnosis, he believed infantile autism was a rare and debilitating condition. Many scientists and parents supported this stance. Their views about infantile autism were influenced by a medical view of impairment and shaped by social expectations that families should have "healthy and normal" children. During this period, any disability was still seen as a problem for the individual or the family to fix, not as a difference that society should value and accommodate. In addition, there were no services or supports for autistic children. Most parents of autistic children were advised to take them to an institution. The social and intellectual changes that led people to support disabled children would take place much later, in part thanks to the efforts of parents like the Rimlands, who raised their children at home and appreciated their children's individuality as they grew up. Their efforts would also lead to a more complete understanding of the condition.

The parents' expertise and activism helped reject the part of the medical model that blamed autism on mothers, led to a greater awareness of autism, and demanded social supports for it. However problematic some of these parents' beliefs may be from our current perspective, this should not prevent us from recognizing and reflecting on what parents such as Rimland and many others did accomplish. Working together at NSAC, they would raise awareness about autistic children's needs and fight for social acceptance and their rights in education.

CHAPTER 5

A MOTHER'S PLEA
FOR INTELLIGENT LOVE

C LARA'S VIEWS ON AUTISM were grounded in her relationship with Jessy. When she read Rimland's book in 1964, Jessy was six years old. When Clara wrote to Rimland in April of that year, she wanted to bring the knowledge she had acquired through "long, detailed, and careful" observation of her own child to bear on Rimland's perspective.[1] A fair and kind correspondent, Rimland became a trusted sounding board for Clara's ideas.

In their correspondence, Clara took Rimland to task for positing a cognitive problem as the cause of autistic children's difficulties with emotional or affective relations. "It is hard to live with such a child, from birth," she wrote, "without feeling that it is indeed the affective impairment that is primary, and that from it all else flows." She told him about Jessy's ability to form abstract concepts even in the total absence of the language needed to express them, evidence that ran counter to Rimland's hypothesis. As an example, she described how Jessy had drawn circular figures before age three, how she was interested in the game "ring around a rosy," and how she had responded to a depiction of the game in a children's book by singing the song. Then, when presented with an image of a geometrical circle, she sang that same song. That is, she had identified "the abstract idea of circularity" from very different instances of it.[2] Clara took Jessy's powerful ability to make such inferences and form abstract concepts as evidence for her view that Jessy could reason well, and that her difficulties lay mainly in the affective sphere.

Rimland responded that, in his book, he had argued that "the affect problem" stemmed from the cognitive one, but he was "by no means completely sold on this." He added that Dutch researcher van Krevelen had found "two cases of Asperger's syndrome in families with autistic children. Asperger's involves affect much more than cognition." Rimland told Clara he would have to work more on this issue.[3] At this point, Asperger's work was still not widely discussed in the United States. Rimland himself had omitted any discussion of that work in his book. Now he realized that the relationship between the two syndromes, Kanner's infantile autism and Asperger's autistic psychopathy, needed to be closely examined.

Shortly afterwards, Clara sent Rimland a ten-page single-spaced typed letter once more addressing the "cognition vs. affect problem," the question of whether autistic behavior, such as desire for sameness and social solitude, had cognitive or emotional roots. Clara's views were similar to Kanner's and Frankl's position that the core of autism was a "disturbance" in the affective realm. But she did not cite any medical literature; she supported her argument with concrete examples of Jessy's behavior. Clara felt confused because Jessy was physically and cognitively able to do many activities, but she did not do them. For example, for a long time Jessy did not go up the stairs. So, the Parks wondered: perhaps she couldn't? But then, one day, they saw her going up the stairs without any difficulty or a moment's hesitation. For Clara, it seemed "as if" Jessy did not want to do certain things. So, Clara asked Rimland how to categorize the cause of such behavior: "Cognitive? or Affective?"[4]

At home, Clara told Rimland, she was continuing her own "do-it-yourself" therapy with Jessy. She was teaching Jessy to read "with startling success." She proudly reported: "Jessy has reached a point now where she *can* learn from people. . . . She is, indeed, very affectionate and responsive now, on a very moving 2-yr old level." During her trip to England Clara had realized that, despite her initial reluctance, Jessy had been able to interact socially and learn from her therapist Marie Singer and from her teachers in a local school in Cambridge. And, just as important, Jessy enjoyed learning with them.

For Clara, Jessy's increasing interest in interacting with them and with other people supported her own view that autism influenced mainly the affective aspects of behavior. She told Rimland: "I think—forgive me my pride—that this is no accident or luck, but has occurred because I took the lack of affect as primary, and . . . worked on that in every way I could devise." She wondered whether one could develop strategies for strengthening patterns of affective contact in autistic children.[5] Clara kept working with Jessy to help her express her own emotions and to relate more to others. "Hello, Mama," Jessy said when Clara entered her bedroom one day while she was drawing. Such a greeting would not usually be a big deal, but Jessy was almost seven years old when, in 1965, she said this for the very first time. Stunned, Clara took a moment to recover. "How long I have waited for those two simple words!," she wrote in her notebook.[6] As a mother, Clara longed for the kind of affective responses that she had experienced with her other children.

Clara also continued taking notes about Jessy's development. Throughout that year, Jessy mastered increasingly abstract social concepts, such as "parent" and "family." Concepts related to human motives and emotions, such as "want" or "enjoy," took much longer. Jessy did not fully understand sentences such as: "The mother wants the children to dig the snow." Clara wrote in her notebook: "*Wants* is the problem, being human & dealing w[ith] affect."[7] For Clara, this too was a sign that the core of autism involved the emotions.

In a progress report that Clara sent to Jessy's pediatrician in January 1966, she emphasized that point. She divided her comments into several sections: "Purely intellectual," "Social," "Speech," and "General behavior." Clara told Gellis that Jessy was an active child: she painted, built puzzles, played with dolls and cars. Her play was repetitive, and she did not initiate new games. She showed steady progress in speech. At this time, Jessy did not use the verb *to be* in any form. She used the pronouns *I* and *you* but always reversed them; that is, she referred to herself as "you." On the social side, Jessy engaged more with warm adults but not with children. Now in her third year in a regular small local school, Jessy enjoyed going to her classes, but ignored the other students.[8]

Under a section titled "Purely intellectual," Clara reported that as soon as Jessy learned color words around five years of age, she spontaneously came up with "blue green" and "pink red." When she learned shape words such as square or circle, Jessy "instantly and with delight" started saying dodecagon and trapezoid after hearing them only once. Clara noted that Jessy could easily acquire number concepts, letters, and simple written words. She did not seem to understand moral or social concepts unless "translated into her own brand of pidgin with most affect situations left out." The process was baffling to Clara. The family "*did not work*" to teach Jessy "dodecagon," which she used instantly "as if it had filled a long-felt need." On the other hand, it took them a long time to teach her "good" and "bad," and they were still working on "love," "sad," "happy," and, lately, "angry."[9]

Jessy's difficulties in learning concepts related to emotions, moods, and feelings reinforced Clara's belief that autism concerned the affective realm. Therefore, her efforts to help her were focused in that area. Rimland disagreed. Clara mounted a pointed defense of her views: "So love-schmove, agreed: You don't get the idea." Clara explained that her approach was not something as "magico-meaningless as bathing the child in love." On the contrary, it was a method to slowly and systematically engage Jessy through small steps, insisting constantly but stopping if she became uncomfortable. Clara asked Rimland to imagine that one could "skinnerize *love*, or affect, or what you will." B. F. Skinner, a well-known American psychologist, had argued that most behaviors could be learned through operant conditioning, that is, by reinforcing desired behaviors with rewards and discouraging undesirable ones with punishments. He also supported the idea of breaking large and complex behaviors into small manageable parts that could be shaped by conditioning.[10]

To a great extent, in childrearing this was no different from the way most parents teach their children many skills. Human babies are born helpless. Infants need to learn practically everything, from walking to being kind to others. Most parents—or in our society, mothers—teach their infants step by step, offering rewards (a smile, a word of praise, a sweet) and sometimes appropriate punishments (a frowning face, a word of reproach, or perhaps no TV or dessert, on occasion). Clara was an intellectual, so she "theorized" her approach in teaching Jessy, but many of her "exercises" were quite usual mothering practices. Clara adapted them to what she viewed as Jessy's own needs and desires at different times.

Clara proposed that Skinner's insights could be used to engage her daughter by encouraging "small steps toward contact with others, starting where the child is." This approach focused on specific behaviors: "if the child responds to tickling, tickle it; if it laughs . . . at being thrown in the air, make sure it is thrown." In sum, start where the child is comfortable and engage her in a playful way. For Clara, the important thing was to "approach *and* retreat." In that way, "contact, because she can retreat from it, is made tolerable, then amusing." Hers was a systematic, loving approach, using creative play to entice Jessy to engage. Clara began using the small-steps approach when Jessy was three. Before then "it did no good, she did not notice me insisting, and I confess it is not my way. But later, it was possible to insist."[11] As she had done with psychoanalysis, Clara adapted psychological theories to develop practices that worked well with Jessy. It was a kind of individualized teaching. Clara tailored these playful exercises to Jessy's comfort level. Jessy learned while having fun.

Success using the small-steps approach also shaped Clara's beliefs about the nature of Jessy's condition. Working with this method, she started to realize that it was not easy to separate what was affective from what was cognitive. As she put it: "Who's to know which, of affect or cognition, worked on in small steps, affected and enlarged the other?" She started to wonder whether the emotional and cognitive aspects of behavior actually built on each other in a seamless process.

Still, regardless of whether her theories were right or not, the important thing for Clara was that Jessy was making progress. She told Rimland: "At any rate, from 5 on she has been reachable by any reasonably warm and intelligent person accustomed to young children, and can learn, step by step still, but far less effortfully programmed. This is no love treatment only; loving *siege*, I said."[12] The basic idea was to access Jessy's world by luring her—lovingly, relentlessly, and intelligently—into ways of acting that connected her more with the people around her. Using her intelligence and her love (could those also be separated from each other?), Clara was helping Jessy to develop her own capacity for relating to others.

More recently, a number of autism activists have challenged this whole paradigm.[13] They ask: Why do autistic ways of relating have to be changed? Who gets to define what is relational, what is love? These are very good questions. They are precisely the kind of reflections that would come out of the work done by mothers and others. As their children grew up, the parents progressively discovered that they had their own affective needs and their own ways of relating. But in the early 1960s, Jessy was a young child. In isolation, she would not be able to learn anything. And she would not be able to teach others, including her own mother, that she had her own way of relating and loving.

Drawing on her extensive notes about Jessy's behavior, Clara started writing a book about her efforts over the previous seven years to teach Jessy everything—from turning on a faucet to reading to paying attention to other people's feelings. "The book," she explained to Rimland, "is to be called *The Siege*: the central metaphor which permeated everything I have done is that of a walled citadel under unremitting, loving attack." She continued, "My book will be mainly about Jessy's growth and the things we have done, and what can be done, by parents, in a family setting." By documenting and examining Jessy's progress, Clara hoped to help other families in similar situations.

Up to that point, Clara had been shocked and frustrated by the lack of published material about methods for supporting autistic children. So, it was especially important to share the ones she had discovered. As she wrote to Rimland: "I had to invent my techniques for myself, and I want to communicate them through the book. What kind of a crazy world is it when a desperate parent, in contact with the best professionals in the country, has to get her help not from them but from Satevepost [*Saturday Evening Post*] articles and biographies of Annie Sullivan?"[14]

In contrast to Rimland, who had written *Infantile Autism* as a scientist, Clara wrote her book as a parent offering her personal experience. She did so for two reasons. One is that she aimed to document her family's journey. Another reason was that she had been made painfully aware of her lack of professional status. After selling an article on British schools to the *Ladies' Home Journal*, Clara sent in another piece entitled "In Defense of Repression." The editor responded: "We couldn't print anything on this subject except from a psychiatrist."[15] Clara got the message loud and clear.

On March 5, 1967, Clara wrote to her mother: "The book is done and off as of last Tuesday."[16] *The Siege: The First Eight Years of an Autistic Child* appeared later that year. It offered an account of the Parks' efforts to understand Jessy's world and to help her understand theirs. It also called for the scientific community to value the parents' work and knowledge.

TEACHING JESSY

The Siege introduced readers to the Park family and the doctors who diagnosed Jessy as autistic. To protect their privacy, Clara used pseudonyms for the children and doctors. Clara identified her husband, David, as a physics professor at a prestigious small college in the northeast, and referred to Jessy as Elly. Clara wrote about how she and her husband, like most parents of children with a poorly understood developmental delay, had embarked on an anguished pilgrimage in search of knowledge and help. They'd gone from the family physician to the local pediatrician, and then to the psychiatry clinic. She recounted how most doctors and therapists had provided little useful advice or services for Jessy. In reflecting on those experiences, Clara did not hide her frustration, but she did not write in anger. She wanted to write a book that was useful to others.

Clara painted her family's life in Williamstown, Massachusetts, as typical for their social class and circumstances. They lived in a small, happy community: "A woman's magazine daydream which happens to be true. Our town is an ideal place to rear children."[17] Clara noted that, as so many American women of her generation, she had focused on being a good mother.

During this period, educated women were encouraged to concentrate on family and children. The cultural messages encouraging "family togetherness" found a receptive audience among the young men and women who had suffered separation and loss during World War II.[18] When, many years later, Clara attended her fiftieth reunion at Radcliffe College, her cohort's trajectory illustrated how child-centric her generation had been. In a letter to her physicist friend Freeman Dyson, Clara reported that many of her classmates had followed the "genuine but undramatic satisfactions of family rather than career or intellectual life." For example, Kate Russell Tait, daughter of the famous British philosopher Bertrand Russell and one of Clara's "class's 2 *summa cum laudes*," raised six children. As Clara told Freeman, she was "typical" of her class, and of "the life of women in that time." Another classmate raised twelve children, another raised nine; Clara's own four was "an ordinary number" among her classmates.[19] As Betty Friedan's *The Feminine Mystique* would reveal in the early 1960s, many of these women felt unhappy and trapped in their domestic roles. Their quest for the "security of togetherness," Friedan pointed out, had turned into a mirage that limited their capacity for individual growth.[20] However, Clara found motherhood rewarding.

As Clara presented it in her book, raising her children had been an enjoyable experience for her, and there is no reason to doubt an account in which she relates with considerable candor other aspects of her life that others could—and would—find easy to criticize. Clara found joy in watching her children grow up: "I had sympathized, and laughed, and rejoiced at the spectacle of a mind unfolding." She busied herself with the many tasks needed to raise children: reading them books, providing them with clay and toys, cleaning, cooking meals, and a myriad of other activities. She used appropriate punishments and rewards in an effort to make her children good people:

"I had tried to make them generous and self-controlled and unsuspicious and good." It was hard work but work she was "terribly proud of."[21]

Then, she got pregnant again. In her book, Clara openly stated that her pregnancy had been unwelcome. Now that her three children were in school, she had been eager to dedicate some time and energy to writing and teaching. Literature had been her longtime passion, and she desperately wanted to return to it.

Clara's account is extraordinary because of her willingness to explore the possibility that she had played a role in Jessy's development. Not by admitting that she did not love her child enough; on that, Clara stood her ground. But she recorded aspects of her life that others might consider important. As she put it, "Every piece of potential evidence must be recorded in this account, not least the evidence that can be used against me. We need to know all we can if someone someday is to understand at last what is relevant and what is not."[22] Thus, she was willing to subject all factors that might have played a role in Jessy's autism to public examination: her disappointment at finding out that she was pregnant; her initial depression; the inner need she felt for books and ideas; her hunger for adult conversation. She did not think they played a role, but she presented them openly, for others to judge as well.

After that discussion, Clara outlined Jessy's early behavior. She knew that individual acts might not be significant. But did they add up to something? As Clara put it, she only had a collection of anecdotes to grasp her child's soul. She believed that, taken together, those anecdotes suggested a picture. As a toddler, Jessy did not explore her surroundings and never reached for objects; she stayed content simply by playing repetitive games on her own. Jessy did not look at other people. In fact, she ignored others and did not respond to their efforts to engage her, with the exception of her mother, who spent many hours with her. For Clara, it seemed as if Jessy deliberately rejected the world. But did she really?

Clara went on to relate her family's search for answers to all the questions raised by Jessy's behavior. Behavior is all one can see. We can see what a child does. But, what does it mean? *Why* does the child do it? Here, we move into the realm of interpretation. Though fully aware of the difficulties of reading a child's mind, Clara said: "We cannot help interpreting." Because Jessy was healthy, and her motor and cognitive abilities seemed fine, her lack of engagement with people and many other things in her environment seemed to be her choice: "again and again it was as if she could but wouldn't."[23] She could turn on a faucet. She had the necessary motor and cognitive abilities for the task. Yet she would not do it. Then, one day, she would simply do it, no problem. It "looked," then, like she had previously been "unwilling" to do it. But why? That was a matter of interpretation. And the Parks kept reminding themselves that they could not be sure of their interpretations. Everything was "as if." Jessy was very young and did not speak much, so it was also difficult to figure out Jessy's own motives.

As Clara saw it, they could not just leave Jessy alone at this early age. She seemed happy, but even that was difficult to ascertain. Clara wrote about how she perceived her daughter as a prisoner: "If smiles and laughter mean happiness, she was happy inside the invisible walls that surrounded her. She dwelt in a solitary citadel, compelling and self-made, complete and valid." For Clara, Jessy's solitary aloofness "denied the possibility of growth."[24] Later, Clara and the whole family would learn about Jessy's own desires and needs, but as a toddler, and with the very limited understanding of autism at the time, the Parks did not think that leaving Jessy alone would be good for her. All parents teach their children the necessary skills to navigate the world until they find a way to do it on their own terms.

As for a strategy, Clara decided to try everything. Clara and Jessy had to forge their way forward together, on a journey neither of them could predict. Clara guided her daughter as much as her daughter guided her: "I learned what I had to from Elly, slowly and painfully, she and I together. . . . I had nothing to guide me but common sense and a still then unverbalized knowledge of three normal childhoods, to which I could add the imperative that an eminent mathematician has given as a two-word definition of the scientific method: 'Try everything.'"[25] She did. She disregarded much of psychoanalysis, but took Marie Singer's good lessons to play with Jessy in games that interested her and construct visual cues to help her anticipate events such as taking a bath. She also used some of Skinner's insights, such as dividing complex behaviors into small steps and using rewards to encourage desired behaviors. She adapted the theories of behavior available in her time to devise practical ways to teach Jessy various skills. In *The Siege*, Clara presented many of the games and practical tools so other parents could see if they helped with their own children.

Today, many autistic advocates would find Clara's approach and the metaphor that guided her, however much love was behind the intent, as inadequate and even harmful. It is worth pausing to reflect on this.

First, let's focus on the metaphor that Clara used in her book, that of a siege to a citadel. One reason some critics find it harmful is because it postulates that there is a "normal" child "trapped" inside an autistic shell. Clara and David probably learned about the citadel metaphor from the staff at the James Jackson Putnam Center. Stephen Shore, an autistic person who went there just a couple of years after the Parks took Jessy, has written about how Pierre Johannet, the medical director of the nursery school, used "the castle" narrative to explain an autistic child's retreat from the world and the need for the psychoanalyst to unlock the doors for the child to come outside.[26]

Influenced by this metaphor and her own experiences, Clara did envision her daughter as trapped in a solitary citadel. At the time, leading psychiatrists and psychoanalysts, from Kanner to Bettelheim, argued that autistic children retreated from the world. Clara also explained in her book that sometimes it also seemed to her family that Jessy chose not to do things that she could do. Thus, she wondered whether Jessy willed her self-isolation. Later, Clara came to see this as incorrect, and medical experts rejected this model as well. But when Jessy was a toddler Clara had little knowledge of autism. The experts had told her how little was known about children like Jessy. Working with a medical model of autism as a retreat into isolation, Clara concluded that the right thing to do would be to help Jessy relate and communicate more with other people. Clara's metaphor of the siege did not refer to the effort to save a "normal" withdrawn child but to the family's work teaching Jessy the skills necessary for her to function in a world she found chaotic. In trying to help her daughter communicate, Clara believed she was opening possibilities for Jessy.

It is also important to note that some autistic people have presented their own experience as being confined in isolation before they improved their relational abilities. In *Ido in Autismland: Climbing Out of Autism's Silent Prison*, Ido Kedar describes his experience of feeling trapped in silence until he was able to communicate with others. Others have described their experience of growing up as an "emergence" from a state of isolation, a state they longed to abandon.[27]

Another reason many would find the metaphor of a siege problematic is that it supports a narrative of the parent as savior, which relegates the autistic person to the role of a victim who is passively saved and cured. But *The Siege* does not fit that mold. To read it that way is to impose our own current perspective on the book. *The Siege* covers the first eight years of Jessy's life, and Jessy is not "recovered" or "saved" or "cured" at the end.[28]

Second, let's address Clara's approach, especially her use of behaviorist principles with Jessy. This will also strike many autism activists as problematic. For them, behavior modification programs do not appreciate and respect the unique ways autistic people relate and think. But we need to keep in mind the historical context and the options open to a mother at the time, as well as Jessy's age and the specific ways Clara made use of behavioral principles. During this period, many children with behavioral or emotional difficulties were sent to custodial institutions. In most of these institutions, they hardly received any attention and the conditions were deeply inhumane, as I relate later. At home, Clara taught Jessy as she taught her other children, by modeling and by using age-appropriate rewards and penalties. That is the way most mothers and families teach their children. Examining how Clara engaged Jessy, it becomes clear that Clara always tried to respect Jessy's boundaries and comfort. And working with Jessy at home, Clara and the rest of the world would eventually learn about Jessy's own ways of thinking and loving.

In addition to presenting the family's journey, Clara criticized the psychiatric and psychoanalytic establishment for not providing adequate support for Jessy and for blaming her as a mother. Simply put, *The Siege* was to a large extent an act of self-defense, and a defense of other parents.

ENCOUNTERS WITH THE EXPERTS

Clara devoted two chapters to her experiences with experts: "The Professionals" and "Professionals as Human Beings." These chapters covered her two very different encounters with psychoanalysis at the Putnam Center in Boston and the Hampstead Clinic in London. During that period of 1962–1963, Clara had also read what the experts wrote on autism. We know they were not kind to mothers. She summarized their views as follows:

> Bettelheim writes that parental rejection is an element in the genesis of every case of childhood schizophrenia he has seen. Beata Rank sets out as her "main hypothesis" that "the atypical child has suffered gross emotional deprivation," and adds that "the younger the child, the more necessary is it for us to modify the mother's personality." Even the wise and humane Erikson, though he remarks that the rejecting mother is the "occupational prejudice" of child psychiatrists, reiterates in the same study that a "history of maternal estrangement may be found in *every* history of infantile schizophrenia."[29]

Although these "were threatening ideas to confront," Clara maintained that they did "not take hold" in her.[30] Yet the experts' assumptions that she had caused her daughter's condition and their condescension toward her at the Putnam Center had affected her profoundly. These clinicians' views had exacerbated the depression she fell into when she became overwhelmed with Jessy's symptoms after they moved to England. Clara did not believe she was responsible for Jessy's condition but she could not help wondering how her conduct and emotions had influenced Jessy.

But Clara was fair in recognizing that not all professionals, including psychoanalysts, were the same. She explained to her readers how different her interactions at the Hampstead Clinic had been. Good therapists such as Marie Singer, her analyst and her friend, had focused on helping her child rather than on following strict therapeutic rules derived from grand theories about the human mind. Clara believed that it would be impossible for therapists who truly cared about children not to teach them something.

Clara also highlighted how important it was for experts to empathize with parents: "What one wants is sympathy, understanding, not tacit but openly given. What one wants is love. Too much to ask?"[31] Sadly, all too often it was too much, because many experts believed that parents, especially mothers, did not deserve it. For many years, Clara had devoted her considerable intelligence to raising her children well. Yet, what she had not understood at first was that this very approach made her suspect in the eyes of many psychiatrists.

In her book, Clara proudly noted that, like many of her friends, she had deliberately used her intellectual abilities in raising her children: "Of professional ability, most of us, we had made motherhood our profession. . . . I was like my friends in putting my full resources of intelligence and intuition into the task of bringing up my children.[32]

Was that really a bad thing?

Following a long tradition that saw feeling and thinking as two separate domains, in the early twentieth century some scholars argued that the female body could not do both maternal and intellectual work. Books or babies, they proclaimed. A woman could not do both—at least not well or without detrimental consequences for her own mental health and that of her children. In the scientific and social debates about "the woman question," taking place after the rise of the feminist movement, the key issue was always whether women's capacity to bear children determined their psychological and moral character. According to scholars such as British sociologist Herbert Spencer and psychologist William McDougall, the female maternal instinct had equipped women, but not men, with the gentleness and altruism required for rearing the young. Nurture, love, and, more generally, the realm of emotion were all women's spaces. As women acquired greater access to higher education and entered the paid workforce in larger numbers, numerous scholars warned that women were losing their natural maternal warmth and instinctive mothering abilities.[33]

As we saw earlier, after World War II, many child psychologists and psychiatrists also argued that mothers "distracted" by intellectual preoccupations would undermine their children's emotional development. Intellectual mothers were cold, refrigerator mothers who were unable to love their children with natural warmth as decreed by women's maternal instinct. But why would a mother's love for books interfere with her loving her children?

In challenging the view that she had caused her child's autism, Clara defended the value of intelligent love. In doing so, she put her finger on a central assumption in autism literature that blamed mothers. All the researchers working on children's emotional development, from Erik Erikson to René Spitz, from Margaret Ribble to John Bowlby, from Leo Kanner to Bruno Bettelheim, claimed that children needed "natural" love—some kind of raw, instinctual feeling that should not be sullied by a mother's other interests. But none of those researchers had explained why this type of maternal love, love that was untainted by intellectual and professional aspirations, is richer and more nurturing than other types of love. None of them had explained why the intellect and the emotions are in conflict with each other.

Clara thought they were not, even in childrearing. In her book, Clara related how, in order to maintain her own sanity while she analyzed and reflected on Jessy's growth, she reminded herself that the qualities that made her suspicious to many psychiatrists—objectivity and rationality—had already served her well in life. And her three older children provided bountiful evidence of her own abilities as a mother. As she put it: "If it is fair to lay failure at the parents' door, as much should be done for success." No doubt, there were moments of despair, of doubts, of wondering if the experts were right after all.[34] But the pride in the thriving children she and David had raised dispelled those dark thoughts.

Clara knew she was a good mother. So when she realized that Jessy's development was not typical, she had no reason to dismiss the tools she had used with success before. Instead, she applied them with renewed energy. Clara's systematic note-taking, her debates with Rimland, and her efforts to engage in discussions with the doctors and psychiatrists show how important it was for her to understand the puzzle of autism and to figure out how to support Jessy.

The Hampstead Clinic had criticized her approach, saying that she took on her daughter's education as a "project." But why should learning and loving be seen as incompatible goals? Couldn't a mother use her mind as well as her heart in raising her child? It was true that Jessy's development had become a project for Clara. But did that make her a bad mother? Would it have been better for Jessy if her mother had simply loved her "instinctively" but did not use her powerful intelligence to understand her needs and develop effective strategies to help her grow?

Clara wrote about her family's journey in the hopes that her account would constitute sufficient evidence against those who blamed autism on mothers. By portraying her stable family life and her dedication to her children—though without denying that raising kids was hard work that required sacrifice and intelligence, and without hiding her intellectual aspirations—she hoped that others could see that the reason for Jessy's autism was not that she was a refrigerator mother.

Clara aimed to show that objectivity and reason are not incompatible with love and can be a valuable part of mothering; further, that intelligent love could be also a way to reach reliable knowledge.

THE AMATEURS

In a chapter entitled "The Amateurs," Clara argued that parents could contribute to advancing knowledge about autism because their love for their children was not an impediment to understanding their condition. She thereby challenged the entrenched barriers between amateurs and experts.

An objective mother may sound like a contradiction in terms. Love is usually considered to be a deeply subjective and passionate emotion, while science is presumed to rest on objective and detached reasoning. This prevailing separation between subjective feelings and objective thinking can be seen in the response Clara received from an editor whom she had met through a friend and who had encouraged her to send her some chapters of her manuscript of *The Siege*. This editor wrote to Clara that the book would be confusing to readers because "the point of view jumps around—sometimes you are the parent, sometimes the reporter on autism, sometimes you are very close to your subject and sometimes detached."[35] In the editor's view, then, Clara should not be both objective and subjective, scientist and mother at the same time. One could not describe and analyze a child objectively while at the same time conveying strong feeling for the child.

But science wasn't always like that. Certainly not so in the field of child development.

"Ask her to look out (for no. 5) when one of her children is struggling & just going to burst out crying." So wrote British naturalist and the father of modern evolutionary theory Charles Darwin in a letter in which he asked his friend and fellow scientist Thomas Henry Huxley to pass a note to his wife, Henrietta. The note included a questionnaire regarding children's facial expressions, and "no. 5" referred to one particular expression in the questionnaire.[36] Darwin wanted Henrietta's observations on her children for his own landmark research on the expression of emotions. He asked many of his friends to collect data through their wives, as he trusted mothers to provide accurate observations needed for reliable knowledge.

Darwin himself had started his studies of the emotions shortly after the birth of his eldest son, William, in 1839. Having recorded his child's growth just as carefully as he described barnacles in another study, Darwin published his observations in one of the first and most detailed accounts of an infant's development, "A Biographical Sketch of an Infant."[37] Today, this 1877 text is considered one of the founding works in child psychology. Charles Darwin could be both a father and a scientist. Nobody at the time questioned whether the great biologist could love his son and also provide an objective account of his development.

Influenced by Darwin, a few years later, in 1882, English-born physiologist William T. Preyer published (in German) *Die Seele des Kindes* based on carefully scheduled and detailed observations of his son's first three years.[38] Its English publication as *The Mind of the Child* led Marion Talbot, a graduate of Boston University, and her mother, Emily Talbot, an educational advocate and secretary of the American Social Science Association (ASSA), to encourage educated middle-class men and women to record their observations of their own children's development. Many women who had graduated from college but found no employment became interested in their proposal. Emily Talbot composed a questionnaire on child observation and in 1882 reported that they had "hundreds of mothers engaged." Emily Talbot solicited the advice of Darwin, who sent his enthusiastic support. That year, Talbot published a report that included six case studies of infant observation and was widely distributed through the ASSA.[39]

Another major figure in encouraging mothers to observe their infants was Milicent Washburn Shinn. She carried out extensive observations of her niece's first seven years and published them, between 1893 and 1898, in her four-volume work *Notes on the Development of a Child*. Thanks to these studies, Shinn was the first woman to receive a doctorate in psychology from the University of California, Berkeley. In 1900, she published *Biography of a Baby*. Encouraged by Shinn and others, some mothers published biographies of their babies.[40]

But a field that had started out by welcoming the contributions of mothers soon considered traditional female attributes as detrimental to scientific inquiry. Male researchers who dominated the emerging professions of psychology and child development dismissed patience, sympathy, and other traits associated with maternal care as interfering with scientific discipline.[41] In evaluating the quality of observations, the scientific credentials of the observer became increasingly important. In addition, the association of modern science with an experimental approach, and the rise of experimentation in psychology in particular, helped to marginalize the "merely" observational approach and skills that had been so influential during the field's early years. Legitimizing child developmental science led to a rejection of maternalist traditions. Male scientists distanced themselves from women and reform organizations that had been instrumental in raising interest in

children's development and welfare. As historian of psychology Ellen Herman has put it: "Twentieth century psychology was a can-do
profession whose supporters pointed with pride to tangible results
far outside of the ivory tower, but they never failed to advertise its
credibility as an experimentally based science and its legitimacy in
the male-dominated academic world."[42] Consequently, child development studies joined many other scientific fields by removing emotions,
and specifically maternal subjectivity, from scientific inquiry.

In the early 1960s, however, some important psychologists began
to reconsider the place of mothers in science, and specifically their
ability to contribute to child development research. In a 1963 paper
on "Problems of Methods in Parent–Child Research," Marian Yarrow, a researcher at the US National Institutes of Health, advocated
enlisting mothers in a nontraditional way. Her studies had shown
that parents' retrospective accounts were not reliable, but Yarrow
proposed that mothers could serve as trustworthy observers in the
present. As she saw it, only mothers had access to certain information about their children, "such as infrequently occurring events, . . .
or interactions in which dimensions of intimacy or crisis preclude the
presence of the researcher." Given the privileged position of mothers
as observers, Yarrow believed researchers could ask them, or even
train them, to provide data about those occasions as well as "data
on the day-to-day rhythms of mother and child interactions." Going
one step further, Yarrow also wondered if mothers "could assume an
experimenter role." In sum, she called for mothers to play an active
role in research, a role that would benefit child development studies.[43] Clara had not read Yarrow, but she put forward similar ideas.

In *The Siege*, Clara passionately *and* thoughtfully rebuked experts who questioned parents' abilities: "Physicians of the soul do
the thousands of afflicted children no service if they undermine the
confidence of their parents in what they can accomplish by intelligent love." Furthermore, she proclaimed: "Intelligence and love are
not natural enemies." As she saw it, "love is a technique as well as
an emotion." Her own work illustrated the value of her position.[44]

What exactly could parents bring to the table? Clara pointed out,
much as Marian Yarrow had, that their special position afforded

parents many advantages. Parents can observe their children in a variety of situations, not just a clinical or therapeutic visit. This gives parents a bigger and more varied data set than the information obtained in "the artificial situation of the therapy hour." In Clara's words: "When you are in twenty-four-hour contact, every experience can be considered for potential usefulness." However, more was at stake than a simple matter of quantity and variety.[45]

The daily contact with their children also allows parents to acquire what Clara called "deep knowledge of the child in context." This advantage could only come from having "intimate knowledge." Parents have extensive familiarity with their child's development from birth. And they know their child's past and its relevance to the present better than any doctor or researcher. Even if a psychiatrist can make independent observations of the child in the present, sound scientific interpretation depends on accessing "the details of the child's history to make sense of what [one] has found."[46]

Clara's point brings us back to the difficulties of interpreting behavior. In the clinic or the laboratory, researchers and clinicians can observe specific behaviors. But what do those behaviors mean for each child? Clara argued that it is easier to understand the meaning of specific acts when one knows a child's history. If understanding a child was akin to exploration, Clara reasoned that only the parents could offer "a map that shows the major landmarks." It is only in that context that one can interpret adequately what specific actions mean for a child.

Close observation of an individual's behavior in context is indeed crucial to knowledge in several fields, including ethology and cultural anthropology. In certain fields many researchers who study behavior would consider observations obtained through intimate knowledge of one's subject to be better than—or at least not worse than—laboratory results. For example, close observation in context had become a hallmark of the young and highly successful field of ethology, the biological study of animal and human behavior. As early as the late 1930s, and especially after World War II, Austrian researcher Konrad Lorenz argued that observations in the natural environment needed to be the basis for the scientific study of animal behavior. For his work in this area, Lorenz shared the 1973 Nobel Prize in Physiology or Medicine with two other great observers of animals in their natural environments, Niko Tinbergen and Karl von Frisch. Their call for close observations of the daily lives of animals was echoed in other fields, including child studies. In fact, many autism researchers quoted ethologists or adapted their focus for the study of children in their "natural environment." Clara did not cite this literature, and she may not have been aware of it, but her views were fully in line with the growing scientific emphasis on close observations of individuals in their natural environments as opposed to relying solely on short interviews or observations in the laboratory.

If understanding the natural environment is important, typically no one was in a better position to do that for children than mothers. Being part of "the context" enabled mothers to understand the significance of specific events in their children's development.

Clara argued further that the circumstances of parents encouraged the very qualities needed for good science: "Living their lives among questions, not answers, they are natural empiricists in a field that—they may be pardoned for suspecting—is not yet ready to press beyond empiricism." This empiricist approach, which rested on close observations, went hand in hand with an appropriately cautious view of speculative interpretations: the deep immersion in the life of the child kept parents from engaging in too much interpretation because they appreciated the complexity of their child's reality and the dangers of making unfounded speculations in that context.[17]

Clara's goal was not to denigrate the knowledge of researchers and therapists, but, rather, to build partnerships. "Let parents into the therapy rooms and the special schools," Clara pleaded. Parents could participate in building knowledge about children and in helping them. In her view, so little was understood about many conditions like autism that "the distinction between amateur and professional has hardly begun to acquire a meaning. There are many parents who, like us, have had no choice but to make themselves experts in their child's abnormality. I have met some of them. They should not have to work alone."[48]

RECEPTION

Little, Brown and Company published *The Siege*. Clara and her editors at this commercial publishing house expected to reach the parents of children with autism and other conditions, social workers and doctors in the field of autism, and also members of the general public interested in child development.

Following publication, readers who wrote to Clara and authors of published reviews noted *The Siege*'s remarkable combination of love and insight, of "wisdom and love."[49] They commented on the hybrid quality of the book, on the fact that this was a unique voice that resisted categorization, and on Clara Park's courage in proposing a union of love and knowledge.

This combination incited different reactions, however. Some showed appreciation mixed with some puzzlement, as seen in a reviewer's comment: "This book is written with an objectivity that is remarkable from one who is so emotionally involved."[50] Or as this one expressed it: "At first reading one is dismayed by what seems to be the ambivalence of Mrs. Park's approach to the problem. . . . By the end of the book one has no doubts that here is a warm human being who has come to terms with adversity by balancing passion with reason."[51] Most reviewers expressed appreciation for the clear account she presented: "Hers is no sentimental, monotonous recital of woe. . . . [She] relates her personal encounter . . . in a sincere and objective manner."[52]

Yet Clara's combination of love and intelligence could be praised even as it was deplored. Here is perhaps the clearest case from one reviewer: "The account is so successful because, although Mrs. Park comes through definitely as a sensitive person, she has the unusual capacity to stand aside and look at herself and her child and interpersonal relationships objectively and analytically. Tragically, it is perhaps this very quality which helped to produce a child of Elly's type."[53] Some reviewers like this one showed a deep appreciation for the book, but still upheld the standard diagnosis and thus blamed Clara.

The parents of autistic children overwhelmingly welcomed her book as a soothing balm for their wounded hearts. In *The Siege*, they recognized the authority of someone who spoke as a parent and who addressed their main concern: helping their children. Many parents wrote to Clara to express their gratitude. A lawyer and father of an autistic son wrote: "Here at long last was someone bold enough to attack the cruel nonsense which is so stupidly, and yet so frequently, inflicted upon the parents of autistic children."[54] Mothers, especially, were grateful to have their experiences brought out into the open and to find an advocate making such a persuasive case about their plight. Frances Eberhardy, a Midwestern mother who defined herself as "the hausfrau type," wished that Clara's book "had been available before," when she was struggling to understand her own child. She congratulated Clara "on a job well done," and also "for explaining to the professionals what it is like to be a parent."[55] Yet another mother simply wrote: "Thank you from the bottom of my heart."[56]

The Siege did not make a big splash right away. Despite the efforts of some of Clara's well-connected friends, her book was not reviewed in the *New York Times*. It was, however, reviewed in local newspapers, and won an award from the National Association for Mental Health. But at first *The Siege* did not win many public accolades from important intellectuals or researchers.

Nevertheless, over the coming years Clara's book became enormously successful. It grew on many readers, laypeople and clinicians alike. People wrote to each other sharing their enthusiasm. After some time, *The Siege* had become a bible for parents of autistic children, who continued, generation after generation, to rediscover the book. It was also translated into French, Dutch, Norwegian, Danish, Swedish, Italian, German, Spanish, and Japanese. Psychiatrist Karl Menninger, at the age of eighty-nine, praised this book that he had "missed" and only read when the second edition came out in 1982. Menninger underscored the "beautiful precision" of Clara's work with Jessy, adding that the story had been "recorded by a masterful clinician and observer and writer."[57]

Challenging the separation of emotions and intelligence, Clara had contested a narrow vision of motherhood and also of science. Here, Clara anticipated feminist critiques of science that in the 1980s pointed out the exclusion of women from science and the absence of women's perspectives. Feminist scholars such as Evelyn Fox Keller questioned the separation of the emotional and the cognitive in science. Scientists, they argued, could not leave aside their own subjectivity. And even if they could, that would not necessarily make them better scientists. Keller proposed a "dynamic objectivity," a pursuit of knowledge that made use of subjective experience and took into account a knower's connection to the world.[58]

Through her own work with Jessy, based on intelligent love, Clara had seen that the dichotomy between the emotions and intelligence actually hindered the understanding of autism. The psychiatric view of autism, rooted in the history of childhood schizophrenia, had been erected upon the conception of a divided self: autistic children had a good or superior intelligence, but no emotions. In her book, Clara Park offered a remarkable analysis of the shortcomings of this view when it came to interpreting her daughter's development. In the revised 1982 edition, Clara made another radical call to rethink the reductionistic categories used to diagnose, name, and treat mental conditions. About autism, she asked: "Cognitive or affective impairment?" She had asked herself that question many times. Now, trusting her own experience, she had a compelling and, from a historical perspective, revolutionary answer: "It is not only unnecessary to choose between them; it is impossible."[59] Understanding Jessy and other children with autism required giving up the simplistic—and unfortunately widespread—dichotomy between emotions and intelligence.

Mothers can love and know. Scientists can know and feel. Science and mothering can be both objective and subjective, while recognizing the multifaceted meanings of both terms and the complexity of their interrelations. Furthermore, in understanding children's development, the cognitive and the emotional are deeply interrelated. That much, a mother could see.

CHAPTER 6

FROM CULPRITS
TO COLLABORATORS

B Y 1964, BERNARD RIMLAND had shown that there was
no evidence for the view that parents caused their children's
autism. In 1967, Clara Park showed that nothing in her behavior
could account for her daughter's developmental difficulties. The battle, however, was not over. The same year Clara's book appeared,
Bruno Bettelheim published *The Empty Fortress: Infantile Autism
and the Birth of the Self*.[1] Here, once more, a major psychoanalyst
and public intellectual blamed mothers for their children's autism.

At the time of its publication, *The Empty Fortress* was heralded
as a major contribution to the understanding of autism. Today, it
is remembered as the best-known exponent of mother blame in the
history of autism. Though he turned to recent research to support
his views, Bettelheim presented basically the same ideas he had already put forward a decade earlier in his 1956 and 1959 papers.
He addressed three fundamental questions of general interest: How
did a child develop a sense of self? Why did a child become autistic?
What was wrong with contemporary society?

Bettelheim argued that infants needed to feel in control of their environment. Otherwise, their emotional development would be distorted. For Bettelheim, even maternal practices such as scheduled feeding times could "dehumanize the infant," because the infant does not develop the feeling that his own actions bring about the important "experience of being fed." For Bettelheim, children lose interest in the world and stop communicating with others if they do not feel that their actions matter in the world.[2]

To support his views, Bettelheim relied on well-known psychoanalysts from this period. He cited Erik Erikson's views about the child's need for trust as a basic first step in development. He also used René Spitz's studies of nurseries. Spitz argued that lack of mother love had led many infants in institutional care to develop severe ailments. Bettelheim relied on John Bowlby's views as well. As we saw earlier, in 1951, Bowlby postulated that the mother was her child's "psychic organizer." Throughout the late 1950s and the 1960s, he continued to emphasize the significance of the mother-infant bond for a child's adequate emotional development.

Just as Bowlby did in his own work on maternal attachment, Bettelheim appealed to research on animals to support his views on human development. He argued that animal researchers had shown the existence of "critical periods" during infancy in which maternal care and love were essential. He also used Harry Harlow's iconic experiments with baby rhesus monkeys raised with artificial "mothers"—dolls made of wire or wire covered with cloth and carrying a milk bottle—as well as Harlow's later experiments raising monkeys in total isolation. According to Bettelheim, Harlow showed that the monkeys raised without their natural mothers appeared fine, but later failed to socialize and mate. By analogy, Bettelheim concluded that the human baby also needed appropriate maternal care and love for proper social development.[3]

During this period, the appeal to animal research to support views about "natural" ways for rearing children was widespread. Konrad Lorenz, who won a Nobel Prize in 1973 for his studies of ducks and geese, defended the existence of early critical periods that determine an animal's future social development. His publications on animal behavior became widely cited by child psychologists and psychiatrists. Bowlby, for example, relied extensively on Lorenz's work and claimed that the latter's studies provided evidence for his own views about the importance of maternal attachment in humans.[4]

When it came to autism, Bettelheim gave the usual caveats about not wanting to blame mothers; nevertheless, he blamed them. He asserted that "the precipitating factor in infantile autism is the parent's wish that his child should not exist." In this literature, the "parent" always meant the "mother." Though he also said that what mattered was the child's subjective belief of experiencing maternal rejection, Bettelheim only discussed cases where mothers had led their children toward those experiences.[5]

To illustrate his views as well as to showcase his therapeutic success, in *The Empty Fortress* Bettelheim provided a riveting narrative of three psychologically troubled children: Laurie, Marcia, and Joey. Bettelheim claimed that their mothers' rejection had driven them into their autistic shells, a conclusion he had reached mainly through interviews with the parents. He also said he had cured seventeen out of forty autistic children. Among these was Joey, the child who behaved as if he were a machine, and whom Bettelheim had described in his famous 1959 *Scientific American* article. Bettelheim proudly reported that Joey was now attending high school.

Bettelheim presented his therapeutic accomplishments as evidence against the position that autism had a biological origin. Though he wrote that some children might be born with a predisposition to the condition, thus accepting the role of some constitutional factors, Bettelheim thought the main causes of autism were psychological. This view, he said, offered more hope. As he put it: "Wherever infantile autism is viewed as an inborn impairment, of whatever variety, the resultant attitudes toward treatment will be defeatist. Among those, on the other hand, who trace the causes of autism at least in part to the environmental influence, outlooks will be more optimistic because of the not always valid but convincing belief that what environment has caused, environment may also be able to correct."[6] Bettelheim rightly pointed out that it is not the case that if something is caused by environmental factors, it can always be changed. Nevertheless, he decided to choose optimism. In this case, his defense of an optimistic outlook for curing autistic children required blaming mothers.

Once again, Bettelheim used his own experience in the Nazi concentration camps to clarify and justify his views. He had witnessed how some concentration camp prisoners had developed schizophrenia-like symptoms when they felt overpowered by a reality they could not change. In a similar manner, Bettelheim resolved, some children retreated into autism because they felt overpowered by an extreme situation they could not control. To help his readers understand this feeling of utter helplessness and the anxiety it created, Bettelheim appealed to the Cold War's pervasive fear of a nuclear conflict declared at the whims of the political leaders.

Bettelheim was widely applauded for his unrivaled therapeutic success and *The Empty Fortress* was praised as a brilliant commentary on modern society. *Newsweek*, *Time*, the *New Republic*, *Scientific American*, the *New York Times*, and the *New Yorker* all reviewed it. Bettelheim made guest appearances on television programs such as *The Hidden World* and the *Today Show*. Many scholars, including the prominent Yale historian Peter Gay and the Harvard medical researcher Robert Coles, heralded Bettelheim as a genius and a hero.[7]

The combination of good storytelling and scientific veneer made for compelling reading. Who would not feel empathy with the three supposedly suffering children and would not cheer when Bettelheim reported his successful therapeutic efforts? Bettelheim became a hero who provided a message of hope: autistic children could recover, and so could humanity. Despite their overwhelming fear of nuclear war, humans could still be agents of their own destiny. For those who did not have the scientific expertise or personal experience to see beyond the narrative, Bettelheim's book had considerable appeal. Yet, while many general readers embraced its message, researchers and parents found little of value.

Clara Park had read an advance review copy of *The Empty Fortress* while finishing her own book. She found the book "theoretically worthless" and Bettelheim's claims about his ability to cure autism "baseless." In addition, Clara believed that none of the children Bettelheim described were probably autistic.[8] Indeed, when they entered the Orthogenic School in the 1950s, the diagnoses for Joey and Marcia were schizophrenia and brain injury, respectively. Only Laurie came to the school diagnosed as autistic.[9]

After Clara shared her criticisms with Rimland, he encouraged her to get into a polemic with Bettelheim. But she refused, believing that Bettelheim would not change his mind, no matter how convincing her arguments might be. On this she was surely right, as Bettelheim did not engage with those who asked for a clarification of his diagnostic criteria or for his evidence of "curing" autistic children (or even clarification of what he meant by that). Rimland sent Clara copies of correspondence in which he had asked Bettelheim for evidence of the effectiveness of his treatments for autism. Bettelheim answered with vague assertions that he was "satisfied with the number of mute autistic children who were clearly autistic and who, because of the therapy received here are now self-supporting successful citizens, many married and have normal children." He refused to discuss anything further with Rimland.[10]

Clara was not surprised. She wrote to Rimland: "For goodness sakes, though, you can't expect a man his age, with a lifetime invested in his point of view, to give it up in the interests of fairness and truth. As [Max] Planck said of a supposedly more genuine science [physics], the older generation isn't converted, it dies." Clara did not want to engage in futile arguments. Instead, she aimed to make her points "by implication," hoping that a strictly personal story would persuade her readers. She told her mother: "There is not much one can do with the theory that the mother caused it except to tell the story in such a way that many readers will find it preposterous. This is more dignified and I think more effective."[11]

Understandably, many mothers were crushed when they first encountered Bettelheim's views, but some raised their voices in opposition. Frances Eberhardy, a nurse at the University of Wisconsin Hospital in Madison, had written about her autistic son to Rimland as soon as his 1964 book appeared. Eberhardy reviewed *The Empty Fortress* for the *Journal of Child Psychology and Psychiatry*. As for Bettelheim's claim that "the precipitating factor in infantile autism is the parent's wish that his child should not exist," she retorted: "In the 7 years that I have been active in a parent group for emotionally disturbed children, I have met no such parent." To drive home the point of how speculative and detached from reality Bettelheim's views were, Eberhardy entitled her review "The View from 'the Couch.'" From a real home, things looked quite different. As for the case she knew "intimately," Eberhardy and her husband had welcomed their firstborn as an "unfolding miracle." A handsome, agile, smart boy, Peter (not his real name) sat and walked at the expected ages. He never put things in his mouth, did not smile, did not cuddle, and rarely looked at people. They thought it was hilarious when Eberhardy's brother remarked during a visit: "That kid has no social instincts, whatsoever."[12]

Eberhardy narrated a far too common story: the visit to a pediatrician, to an audiologist, and finally to a psychiatric social worker who surprised them by asking many questions about Eberhardy, and none about her son. We are familiar by now with the expert's explanation: How could she expect her son to be warm when she was cold to him? When Eberhardy asked for suggestions or materials to read, the psychiatric social worker didn't recommend any because she "sounded like a school teacher already." She was accused of using an "intellectual approach to motherhood."[13]

There were more condescending doctors and unhelpful theories as Eberhardy alternated between crushing guilt and resentment for being treated as a child. Finally, Leo Kanner himself diagnosed her son as autistic. Since Peter began talking at an early age, Kanner believed the prognosis was good and recommended a specialized boarding school in Pennsylvania. Peter spent nine years at the school, with home stays during holidays and summers. Sometimes, the awareness of his differences and the way some people misunderstood him made Peter feel "out-of-tune" or "all mixed up." But his excellent ear for music was a source of happiness and enabled him to choose his own vocation and a job tuning pianos.[14]

When she wrote this review, Eberhardy had not yet read Clara's book. However, she too called for experts to treat parents with kindness, pointing out that raising a child was a hard job, and experts made mistakes too. She pleaded: "We need your support. . . . We need techniques. . . . Let us not belittle parents, their observations, their abilities. Whoever else works with our children, we are their principal contacts with the world."[15] In her review, Eberhardy adopted the same strategy Clara used in *The Siege*. She did not engage Bettelheim's claims. She offered nothing but her personal story to persuade her readers. It was enough.

Many psychologists and medical doctors working on autism also found fault with Bettelheim's book. John Wing, an English researcher of autism and father of an autistic child, pointed out that Bettelheim did not provide sufficient information to properly evaluate his claims about diagnosing autism and his therapeutic success. He also did not provide evidence for his assertion that the children he wrote about had been rejected by their mothers. And Bettelheim did not explain either why many children who had been rejected by their mothers did not become autistic. Though Bettelheim had praised and used Harry Harlow's work, Harlow started his review of *The Empty Fortress* saying that the book was "relatively empty from cover to cover." His assessment was straightforward: "Seldom has an author said so little, about so few cases, in so many words." In a letter to Dutch researcher Arnold van Krevelen, Leo Kanner noted that the *Empty Fortress* was "full of psychoanalytic speculation." In the first case presented in Bettelheim's book, Kanner had counted 146 instances of such speculation, as seen in Bettelheim's use of words and phrases like "seems to, it is possible to speculate, suggest, assume."[16]

In his 1969 address to the National Society for Autistic Children meeting, Kanner repeated this criticism, referred to Bettelheim's book as "the empty book," and acquitted the parents. Present in the audience were Clara Park, NSAC's president Ruth Sullivan, Margaret Dewey, and many of the mothers who had suffered, as Clara would put it in a book later, "a kind of pain that only those can understand who have lived it." This was an unbearable pain because one felt attacked "where you're most vulnerable, in your pride in your home and the wish and need to believe that you've done the best you could for those you love."[17]

Although *The Empty Fortress* became a bestseller and Bettelheim's self-proclamation as an autism expert brought him much
clout with laypeople, autism researchers and parents of autistic children knew better. Bettelheim's grandiose pronouncements about the
birth of the self rang hollow. His descriptions of the children were
good storytelling, but those with real knowledge of an autistic child
did not find them believable.

In addition to the criticisms put forth at the time, a close reading of Bettelheim's book reveals poor scientific practices. For example, Bettelheim based some of his arguments on Bowlby's work, but
Rimland, in his 1964 book, had already noted that Bowlby's views
had been extensively criticized. In addition to the critiques cited by
Rimland, there were others. In 1961, psychologist Lawrence Casler
published a devastating critique of Bowlby's work showing that
many of the studies he relied upon overlooked the role of critical
variables and relied on small or invalid samples.[18]

That year, ten years after the World Health Organization published Bowlby's famous report on maternal care and mental health,
the WHO issued another report that included thorough examina-
tions of Bowlby's ideas from anthropologists such as Margaret
Mead and other leading sociologists and psychologists. These critics
pointed out that Bowlby had unduly extrapolated from research on
children raised in institutions—who were missing much more than
mother love—to develop his views about children in everyday home
life. Bettelheim also ignored major criticisms of Spitz's work that
exposed his failure to use adequate controls and analyze the impact
of many factors affecting those children living in the institutions he
studied, including diseases and lack of sensory stimulation. Therefore, Spitz's conclusion that the children withered away because they
did not receive adequate maternal care was not supported by his
limited analysis of only one factor among the many that influence
a child's psychological development. Bettelheim also cherry-picked
aspects of some scholars' research that supported his views while ignoring others that did not. For example, Harlow could not be taken
as saying that mothers were essential for an infant's psychological
development because he claimed that peers were more important

than mothers in primate socialization. Furthermore, Harlow worked on rhesus monkeys. Though he believed his results could be extrapolated to human infants, leading psychologists had also criticized this extrapolation. Bettelheim failed to mention any of those criticisms.[19]

In addition, Bettelheim's accounts of the children were highly speculative and inconsistent. Take the case of Joey, the child who behaved as if he were a machine. In his 1959 article Bettelheim said that even before his birth, Joey's mother "had already excluded Joey from her consciousness." In his 1967 book, though, he said that she had "enjoyed the thought of becoming a mother, of having a baby who would make her less lonely." The book depicted her as ignoring the baby after his birth.[20] To explain how Joey became obsessed by machines, Bettelheim related how Joey's mother, when going to an airport, was overwhelmed by feelings about a past lover and anxiety about her husband. This experience supposedly caused Joey's attachment to machines, as he perceived at the tender age of eighteen months that machines had a power over his mother that he did not.[21] But how could an infant react to his mother's anxiety by concluding that machines were more powerful than humans? And how could Bettelheim possibly know that Joey drew that conclusion at the time? The methods Bettelheim used to understand Joey's personality were also unclear. At one point, Bettelheim claimed to be following a process "deductively," only to later recognize that "we can only speculate."[22]

Now, how could ideas that we now find blatantly wrong have seemed so reasonable at one point?

The Empty Fortress became so successful in large part because it presented a morality tale about the dangers of living in an uncaring society. Bettelheim warned his readers that in a mechanical world without warm human relations, a child would try to survive by "retreating" into his own world.[23] By appealing to the potential of autism to reveal profound mysteries about the formation of the self and the perils of a dehumanized modern world, Bettelheim captured the reader's imagination.

In the midst of the Cold War and a frightening nuclear arms race, Bettelheim's call to pay attention to human relations resonated

deeply. Combined with his claims that many autistic children treated
at his school had improved greatly and many others ceased to be
autistic, his message gave hope to his contemporaries: if autistic children could come out of their cocoons, humanity could also find its
way to construct a more humane society where people did not fear
for their lives, a world in which they could be masters of their own
fates. Thus, Bettelheim delivered a message of hope at the expense
of autistic children and their families.

Bettelheim's allegations against the mothers of autistic children
were accepted by many despite his lack of evidence because they
reinforced the widespread concern in American society about the
alleged damage done by mothers who worked outside the home.
Blaming mothers for social ills and especially for children's problems
had a long tradition in American society and, as we saw earlier, was
pervasive in psychiatry after World War II and during the 1950s.
In the 1960s, rising consciousness about gender inequality following the 1963 publication of Betty Friedan's *The Feminine Mystique*
and the formation of the National Organization for Women in 1966
advanced the second wave of the feminist movement in the United
States. Women started demanding greater equality at the workplace
and also at home. Identifying mothers as responsible for their children's mental health worked against these developments, implying
that women needed to stay home, thus reasserting the importance of
traditional gender roles at work and home.

The view that mothers played a key role in the origin of their
children's autism persisted during this period, especially among
those scientists who believed nature had decreed separate roles for
men and women in childrearing. Disrupting those roles, they argued, would have serious negative consequences for society. For example, as John Bowlby saw it, autism was due to a "combination
of two or more" of these three factors: genetic, brain damage, and
inappropriate mothering. To back his views about the importance of
"natural" mothering Bowlby used Konrad Lorenz's work on ducks
and geese as well as the work of animal researcher Niko Tinbergen,
who shared the 1973 Nobel Prize with Lorenz for their work on
animal behavior. In a peculiar turn of events, in his 1973 Nobel

acceptance speech for his work on seagulls and fish, Niko Tinbergen used Bowlby's ideas to advance the view that modern civilization had disrupted the natural patterns of mothering, and those disruptions played a causal role in childhood autism. Several parents and autism researchers strongly criticized this position.[24]

Child psychoanalysts who had blamed mothers before also remained influential. Clara Park discovered this at the 1974 meeting of the International Association for Child Psychiatry and Allied Professions in Philadelphia. Elizabeth Irvine, a British social worker who had been impressed by *The Siege*, invited Clara to participate on a panel called "The Positive Value of Parents." Clara was elated, until she saw that the program included, as she scribbled on a press release announcing the conference, "All the bad guys!" The "Great Pioneers" panel at the conference included Bruno Bettelheim, Erik Erikson, and Margaret Mahler.[25] In the United States one could hardly find a more influential group of psychoanalysts who had blamed mothers for their children's conditions. Irvine told Clara not to worry, however. She would not have "to confront Bettelheim et al.," since they were not likely to attend a panel about what parents had to offer.[26] Indeed, they did not.

At this conference, Clara realized that mothers were also under suspicion due to new theories that while recognizing that biological factors played a role in autism also looked for supplementary psychogenic influences. This inevitably led back to mothers. In a letter to Margaret Dewey after her trip, Clara said that, since parents talked to each other so much, they had failed to notice that not everybody was convinced about the biological roots of autism.[27] Their fight was not over.

And yet, there was some progress. In her conference paper, Clara spoke her mind: "Ten years ago I would not have dared to speak to you on 'The Positive Value of Parents'—nor would I have been invited." Back then, acknowledging that her child was autistic "would have been to display myself as a 'refrigerator parent,' whose emotional emptiness was demonstrated by the indubitable fact that I observed my child's abnormal behaviour, and tried to do so objectively." Now, Clara remarked, the inclusion of her panel at a professional conference suggested that there was "a *frail* new willingness to recognize the capacity of parents for doing things right."[28]

Encouraged by the incipient willingness to listen to them, the parents of autistic children in the early 1970s led the way to a crucial development in the field: a move from theories to practices, and from parents to children. Rather than using autism to reflect on motherhood or on the problems of modern society, it was time to focus on helping autistic children develop their abilities.

PARENTS AS COTHERAPISTS AND COLLABORATORS

Among the child psychologists who concentrated on teaching autistic children in the United States, two became particularly influential: Eric Schopler and Ivar Lovaas. Though they adopted different approaches, they both discovered that they needed to collaborate with parents in order to reach their goals.

Eric Schopler was born in Fürth, Bavaria, in 1927. In 1938, his family immigrated to Wisconsin and later moved to Rochester, New York. Just after finishing high school in 1945, Schopler was drafted into the US Army. He later worked as a psychiatric social worker in different institutions and obtained a PhD in child psychology at the University of Chicago in 1964. Upon taking his first academic job at the University of North Carolina at Chapel Hill in 1964, Schopler and his colleague Robert Reichler started the Child Research Project, an outpatient program for the study and education of children with various conditions, including autism.

In the late 1960s, Schopler and his student Julie Loftin investigated the claim that the mothers of children with autism showed "disordered thinking." Their joint 1969 publication of the results noted how parents such as Clara Park had recently contested the view that they were "refrigerator parents" while some research using the Object Sorting Test, in which individuals sort objects following previously provided patterns or rules, showed impaired thinking in the parents of psychotic adults and children. Schopler and Loftin tested the parents in different situations, telling them that the test had different purposes. The results showed that parents (particularly the mothers) suffered from "disordered thinking" only when they were in situations where they felt they were being evaluated "about the anxieties, guilt and confusion" resulting from their experiences with their psychotic or autistic child.[29] This corroborated what Clara and Ruth Sullivan had been saying about their frustrating experiences with experts who were predisposed to be suspicious of them: no mother could be relaxed and warm when she was standing trial.

Greatly impressed by *The Siege*, Schopler invited Clara that same year to give a talk at a conference he had organized. This would be Clara's first talk about Jessy. In 1971, Schopler published an article entitled "Parents of Psychotic Children as Scapegoats." As the title indicated, he maintained that psychiatrists and psychologists had used parents as scapegoats to cover their own inability to understand and help their children. His main references were the writings of all the parents who had provided insightful analysis of autism, including Frances Eberhardy and Clara Park. Schopler recognized early on how much researchers and clinicians could learn from parents.[30]

From then on, Schopler and Reichler encouraged parents to become cotherapists. In a 1971 paper that became widely influential, they proposed a "developmental therapy" in which parents would play a major role in improving the "adaptation between the child and his family."[31] The parents first watched trained therapists work with their autistic children through a glass window. Then, the parents and therapists talked about what worked and what did not. The parents also shared their techniques and experiences. Although most parents did not have formal training as therapists, Schopler and his colleagues recognized their valuable input. At this time, Schopler and Reichler still said that the way to help autistic children was by rebuilding their relationship with their mothers, but they now welcomed these mothers as collaborators.

Clara, who often noted that it was easier to catch flies with honey than with vinegar, eagerly joined forces with Schopler. As editor of the NSAC newsletter, Clara assisted Schopler by promoting his views among the parents and publicizing events he organized. Over time, the honey worked. Schopler became more and more impressed by parents' contributions and involved them in his conferences and other projects.

Parents became instrumental in the success of Schopler's major endeavor. In the early 1970s Schopler kept Clara informed about his efforts to develop a center for research and treatment of autistic children.[32] Established in 1970, the North Carolina chapter of NSAC lobbied the state legislature for funding this project. In 1971, Schopler and the chapter's president, Frank Warren, whose autistic son George had learned to talk after participating in Schopler's program, convinced Democratic State Senator Charles H. Larkins Jr., to introduce a bill in the General Assembly that recommended funding for a public program to carry out research and provide therapy for autistic children. Several endorsements accompanied the bill, including one from Leo Kanner and one from NSAC's president, S. Clarence Griffith Jr. After the bill passed, the University of North Carolina established a center for the Treatment and Education of Autistic and Related Communications-Handicapped Children, or TEACCH, in 1972.[33]

The creation of TEACCH was a landmark development in the history of autism. It was the first program receiving extended funding for autistic children from a state government. Furthermore, this funding went towards establishing a statewide program of training and education, not merely a grant for research or a specific project. With three initial centers and its headquarters located at a major research university, the prospects for its continuity were strong. And TEACCH welcomed parents.

Collaborating together at TEACCH, parents and psychologists such as Schopler and later Gary Mesibov developed teaching programs and services for autistic children. Including classes in music and arts, they sought to build on their special skills and strengths. For each autistic child, they set individual goals based on a profound knowledge of the cognitive strengths of the child and his or her family situation. Those goals respected the different ways autistic children perceive the world.[34]

The give and take between therapist and parent, which had been so vehemently denied to Clara and other parents only about a decade earlier, became the hallmark of Schopler's approach. Schopler even required parents to keep "daily logs," thus institutionalizing the practice Clara and many other parents had started on their own years ago. Earlier, many psychiatrists had criticized this practice, which was useful to understand the particularities of each child, as a sign of the mother's cold objectivity and intellectual approach to childrearing.

Schopler encouraged collaboration in other venues. For example, in 1974, as incoming editor of the *Journal of Autism and Child Schizophrenia*, he started publishing a new column entitled "Parents Speak," conceived as a forum for dialogue between parents and professionals. Mary S. Akerley, NSAC's president at the time, penned the introduction, noting that the Society saw this column "as a way to contribute to the clinical picture of autism" by providing the "parental perspective" necessary for a "comprehensive view."[35] This initiative made some professionals nervous, however. In another new section in the same volume, "Questions, Answers, and Comments," the first question printed was a query to the editor by an editorial board member of the journal, British psychoanalyst E. James Anthony. He worried about the new policy of including parents as contributors because "the scientific level might well be lowered as a result." Schopler replied that, in his view, "an attempt at reasonable dialogue over scientific and clinical material" would "enhance the scientific level rather than diminish it."[36] Schopler and Gary Mesibov also invited parents to write articles in the books they edited about different aspects of autism. Clara Park, Margaret Dewey, and other parents became regular contributors. Their participation was not simply seen as anecdotal.[37]

Parents had become welcome collaborators in the effort to understand autism and improve the lives of autistic people not only by providing adequate support and services for them, but also by changing society's perception of autism. For Schopler and his collaborators, autism was not a mental illness but a lifelong developmental disability. Making this view official, in 1979, Schopler renamed the *Journal of Autism and Childhood Schizophrenia* as the *Journal of Autism and Developmental Disorders*. His longstanding collaboration with parents had led to important programs that adapted teaching styles to the characteristics of autistic people, to a better appreciation of their strengths, and to joint efforts to bring about social change for autistic people's acceptance.

Other psychologists were also traveling the road toward collaboration with parents, including Ole Ivar Lovaas.

Lovaas was born in 1927 near Oslo, Norway. A talented violinist, he moved to the US with a music fellowship from Luther College in Iowa. But World War II and the Nazi occupation of Norway when he was a teenager left a deep impression on him. He turned to psychology to understand human behavior, earned his PhD from the University of Washington in 1958, and in 1961 he became a psychology professor at the University of California, Los Angeles.

By all accounts, Lovaas was a man of boundless energy who did not fear professional or physical challenges. He loved playing handball, skiing, and sailing. His former students remember him as a charismatic teacher, amusing them with all sorts of stories with his loud, tenor voice and strong Nordic accent. Beneath the public persona, however, one encountered a man with changing moods who could be harsh to others. Lovaas's work on autism and his personality brought him many admiring followers as well as fierce critics.

Lovaas's therapeutic approach aimed at teaching or modifying specific behaviors using principles associated with behavioral psychologist B. F. Skinner. For Skinner, all behavior can be taught using appropriate rewards and punishments. Known as Applied Behavior Analysis (ABA), Lovaas's approach first required "breaking down" a behavior into manageable components. The second step consisted of enticing a child to learn a behavior by using things such as sweets or small sips of juice as rewards. Lovaas's early work focused on teaching language to autistic children in a laboratory setting.

The application of ABA methods required intensive work with each child. During a whole year, Lovaas and his group devoted six hours a day, five days a week to one girl: Beth. Since age three, Beth had banged her head against walls and furniture; she pinched and slapped herself; once she set her hair on fire by sticking her head into the electric wall heater. Her body was swollen and bruised, her skin discolored.

Lovaas mostly used positive reinforcement, through rewards, but he also used aversive tools—punishment or unpleasant stimuli— in order to eliminate children's self-inflicted harms or aggression toward others. Unfortunately, offering sympathetic comments to Beth during her self-destructive behavior actually increased its frequency and magnitude. Through a combination of reinforcements and punishment, the team helped her control her injurious actions.[38] Aversive stimuli included unpleasant slaps on the thigh, shouting, and, in some cases, low-level electric shock.

"Screams, Slaps and Love: A Surprising, Shocking Treatment Helps Far-Gone Mental Cripples." That was the title of a 1965 *Life* magazine piece on Lovaas and his work with four children between the ages of seven and nine: Pamela, Ricky, Chuck, and Billy. The authors, Don Moser and Allan Grant, noted that seven-year-old Billy, "like so many of the thousands of autistic children in the U.S., would go into gigantic tantrums and fits of self-destruction, beating his head black and blue against the wall." The article emphasized that Lovaas was not interested in causes, but results: "You have to put out the fire first before you worry how it started."[39]

In explaining how Lovaas put out fires, *Life* focused on the most dramatic, controversial part of his treatment: the shock room. The article declared that the "most drastic innovation" in Lovaas's techniques was "punishment. . . . His rarely used last resort is the shock room."[40] But the words "rarely used last resort" in the sentence are muted as they appear in a small column of text next to big photographs in which Pamela, in her capri pants, flower shirt, and ponytail, looks with terror at the floor beneath her bare feet. Here in the shock room she is walking on a floor laced with metallic strips, and with two electrodes on her back. Lovaas is teaching her to read. When she gets distracted and stops reading, Lovaas yells "No!" and turns on a current high enough that she screams.

On the next page, which shows therapists playing with the children, the reporters noted how they demonstrated affection as a way to teach children: "Even more than punishment, patience and tenderness are lavished on the children by the staff. Every hour of lesson time has a 10-minute break for affectionate play." But the word "love" in the article's title comes third, after screams and slaps. The article's discussion of love as a central tool in Lovaas's behavioral therapy was muted amidst the children's screams.

After "some 90,000" interactions using food and affection for rewards, seven year old Billy was able to talk and use some language for communication. The "big breakthrough" for Chuck, who was also seven, was giving "a simple friendly hug" to the therapist, an event that his mother watched in delight through a one-way mirror. Pamela, age nine, had started to read, though when left on her own she reverted to her "bizarre autistic ways." And Ricky, age eight, improved his communication skills, on one occasion telling the members of a UCLA seminar: "I am 4 feet 3 inches tall and I'm wearing black and white tennis shoes!"[41] The authors left it up to the readers to decide whether using punishment to teach these children was justified. But it would be difficult for a reader to forget Pamela's big, open eyes, as she waited in terror for the next electric shock.

In several of his writings, Lovaas addressed the ethical concerns about using punishment, arguing that the ability to reduce aggressive and self-destructive behavior justified its use in a controlled manner.[42] However, the controversy would not go away.

Almost a decade after the *Life* article, a 1974 interview in *Psychology Today* focused public attention once again on ABA's use of punishment. Lovaas argued that aversives were a tool that only a loving teacher could use in a very controlled way in specific cases, such as to avoid self-mutilating or aggressive behavior. The interviewer, Paul Chance, entitled his biographical sketch of Lovaas "Poet with a Cattle Prod," and described him as "a poet who is not afraid to get his hands dirty."[43]

Others tried to present the kinder face of behavioral modification. That same year, in a piece for the *New York Times*, Robert Claiborne defended "behavior modification" in helping children with autism—counter to the growing concern over ABA created by Stanley Kubrick's 1971 now classic film *A Clockwork Orange*. In this film, researchers use extreme conditioning techniques, including strong electroshocks, to rehabilitate a sadistic criminal. Claiborne argued that rewarding certain behaviors and discouraging —even punishing—others was what parents had been doing for ages to educate their children. He supported the work of "pioneers" such as Lovaas who "have taught self-control to children who previously had to be kept in straitjackets to prevent them from mutilating themselves."[44] If the name Robert Claiborne sounds familiar, it's because we've met him already; he was Clara Park's brother.

In the mid-1970s, Lovaas and his colleagues assessed the results of using ABA treatment for seven years with twenty autistic children. They reported significant gains, but they also found that gains in language and social interaction were subsequently lost in many cases, as the children often reverted to their pre-treatment baseline behaviors. Three variables made a difference: how early the intervention started, how intensive it was, and how much the family was involved.[45] For example, Rick and Pam, two autistic children, regressed when they went to a state institution after being discharged from the UCLA program. However, children who went home and had parents who continued the therapy fared much better. These results led Lovaas to shift his focus from the lab to home-based interventions, and from professional therapists to parents.

Parents became increasingly important in the effective use of behavioral therapy for two reasons. First, as Lovaas and his colleagues noted, putting an ABA program in parents' hands assured "generalization of the treatment effects to the child's natural environment" and helped "maintain the treatment gains."[46] Second, parents were also needed in order to tailor ABA treatment to the characteristics of each child. Because of the diversity of children included under the diagnosis of autism, Lovaas and his colleagues proposed to pay more attention to individual differences in applying ABA. They emphasized that behavior therapy resembled procedures used by teachers such as Anne Sullivan as well as parents such as Clara Park. Lovaas confessed to be "struck" by the similarity of the methods used by these teachers, and by their comprehensive and meticulous commitment in their use.[47]

Lovaas and his colleagues also rejected the disease model of autism and emphasized the need to work on specific behaviors that could help a child to live an independent life, as explained in their 1981 book *Teaching Developmentally Disabled Children: The Me Book*.[48] The book presented a program of environmental reform: "Our task," said Lovaas, was "to construct a special environment, one in which the disabled child could learn."[49] The book chapters guided the reader to help the children learn a variety of behaviors: sit, pay attention, give a hug, stop self-stimulatory and disruptive conducts, imitate, acquire basic language skills, and follow verbal instructions. Lovaas and his collaborators also focused on the acquisition of diverse cognitive and social skills such as drawing, writing, and playing, and independence-building skills, such as dressing or bathing. Children learned these skills best in their homes and schools. Thus, Lovaas concluded: "The parents and teachers became the child's primary therapists, and we became their consultants."[50]

Lovaas's work on ABA became well known. He engaged in public debates passionately. And he built an influential treatment center. Much of his success was due to the support he received from parents. Later in his career, Lovaas recalled a dinner with Bernard Rimland and five other parents of autistic children in 1964 as a turning point in his relationship with parents. Rimland and other concerned and active parents convinced him that the only way to "break the stronghold exercised by psychodynamic therapists over treatment" was "through joint action."[51] They all agreed on one thing: therapy first, theory later. Lovaas welcomed parents as co-therapists from the beginning, and later considered them the primary teachers for their children.

However, Lovaas's behavioristic approach was controversial from the start and only became more so over the years. Early on, some parents found ABA very effective, while others did not. Rimland was one of the first parents to support Lovaas. Rimland and his wife, Gloria, had been advised to put their autistic son Mark in an institution. At seven, Mark was in diapers. He started using language to communicate with them at eight and a half. In 1964, during his year at Stanford's Center for Advanced Study in the Behavioral Sciences, Rimland visited UCLA to see if Lovaas's approach could be used with his son. After Rimland met Lovaas and observed his methods, he and Gloria started using applied behavioral therapy to teach their son. Mark learned to read very quickly. He made sufficient progress socially that he was able to live at home with his parents and siblings and attend a nearby school.[52] Rimland became a stalwart supporter of ABA. Other parents were extremely disappointed. Josh Greenfeld moved with his wife and two sons from the suburbs of New York City to Los Angeles in order to have Lovaas work with his autistic son Noah. But according to Greenfeld, Lovaas lost interest in Noah as soon as he saw that he was not making much progress.[53] ABA did not work for every autistic child.

Lovaas's use of aversives became enormously controversial among parents as well. During the mid-1970s, thanks to the backing of Rimland, the Parks, and some other parents, the National Society for Autistic Children gave qualified support to the use of aversives for difficult cases in which children severely injured themselves or others. Although he had many disagreements with Lovaas, at this time Schopler also defended the view that punishment might be necessary in some cases. As time went on, however, this became an increasingly divisive stance. Some parents resisted ABA because they didn't want to use punishment to teach their children.

ABA has remained deeply controversial to this day. Several accounts have praised it, and thousands of families still use it in North America. However, autistic advocates and allies have also presented poignant criticism. They flatly reject the use of punishments as unethical. In addition, they consider the whole ABA approach to be dehumanizing and infantilizing because an external authority tries to change a person's behavior through rewards and punishments. Many of them also criticize it as ineffective. In many cases, it is also misguided since it is often used to change behaviors that are not harmful (such as hand flapping). Furthermore, the critics have argued that the goal of ABA treatment is to make autistic people behave more like non-autistic people. As such, it supports a normative model of behavior for all individuals, rather than respecting autistic differences.[54] These are important critical perspectives that are still debated today and get to the core of what the objectives of any therapeutic program regarding autism should be.

However flawed some of these therapeutic approaches are considered today, in the 1970s, the teamwork between parents and psychologists brought about two important changes in the history of autism in the United Sates. First, it was a major gain for parents, and especially mothers, who had started as co-patients and went on to become collaborators. This represented a profound improvement over previous approaches. Bettelheim thought removing autistic children from their mothers' care was an essential step for the children's improvement. Many psychoanalysts included parents in the children's therapeutic sessions, but they also treated mothers for their pathologies in separate sessions. Lovaas and Schopler, in contrast, welcomed parents as equal partners.

Second, this collaboration also transformed the way autism was generally conceived. As co-therapists, the parents' practical work— focusing on teaching autistic children specific skills—was key to the reconceptualization of autism from a mental disease to a developmental condition.[55] From that perspective, parents placed less emphasis on finding a cure, and more emphasis on teaching their children coping skills and finding supports that helped them learn in their own ways.

To a great extent, this shift was possible because many parents, including Clara Park, did not simply "apply" psychological theories or general therapeutic models. Becoming part of their children's education allowed parents to reshape the programs and techniques in ways that were better adapted to their children's individuality and specific needs. From the inside, parents could provide a better critique of the limitations of those programs.

Working with supportive psychologists, parents focused on cultivating their children's skills and engaging them in their own development. Through that joint work, concentrating on how to teach children on the basis of their individual needs and their special strengths, researchers and parents continued to uncover the children's ability to learn, as well as the wide range of diversity among autistic children. This would have tremendous consequences.

CHAPTER 7

FROM CUSTODIAL
CARE TO EDUCATION
FOR AUTISTIC CHILDREN

C LARA PARK AND OTHER MOTHERS WHO, in the 1950s
and early 1960s, decided to teach their autistic children
at home went against common medical advice and social norms.
During that period, many child psychiatrists and pediatricians still
recommended custodial care for a child with behavioral difficulties
or cognitive disabilities. Often, the rationale was not that it would
be better for the child, but that it would be better for the parents
and the siblings. For a variety of reasons, many parents followed
that advice. Sometimes, they did not even mention to others the existence of their disabled child. For example, in 1944, psychoanalyst
Erik Erikson and his wife put their fourth child, Neil, who was born
with Down's syndrome, into an institution without ever telling their
other children.[1] Two decades later, in 1966, the famous playwright
Arthur Miller institutionalized his son, Daniel Miller, also born with
Down's syndrome. Miller, who had written so insightfully about

prejudice, did not even bring his son home from the hospital when he was born, and did not mention him in his autobiography.

In 1962, two years after her brother John F. Kennedy was elected president of the United States, Eunice Kennedy Shriver broke the silence surrounding this topic by publishing a moving account of her older sister, Rosemary, in the *Saturday Evening Post*. Rosemary had been born with a mild cognitive disability. She was raised at home and participated in family life and travels. However, in her early twenties, after she hit a member of her family, she was subjected to a lobotomy that left her practically mute and catatonic. She spent the rest of her life in custodial care. Eunice Shriver's article called for fighting public prejudice and advocated the deinstitutionalization of children and adults in custodial care. She encouraged families and all citizens to focus on the abilities of people with developmental delays and to include them in all aspects of community life.

Senator Robert Kennedy—one of Eunice and Rosemary's brothers—visited the Willowbrook State School for children in Staten Island, New York, in 1965. He was shocked at the conditions. Willowbrook was the largest state-run institution for people with mental disabilities in the United States. It had opened in 1947 and was designed for a maximum of four thousand people. In the mid-1960s, it sadly (but literally) warehoused six thousand children and adults in deplorable conditions. Though a social worker, newspaper coverage, and a television station alerted the public to the inhumane situation there, the institution remained open until 1975, when it closed as the result of the activism of parents, social workers, and journalists.

Willowbrook may have been a particularly extreme case, but many other institutions were little better. In his moving and insightful account of living with a disability, *Brilliant Imperfections*, Eli Clare recalls how his parents took him to be examined at a different custodial institution, the Oregon Fairview Home, in 1966. Fortunately, he says: "If my parents did nothing else, they didn't leave me there." Having learned more about the inhumane treatments at this institution over the years, he confesses that Fairview still haunts him. Only many years of activism led to the deinstitutionalization of children during the 1970s and 1980s as well as the closing of institutions in which, as Clare puts it: "Sisters, fathers, cousins, and aunts vanished from their home communities."[2]

The Parks had also been advised to put Jessy in an institution, but they did not. Together with other families who raised children with disabilities at home, they helped to transform a culture that did not welcome children who behaved in ways that society did not accept. Although they were middle-class families who had been expected to build "normal" families and have perfect children, the Rimlands, Sullivans, Deweys, Parks, and many other parents of autistic children did not hide them away.

Working with their children and teaching them, these parents provided convincing evidence that autistic children had the capacity to learn. They did so, as Clara had said, by working first through trial and error and later with the support of psychologists such as Lovaas and Schopler, selectively borrowing and adapting techniques that worked well with their children.

An inveterate pragmatist, Clara rejected the view that Lovaas's operant conditioning–based behavioral therapy (later called Applied Behavior Analysis or ABA) treated children like trained laboratory animals. She didn't let anyone box her into an absolutist view concerning ABA, either on the side of those who supported it or on that of its vehement opponents. On May 28, 1969, she wrote to Schopler that "an element of the irrational enters into both positions."[3] In addition, she had just seen a film where children were taught using behavioral therapy and was impressed.

Clara was referring to UCLA psychologist Frank M. Hewett's 1965 twenty-minute documentary *Autism's Lonely Children*, one of the earliest portrayals in film of two children with a "severe emotional disorder called autism," a "withdrawal from the human world." In a room full of toys, one of the children, Marty, throws a stick down over and over and over again. Four-and-a-half-year-old Peter grinds down pencil after pencil after pencil. Hewett then works with each child in a teaching booth. He asks some simple questions: What's your name? He asks the child to imitate him as he touches his ear, claps his hands, or repeats a sound such as *bee, bee, bee*.

When the child does so correctly, he receives a piece of candy. When the child does not answer after repeated attempts, Hewett lowers a screen between them, leaving the child alone in the dark for a few moments. We never see the kids in apparent distress in their interactions with him. At one point, Marty spontaneously kisses Hewett on the cheek. As Clara noticed, Peter and Marty had developed a comfortable relationship with Hewett. Toward the end of the film, Hewett shows Peter's parents how to use picture cards to teach their son new words: *food, mama, water, key*. Using candy and praise, Peter's parents teach him new words. Up to then, his vocabulary had been limited to only fifteen words.[4]

Clara told Schopler that Hewett's film had drawn her attention to two important aspects. First, it illustrated how behavioral therapy could help these children develop new behaviors, "probably more efficiently and quickly than more haphazard and less intensive methods." Second, she also noticed that it had another beneficial effect: it helped the child develop a relationship with another human being in a way that the child seemed "able to accept." In this way, the therapy facilitated the "establishment of a personal relationship with him."

For Clara, behavioral therapy did not require treating autistic children as laboratory animals taught to perform tricks for rewards, like Skinner's pigeons. In fact, she suggested to Schopler that this method could be used in a way that made developing a relationship with the therapist a reward for the child. In that way, autistic children could learn to relate to other people in nonthreatening ways.

In sum, Clara saw no need to choose between the approaches of Schopler and Lovaas. A mother could and should use both, as long as it helped her child. Clara knew about Schopler's techniques (which sometimes included behavioral methods). She also heard Lovaas talk at conferences and, like many parents, borrowed selectively from his approach, adapting it in ways that seemed to work best for Jessy. As the editor of NSAC's newsletter, she made a point of reporting on different approaches and therapies. As she explained to Schopler, she did not "want the Newsletter to become the prisoner of any one method of treatment—*or* education, if the word makes any difference."[5]

Clara's aim was to teach Jessy, like any mother teaches her children. Because of Jessy's disability, Clara had to search among the available options at the time, seeking advice first from psychiatrists and psychoanalysts and later from psychologists. Despite her rejection of psychoanalysts' explanation for autism and the blame they placed on her, she focused on learning what she could from them in order to help teach Jessy the things she needed to learn. Working with psychotherapist Marie Singer, she realized that it was possible to overcome differing opinions on theory and jointly develop practical exercises that helped her daughter. When she later encountered the views of Schopler and Lovaas, Clara again concentrated on extracting the bits and pieces of their therapies that helped her devise ways to teach Jessy, in a comfortable way, the skills she needed.

First, safety: every child needs to learn that it is not safe to run into the street or touch the stove. Second, toilet-training. Third, some basic rules for living with others: not pushing or hitting your siblings, other children, or your teachers. Like other parents, and as she had done with her other children, Clara used rewards and, sometimes, appropriate punishments. In psychological jargon, these techniques come from behavioral therapy, though most of the time they are simply the strategies parents use naturally—for example, giving a sweet as a reward or withholding dessert as a penalty or punishment. Clara needed to use this method in areas in which Jessy had more difficulty learning.

By 1964, Clara had already told Rimland that she was trying to "operationalize love," using tickling and tossing her child in the air as rewards, and working with "small steps" to help Jessy make contact with others. By using reinforcements, Clara even tried to teach Jessy about emotions.[6] Today, some autistic advocates criticize the attempt to intervene in teaching an autistic person how to relate because they see this as an attempt to impose a neurotypical way of relating on the autistic child. Jessy, they would claim, has her own unique way of feeling and relating, and it should be valued. But when Jessy was a child, Clara did not know that. And neither did anyone else. The work of Clara and other parents helped to show that many autistic people find their own way of relating satisfactory and meaningful. That was a lesson Clara learned from Jessy through her deep engagement in Jessy's education.

For a few years, the Parks family made more systematic use of what one might call a homemade and very creative program inspired by operant conditioning. This program, based on rewarding desired behaviors, reduced and even put an end to some behaviors, such as screaming or pushing others, that had inhibited Jessy's learning and her relationships with classmates since her early days in school.

Jessy enjoyed going to school, but school had never been smooth sailing for her. In the earlier grades, she did not want to share crayons or join group activities. She grimaced. She screamed. Sometimes, she pushed others. Her teachers complained about her disruptive behavior. Overall, in the classroom, other children avoided her and she kept to herself. In high school, some of these things only got worse.

On a cool, early morning in the fall of 1971, Jessy boarded a bus to Mt. Greylock High School. She was thirteen years old. The social environment encouraged uniformity. Surrounded by teenagers following the latest fashions, Jessy stood out in her pink jacket and green mittens. Unlike other students who arrived to high school with friends, Jessy arrived alone. In the cafeteria, nobody sat with her. In the noisy hallways, with students darting around to a classroom or the gym, Jessy stood overwhelmed by the noise, covering her ears.

Shunned by other students, Jessy dealt with the sensory overburden by engaging in behaviors that made her more conspicuous. She stood in the hallways alone. She flapped her arms, wailed, and screamed. The other kids kept their distance from her. It did not help when she pushed others and cut in line. Nor when she approached people to smell them or touch their clothes. Jessy was generally pleasant, polite, and kind, but sometimes she interrupted people. Once she pushed a teacher against a wall. Some classmates made fun of her. Some kids bullied her. A few called her "retard." Jessy's behaviors made her stand out in a school environment that still praised uniformity and conformance, at a time when no disability was valued or even accepted.

However, a pair of seventeen-year-old identical twin sisters, Anna and Diana, found Jessy intriguing. One day Jessy came into their art class. While she painted, the teacher asked her what colors she was using. She did not answer. She covered her ears, mumbling "Mm-chello." When Jessy left, Anna asked the teacher about her. He said Jessy was autistic.[7]

Anna and Diana, who had only a few classes left before graduating, took the time to get to know Jessy and help her in school. They did so intensely. In art class, they worked with Jessy, sketching, drawing, and painting. They helped her understand directions, ate lunch with her, and modeled what to do in gym class so that Jessy could follow the rules and participate in team sports. Jessy shadowed them, imitating their moves. They became friends. Soon, Anna and Diana also became her informal teachers. Eager to support Jessy, they just needed the right tool for the job. And it arrived in an unexpected way.

It all started by chance, when a family with an autistic son visited the Parks. A watchlike gadget on the boy's wrist caught Jessy's attention. It was a golf counter, a tool that golfers use to keep score. When the boy did something good, he clicked it and gave himself a point. At the end of the day, if the boy had reached thirty points, his parents gave him a small reward.

Jessy immediately wanted one. This mechanical gadget had numbers, was predictable, and was easy to use—just the qualities that a child like Jessy, who was entranced by exactness and arithmetic, appreciated. Clara got a golf counter for Jessy, who could hardly wait for it to arrive in the mail.

Clara then made "a great invention," one that truly transformed the way the Parks used behavioral therapy: the contract. In collaboration, Clara and Jessy wrote a weekly contract and decided which specific words and actions were to be rewarded, such as "saying please" or "answering when spoken to."[8] Together, they decided how many points Jessy would get for each desirable behavior. For example, at the beginning, if Jessy reached a hundred points by the end of the day, she would get a popsicle. Each contract was, as her husband, David, put it, "a negotiated agreement and contained nothing" that Jessy did not approve. Jessy kept track of the points herself. Clara administered the rewards.[9]

Clara and Jessy also modified the system over time in mutually agreed upon ways. At first, there were only rewards, but later they introduced also "penalties," that is, deducting points for actions that they both concurred were not nice. Any actions that were not part of the contract were not rewarded or penalized. Some deductions were never necessary. Jessy and Clara had set a deduction of "1,000,000 points for calling attention" to somebody's illness or disability. Jessy never had to make that deduction.

Jessy enjoyed setting goals for herself and loved the contracts. Although she did not particularly like reading, she read over the contracts often. At first, they contained only a few items, but Jessy kept making them longer. Clara convinced her to stop at "two closely written pages." Over time, it became clear that Jessy did not even care about the specific rewards. The day when Jessy reached 145 ½ points, considerably more than the one hundred points needed for a popsicle, Clara realized that the points themselves had become rewards for Jessy.

This became clear when they drew up a contract for swimming. Clara had taught Jessy how to swim, but on her own she would only venture a few feet into the water before turning around and reaching for her mother's outstretched arms. So Clara and Jessy agreed to set a reward of a thousand points for swimming the length of the pool. Clara hoped Jessy would do so by the end of the year—advancing slowly, gradually learning to go a bit more, and then a bit more until reaching the end. Soon after making up the contract, they went to the pool one evening. Clara described what happened next: Jessy "walked up to the deep end of the pool, jumped in, and swam the 75-foot length *eight times*."[10]

The method was less useful for learning more abstract concepts such as "doing something to help" around the house. For Jessy to understand it, this broad idea had to be broken down into specific activities: vacuum the house, do the ironing, cooking, etc. Then, using the points method, Jessy soon learned to perform these activities, as she put it, "without told."

David reported about this program in the pages of the *Journal of Autism and Childhood Schizophrenia*, so that other parents could learn from it. He highlighted the aspects that they believed made it work. First, Jessy had to concentrate only on a few things at a time. Second, the plan made no impossible demands. Third, "the child was surrounded by success." Many of the behaviors that Clara and Jessy put in the contract had caused Jessy pain and frustration for years. Now, she was happy they were gone. Fourth, Jessy was responsible for the program too as she was an active and eager participant in its design and implementation. Lastly, the program played on Jessy's strengths: her interest in counting, systems, ritual, and her transparent honesty.[11]

Another advantage of the program was that Jessy could design contracts with other people in her family and also with her friends. Jessy's brother and sisters began to use it to help Jessy learn more new things. And so did Anna and Diana. Jessy received points for trying new foods, and she asked for ice cream and chocolate, two of her favorite sweets, as rewards. It was only a short time before she went from insisting on salads with only four ingredients to eating almost anything.

Jessy, her brother Paul, and the twins also introduced a new and important modification to their homemade behavioral program: they all became participants. Together, they wrote contracts for each other. After all, Jessy was not the only one who needed to learn or change some behaviors. Thus, in 1973, they all collaborated in writing some contracts for the summer they were spending together in the Parks' house on Block Island, just off the southern coast of Rhode Island. When they bought it some years earlier, it was such a wreck that Jessy called it the "mess house." But the family enjoyed renovating it and spending the summers there. That year, the twins joined them. In their summer contracts, Anna got points for trying new foods. Diana lost points for not exercising. And Paul lost quite a few for using "Bad Words."

This democratic approach encouraged all of them, and helped Jessy eliminate a verbal tic that made her speech difficult to understand. At the end of every sentence, she added a "hello." For example, she would say: "I like pizza, hello." When David and Clara left on a trip to Japan, Paul and the twins thought it would be nice if by the time they returned, Jessy had gotten rid of her "hellos." Jessy agreed to deduct a hundred points for each unnecessary hello. It was difficult because Jessy said the hellos so often that she had lost thousands of points within an hour.[12] She seemed quite unhappy at the end of the first day, but they all persevered. By the time David and Clara returned, the "hellos" were gone. With this program, Jessy was able to achieve her goals more effectively than many others. Although some of her house companions tried the points system for exercising more or eating fewer sweets, none of them had Jessy's determination and honesty.

At some point, Jessy and one of her teachers agreed that Jessy could work for "praise," not for points. Her parents were not sure this method would work. However, Jessy was willing and indeed eager to do it. After being told: "Jessy, that's good, that's wonderful!" she would smile and say: "Is this praise? Is this praise?"[13] Her family and friends felt also rewarded by her happiness. Smiles and praise are powerful reinforcements. They work on all of us.

According to her father, not only had Jessy enjoyed the program, she also welcomed the changes it brought about. "She has told us so herself," David concluded in his report about their homemade program based on the principles of operant conditioning.[14]

Though inspired by Skinner's ideas, the program the Park family had developed departed significantly from the standard view of ABA as an intensive program of behavior modification imposed by an external authority. Jessy set her goals, chose her rewards, and agreed to the "punishments" or penalties. Their program did not try to eliminate autistic behaviors such as rocking or flapping but focused on behaviors that Jessy said she wanted to change because they made her feel anxious or interfered with other things she wanted to do. Because the program was designed to use elements she liked—specific goals, fixed rules, precise rewards—Jessy expressed that she wanted to participate and provided input in its development.

Thus, the way the Park family used the behavioral approach cannot be said to follow a medical model that privileges scientific expertise, assumes that disability has no inherent value, and sees autism as something to overcome. In a collaborative way, they all designed the contracts and modified the program in light of their own experiences; they focused on behaviors that each of the participants, including Jessy, wanted to change, without any external authority imposing goals on them.

Reading about a therapy or a teaching program in the textbooks or the academic articles, we often encounter a one-model-fits-all scheme. Yet, in real life, parents were changing and adapting activities and programs to suit their own children. Those adaptations, carried out in the domestic space by individual families, are rarely documented and published. But we cannot undervalue how common and significant they have been in the history of autism.[15]

The insights gained through these practices that families developed on their own are also knowledge, experiential knowledge, that was often shared and transmitted to others. This happened in their correspondence, discussions during their meetings, or through information provided in the NSAC newsletter. For example, after reading about the Parks' experience with their contract in the NSAC newsletter, Elizabeth M. Flagler, the mother of an autistic son, wrote to the Parks that she was going to try it with him. She, too, was avoiding using this method to "eradicate" her son's autism since, as she put it, "the mainstream is not the goal we are aiming for."[16]

Teaching their children, the parents and families of autistic children made a crucial discovery: autistic children were able to learn. That knowledge led them to fight for their children's education.[17] Society also needed to change in order to support and value their education.

THE RIGHT TO AN EDUCATION

As a teacher, Clara had seen firsthand how education could change one's possibilities and sense of self. For the Parks, it was clear that Jessy needed to attend school, though getting her accepted was a struggle. On several occasions, the school said Jessy could not continue. Because some teachers and classmates found her behavior too disruptive, her prospects for continuing in a public school were uncertain. Clara and David even inquired about sending her to a boarding school. But they fought continuously, and, at the end of

1969, the local school system allowed Jessy to continue, though on a part-time basis and taking only some classes. But things were about to change.

In the early 1970s, a series of developments made special education a legal issue. An investigative report called *The Way We Go to School: Children Excluded in Boston*, published by the Task Force on Children out of School in 1969, had shown that thousands of children received an inferior education or were systematically excluded altogether from the public education system. Using this evidence, activists fought to change this state of affairs. Eventually, their efforts led the Massachusetts state legislature to pass Chapter 766, the first state-level special education law in the nation's history, in 1972.[18] Clara became involved in advisory and review activities for special education in Massachusetts after this law was passed.

Meanwhile, in 1971, the Pennsylvania Association for Retarded Children (PARC) had also challenged laws excluding "children of school age who deviate from the average in physical, mental, emotional or social characteristics to such an extent that they require special educational facilities or services" from attending school. The lawsuit was settled in US District Court in early 1972, thereby ending the common practice of denying those children access to free public programs of education and training.[19]

It was a watershed event. In 1974, Clara published "Elly's Right to Education" (Jessy was still Elly for the public), an article that made clear how important this victory was, not only for autistic children like her daughter but also for all children who did not fit the standard norms. Most of these norms had been established through mental tests that, while aiming to measure some "natural" cognitive abilities, relied on faulty assumptions, racist beliefs, and sociocultural biases.

To illustrate how difficult school access for autistic children had been up to that point, Clara recounted how Jessy's schooling had been a long process marked by anguish, instability, and numerous returns to square one. It included a few years of private school, arguments with public school administrators, months-long periods of

Jessy being sent home because she was too disruptive or did not fit in with the other kids. In the school system, nobody had a good plan for Jessy. As Clara put it: "Children weren't supposed to be emotionally disturbed for more than two years. They were supposed to get well after that, or disappear." A residential school is what the local schools always proposed to them, an institutional solution for what they considered the Parks' private problem. Then it would be "out of sight, out of mind."

But the Parks, like many other parents and activists, believed that all children had a right to an education, and that society was responsible for providing it.[20] They did not give up, and Jessy was allowed to go back into the school system, at first part-time, then as a full-time student. She was in a class for the "educable retarded," where she was taught by teachers with training in special education. Clara revealed how at one point, the psychologist who tested Jessy at the school said she was a lost case, an autistic-turned-schizophrenic who instead of mathematics should be taught at most to "handle her periods." Wisely, Jessy's teachers did not heed that advice.[21]

Like other autistic children, Jessy had a *right* to be in school. And through the judicial system, the US government had determined that she deserved publicly supported education just as much as any other child. Jessy, her mother proudly said, "would be in school, and still be at home with us, because we loved her and taught her and played with her and worked with her, and we didn't want to send her away."[22]

And other children with disabilities had a right to schooling as well. Her journey with Jessy had taught Clara that the fight to make society value and support a child with a disability could not be only about autism. For her, coalition building with other advocacy groups was not just a strategy to gain political power, though that was important too. Clara believed that society needed to value all disabled people and welcome them in all areas of community life, starting with educational institutions and programs.

In a 1976 book, *You Are Not Alone*, which Clara wrote to offer practical advice to the parents, she highlighted this message of hope,

citing the psychologist she had seen using behavioral methods in a
documentary, in what she perceived was a humane way:

> Until recently, more often than not, it has been possible for school
> administrators to tell us that our children are too handicapped—
> whether emotionally, or physically, or mentally, or in combina-
> tion—for schools to teach them. If they say that to you—and it's still
> very likely they may—you can quote Dr. Frank Hewett, Professor
> of Education and Psychiatry at the University of California at Los
> Angeles. Tell them that "every child is ready to learn *something*,"
> and that it's the school's business to find out what and how. But
> since 1972, you have had more than words behind you. You have
> had law.[23]

She was right. Just recently, the fight for the educational rights
of all children paid off. The 1972 District Court's decree became
codified in national legislation as the 1975 Education for All Handi-
capped Children Act. This law required public schools that accepted
federal funds to provide equal access to education for children with
physical and mental disabilities. In 1990, and thanks to the efforts of
parents, the revised act—renamed the Individuals with Disabilities
Education Act (IDEA)—specifically referred to autism as one of the
disabilities covered.

On the basis of their practical work with them, the parents who
raised their children at home acquired enough knowledge to contest
a dismal psychiatric diagnosis and to challenge the social limits on
what their children could do.

Working with their children in an intensive and continuous way,
with the help of supportive teachers and psychologists, parents also
discovered another important fact about their children: they varied a lot.

DIVERSITY WITHIN "AUTISM"

From the start, parents had a difficult time obtaining a definite diagnosis for their autistic children. This was due to several factors:
the diversity of terms employed (atypical children, infantile autism,

childhood schizophrenia, autistic psychopathy), the uncertainty about whether infants would "outgrow" certain behaviors, and the fact that some of the behaviors characteristic of autism are also seen in children who have other conditions. As a result, by the end of the 1960s, clinicians still had not been able to agree on a standard set of diagnostic criteria.

But there was another reason why diagnosis was difficult: the category of autism included children with a wide range of behaviors and abilities. In the 1970s, epidemiological work, follow-up studies of autistic children diagnosed years or even decades earlier, and the work of parents made it clear that the category of autism encompassed a very heterogeneous group of children.

Epidemiological studies aiming to figure out how many children were autistic revealed that there were many "types" of autistic children. In 1967, Victor Lotter, a member of the Social Psychiatry Unit at Maudsley Hospital in London, published the first estimate of "autistic conditions" in the world. He looked at children from ages eight to ten in Middlesex, in the Greater London area.[24] Working first with John Wing, the researcher who had written a negative review of Bettelheim's book, Lotter started with a list of criteria published in 1961 by a committee of British experts led by psychiatrist Mildred Creak.[25] Wing and Lotter replaced some vague criteria on that list with observable behaviors and measurable abilities.[26] Using their modified questionnaire, Lotter identified 135 "possible" cases of autism. Then, he gave intelligence and social maturity tests to those children, collected behavioral descriptions from their teachers, nurses, and mothers, and also met with each child. Analyzing those materials along with medical records, Lotter calculated a score for each child that identified thirty-two children as "autistic," corresponding to a rate of 4.5 cases per 10,000 in the Middlesex population.[27] Lotter also pointed out the existence of "great differences" between autistic children and suggested establishing subgroups.[28] Other researchers, such as Michael Rutter in England and James Anthony in the States had also proposed this.

Progress in refining diagnostic criteria was slow. Criticizing the state of confusion, Rutter proposed restricting the term and reserving the diagnosis of autism for "a severe disorder beginning in infancy," characterized by disturbances in interpersonal relationships. These were expressed as "an impression of aloofness and distance, an apparent lack of interest in people, a failure to form enduring relationships, avoidance of eye-to-eye gaze, . . . and a lack of sympathy or empathy for other people," among other symptoms.[29] Leo Kanner and Bernard Rimland had defended this position all along in their numerous attempts to establish strict criteria for "infantile autism."

Kanner, Rimland, and Rutter also held similar views about the parents of autistic children. Rutter argued that a "high proportion of the parents of autistic children are of above average intelligence and of superior socioeconomic status." Rutter noted that Lotter had found this result in his epidemiological study and thus proved that such a conclusion was "*not* an artefact of referral policies to clinics."[30] This had been a contested issue, though. Clara Park had told Rimland that other factors could explain why mostly educated and affluent parents had their kids diagnosed as autistic. For her, the reason was not that only these parents had autistic children; it was that they were more likely to have their children diagnosed as such.

Stereotypes about the parents of autistic children, and assumptions about class and race, were surely affecting diagnosis. Carolyn Betts was a poor Black mother when she gave birth to her son Jeffrey in 1970. In her memoir, she recounts how it took several years for him to "earn" a diagnosis of autism, after having received other diagnoses, including brain damage and childhood schizophrenia. Clara believed Betts's difficulties in obtaining the appropriate diagnosis were due to the professional assumptions about the social background of autistic children. Edward Ritvo, an autism researcher at UCLA, argued that several kinds of "referral bias" were responsible for the widespread belief about the parents being highly intelligent and mostly affluent. Assumptions about parents directly affected the criteria for diagnosis and, consequently, the prevalence numbers obtained by researchers. More importantly, they affected which children and families received support, and a correct diagnosis. To this day, we still know little about how social and racial biases influenced the history of autism. We do know that racial, gender, and class stereotypes still have a detrimental effect on autistic people and their lives.[31]

In the late 1960s, most debates about diagnosis centered on three fundamental issues that had been contested for about three decades: Was autism connected to childhood schizophrenia? Was there only one type of autism, or more? And what was the relation of autism to cognitive disability?

The relationship of autism to childhood schizophrenia had been confusing from the beginning. Psychiatrists first used the word "autism" to refer to a symptom of adult schizophrenia. Then, Kanner and Asperger postulated autism as a separate condition from childhood schizophrenia. Many psychiatrists used the terms "autism" and "childhood schizophrenia" interchangeably. Others, such as Lauretta Bender and Louise Despert, argued that autism was the earliest onset of childhood schizophrenia, a position that Kanner took on and off in his writings. In 1964, Rimland argued that infantile autism and childhood schizophrenia were two separate conditions, with different origins and different courses. By the late 1960s, this position represented the majority view. However, as late as 1968, the American Psychiatric Association's Diagnostic and Statistical Manual of Mental Disorders (DSM-II), which classified all accepted mental disorders, did not include autism as a condition; it only listed "Schizophrenia, childhood type."[32]

Was there only one type of autism, or were there more? Even the best-known proponents of autism as an independent condition did not agree, as seen in a special 1968 issue of Acta Paedopsychiatrica, celebrating the twenty-fifth anniversary of what its editor, Dutch child psychiatrist Arnold van Krevelen, called the "birth year of autism."[33] In that issue, van Krevelen republished Kanner's 1943 paper along with a new paper by Asperger.

Asperger published a new paper in which he compared his notion of autistic psychopathy to Kanner's diagnosis of infantile autism. He argued that, despite many similarities warranting the term "autism," the two "disturbances differ widely." In his view, whereas Kanner's children suffered from some psychotic state, "Asperger's children," as he called them, were endowed with very high intelligence and developed full speech. In addition, their disturbances were not as strong as those in children with infantile autism, which meant they had a better social prognosis. "Asperger's children," he noted, often did extremely well in their professions.[34]

So, twenty-five years after their first publications, Asperger defended the view that infantile autism was a condition different from autistic psychopathy. Kanner also saw it that way. But the question about the cognitive abilities of "Kanner's children" and "Asperger's children" was not so simple.

What was the relation of autism to cognitive disability? In his review paper Rutter claimed that there could be "no doubt that many autistic children function at a mentally subnormal level."[35] Yet, he noted that many researchers, including Rimland and Kanner, would not agree with his statement. Asperger had identified children with severe cognitive disabilities in his first paper on autism in 1938, though he did not mention these children in his 1943 article. He did not mention them in his 1968 paper either. Thus, "Asperger's children" were all endowed with very high intelligence because Asperger, who had originally posed the existence of two groups of children with autism, did not mention the group with intellectual disabilities. Kanner claimed that most children he described in his 1943 paper looked intelligent and had good cognitive "potentialities."[36] That is, they had the potential to learn, at least in some areas.

When Kanner published his first papers on autism, other clinicians in the United States pointed out that one could not clearly separate autistic children from children with intellectual disabilities. In their 1951 paper, "The Inadequacy of Present-Day Concepts of Mental Deficiency and Mental Illness in Child Psychiatry," the director of the Massachusetts School for the Feeble-Minded, Clemens E. Benda, together with Malcolm J. Farrell and Catherine E. Chipman, pointed out that the term "idiot" was originally used "for all exceptional children who were not able to make a proper community adjustment." If one looked only at behavioral patterns, "the idiot is almost, *by definition*, an 'autistic' child." Thus, they noted that institutions for the "mentally retarded" housed many autistic children who had been diagnosed as "idiots." These researchers believed that the criteria being now introduced to divide these children into "autistic" and "mentally deficient" were no longer valid.[37]

For Kanner, the strict separation of autistic children from children with cognitive disabilities became increasingly problematic when he discovered that the children he saw in 1943 had developed in very different ways. In 1970, he published a follow-up study of the eleven children in his 1943 paper. By this time Donald—the first boy Kanner diagnosed with infantile autism—was a thirty-six-year-old bachelor. He had obtained a BA in French, was working as a bank teller, lived with his parents, and played golf several times a week. He drove his own car and led a fairly independent life. In contrast, some of the other children had ended up in state hospitals. Although they had previously astonished adults with their feats of memory and other skills, now as adults they lay in self-isolation in a "nirvana-like existence." Those who could still be tested had IQs that had dropped to "figures usually referred to as low-grade moron or imbecile" ("imbecile" and "moron" were terms still commonly used by experts to designate different degrees of "feeblemindedness").[38] While Kanner did not use these results to reflect on the relationship between mental abilities and autism, he did note that they revealed considerable heterogeneity within his first group of children. Kanner concluded his review with a question: "It is well known in medicine that any illness may appear in different degrees of severity, all the way from the so-called *forme fruste* to the most fulminant manifestation. Does this possibly apply also to early infantile autism?"[39] He also ended another follow-up study published in 1971 wondering: Could early infantile autism manifest itself in different degrees in different people?

As studies in this area intensified, researchers confirmed the striking variation among autistic children. This discovery fueled further discussion about whether Asperger's notion of the "autistic psychopath" referred to the same condition as Kanner's "infantile autism" or not. In a 1971 paper published in the new *Journal of Autism and Childhood Schizophrenia*, the Dutch psychiatrist van Krevelen claimed, once more, that the "two clinical pictures differ considerably." For him, the conditions were "unmistakably" different because Kanner had described "psychotic *processes*, characterized by a *course*," whereas Asperger had described "*static*" personality "*traits.*"[40]

For mothers, whose expertise was based on daily contact with their children and their personal knowledge of other autistic children, the issue was not so clear. Clara asked her friend and active NSAC member Margaret Dewey for her opinion on van Krevelen's paper. Dewey answered that she did not care much for his attitude as it shut down debate by appealing to what he found "unmistakably clear." She also did not agree with him. The older autistic children she knew all had "aspects of the Asperger syndrome if they have speech, regardless of how early they showed autistic symptoms and the surety of this diagnosis." Dan Eberhardy, the son of the nurse who had written the critical review of Bettelheim's book, seemed to fit the description of Asperger kids provided by van Krevelen even more than her own son Jack did. Yet Dan "was clear cut autistic as an infant."[41] In fact, Leo Kanner himself had diagnosed Dan Eberhardy with infantile autism. Dewey had told Clara earlier how similar Dan was to her own son. She and Frances Eberhardy called their sons "long-distance twins" because "their talents, mannerisms and interests are so much alike." Dewey described them as "slow perfectionists as [piano] tuners, naïve, morally upright, rigid and sympathetic to the underdog."[42]

By comparing the evolution of their children with one another over the years mothers were able to appreciate that autistic "traits" were not necessarily static, as Kanner's follow up studies had also revealed. And, if they were not static, then there was no clear-cut separation between Kanner's and Asperger's syndromes. As an infant, Dewey's son Jack was exactly like the kids described by Kanner. In fact, she had identified her son's condition when she read Kanner's first paper. Now, Jack had a job tuning pianos. He was also able to have conversations about that topic, about music more generally, and about other subjects of interest to him. Dewey also told Clara about another puzzling case. At the 1969 NSAC conference, Kanner told her that only one child in his original group had married. Dewey imagined that the young man must have become "socially smooth enough to attract a girl." So, Dewey wrote, his social development raised the question: "Was this young man then not a real case of Kanner autism?"[43]

Dewey described other cases she knew, underscoring the different developmental paths in autism from childhood to adulthood. For example, one boy, Jim, who was now 20, "got through school in regular classes, talked earlier and better than [her son] Jack, has a higher I.Q., does college level Math but fifth grade reading comprehension at age 20." And Jim's brother, Randy, "has never talked at age 16 except for a few baby-talk words he recently acquired. He seems to be severely retarded." Yet "Doctors call them both autistic and are baffled by the differences."[44] In the autistic children she had met, Dewey did not see the sharp differentiation between the two syndromes that van Krevelen proposed. Moreover, some kids who had been diagnosed as fitting in one category now belonged in the other.

In the clinic or the psychiatrist's office, experts could fit their observations into neat, static categories. Using their tests for determining a person's "mental" ability and "social" development, they often assumed uniform stages of development and put children into fixed categories. Because the mothers observed processes, however, they could see development and change. Dewey's point is worth underscoring because it challenged the dichotomy between Kanner's and Asperger's types of autism.

In 1981, British researcher Lorna Wing published an influential article that is widely credited with introducing Asperger to the English-speaking world, as well as proposing the idea that autistic features are on a continuum (what is referred to today as the autism spectrum). Wing rejected the concept of "autistic psychopathy" and renamed it "Asperger's syndrome." She argued that autism encompassed a triad of impairments involving language, imagination, and repetitive activities. Wing posited that each autistic behavior had a range or spectrum of expression, as it "can occur in varying degrees of severity, and in association with any level of intelligence."[45]

The notion of a continuum of autistic behaviors was not a new idea. In the early twentieth century, Bleuler said that all of us engage in different degrees of autistic withdrawal and autistic thinking. In his 1943 paper, Kanner also recognized individual differences in the degree and development of autism, a fact corroborated by follow-up studies in the 1970s.[46] In the United States, in part thanks to van Krevelen's writings on Asperger, Rimland and several mothers of autistic children had been discussing these issues for years. Yet, it took a while for this idea to take hold. Why was that the case?

In my view, it had little to do with whether Asperger's paper was widely known or not; rather, it had more to do with knowledge that came from lived experiences. In her proposal of looking at autism as a continuum, Lorna Wing was drawing not only on her scientific research but also on her knowledge as a mother of an autistic child. Wing and her husband, John Wing, often corresponded with Clara, Dewey, and other parents of autistic children. When Wing introduced the idea of the continuum, she was putting a name on a known reality among the parents. Many of the families knew each other personally. They traveled to conferences with their children, saw both their own and other autistic children grow up, and compared notes about their development. In fact, as Eyal and his colleagues put it, the parents had constructed the "niche" in which the idea of an autism spectrum could thrive.[47] Parents, autistic people, and researchers could now adopt a notion whose significance had not been appreciated earlier.

IN THEIR OWN VOICE

As soon as Rimland put many families of autistic children in contact with each other in 1964, they began visiting each other. Many of them also attended NSAC's annual meetings as families, bringing their children. The families socialized after the professional sessions. These exchanges gave the parents a sense of community, but the meetings also enabled autistic children to meet each other and develop their own sense of community. In some cases, this was the first time that an autistic person met another. For example, when the Sullivans visited the Parks as early as 1965, their son Joseph met Jessy. Margaret Dewey's son Jack met Jessy in 1972. He told his mother that now he knew autism was "a real thing," since until then he had read about autism only in books. He was twice Jessy's age, but he understood her behavior and recognized himself in her. He was very happy to have met her.[48] Through his parents, Jack also met Frances Eberhardy's son Dan on several occasions, and they enjoyed each other's company. They shared a strong interest in music and felt they understood each other.

In their frequent correspondence with each other, Clara, Ruth Sullivan, Margaret Dewey, and other mothers discussed how they were learning to better hear their growing children's own views. For example, one day, Joseph Sullivan went into a tantrum about something. His mother could not discuss it with him because he was so upset. So she decided to write a question for Joe. He responded by writing the answer. It worked! She had found a new and helpful way for him to communicate his concerns to her. As she explained to Clara in a letter: "The change in mood was dramatic. He stopped shouting, and even stopped talking. He stood over my shoulder as I wrote, then quietly took the paper and held it up against the door to write his answer. He handed the paper back to me without a word; I answered, then he wrote another question. The episode finished quietly." Ruth Sullivan included a copy of their written conversation and her reflections in a letter to Clara: "I wonder if it is possible that during excited periods he cannot process verbal input as well as usual. Our written exchange seems to satisfy him."[49] Ruth Sullivan and her son Joseph had found a way of communicating that worked for both of them. He could thus make his desires known. Clara also tried this method with Jessy. It worked as well, and it became a good way of hearing Jessy's own views on many issues.

Clara and other parents also started including the voices of autistic individuals in the National Society for Autistic Children's newsletter, first through stories Clara told in a column entitled "How They Grow." When they first began writing about their children, the mothers changed their names to protect their identities. But when their kids became young adults, some of them wanted their names and experience recognized.

Thus, when Clara included a story about Margaret Dewey's son Jack using the name Dick, he read it and asked his mother: "Why did you change my name?" Dewey explained the reason, but Jack retorted: "Is autism something I should be ashamed of?" Dewey asked her son, who had always been interested in music and had a job as a piano tuner, whether he would want people to know he had been an autistic child if he became a successful composer. His response left no doubt: "Yes, because then people would treat autistic children better and give them a chance to develop their talents."

Margaret Dewey told Clara: "Henceforth in Newsletter Dick shall be Jack Dewey." Clara could not be happier: "It's marvelous, + pleases me so much. Tell Jack that his experiences are of help to many people + several of the letters I've had specifically mention his remarks. Jack Dewey he shall be."[50]

On other occasions, autistic people wrote their own articles for the newsletter. For example, Jessy published a piece in which she offered advice to other autistic people about how to submit a job application. James Flagler of New York contributed several times. Among other things, he published "How I Feel," an essay he wrote as a freshman at LaGuardia Community College in New York City.[51] Newsletter articles by autistic people helped them connect and find out they were not alone.

Clara encouraged Jessy to present her own views about her autistic experience. In a 1974 letter to John Wing about how there was only "inchmeal" progress in the field of autism, Clara said that she and Jessy were going to Smith College to give a lecture about autism. In the past, Clara had always talked *about* Jessy. But this time, when the college invited her to speak, she suggested including Jessy, who was now sixteen and who she thought would be able to handle some questions—"If the answers are weird they'll learn so much the more." Clara added: "Progress is slow and the destination even more uncertain for her than for the rest of us, but she couldn't have done this 4 years ago. There's that."[52]

The inclusion of Jessy at Clara's lecture was actually revolutionary. Not only did it show Jessy's social progress but Clara's as well. Clara had realized that her descriptions of Jessy's world could only provide a partial picture. Jessy had her own views. Her voice deserved a hearing. Other parents also realized that autistic people deserved to tell their own stories.

Parents began encouraging autistic people to present their own views at the National Society for Autistic Children conferences. These venues were comfortable and welcoming for them because they had attended as children with their parents. They also knew the other families and kids in attendance.[53] As early as 1970, Dewey's son Jack was interviewed in a panel at the annual conference. Autistic people became a larger presence as participants as well. Temple Grandin, an autistic person and scientist who became famous for her work in designing more humane facilities for animals, gave her first talk at an NSAC annual meeting after talking with Ruth Sullivan. They had met by chance in an airport in 1980 on their way to the NSAC annual meeting in Chicago, and Sullivan encouraged her to speak about her life. In the 1981 meeting held in Boston, Grandin participated in a roundtable discussion on adults with autism organized by Ruth Sullivan.[54] In 1988, Grandin became the first autistic person to serve on NSAC's board of directors (by this time, the society had changed its name to Autism Society of America).

As other societies emerged, some of them also invited autistic people to serve on their boards, though the road to inclusion was never smooth, as parents and autistic advocates came to disagree with each other and among themselves on a variety of issues regarding research, treatment for autism, and the legitimate representation of those autistic people who are not able to communicate their own positions on such topics.

Some of the mothers who had fought hard for their children's rights to become part of the community at all levels now realized they needed to step aside. Having advocated the rights of their children, encouraged them to express their own views, and helped them to develop their own interests, the parents also realized that they needed to let them speak in their own voice. In a letter, Margaret Dewey told Clara about her son's increasing self-awareness. After a difficult adolescence and a couple of distressing years in college, Jack had a job and his own place. Therefore, Dewey was planning to disengage herself from the National Society for Autistic Children. As she told Clara, she did not want "anybody (Jack included) to feel that I 'need' his autism for my own activities."[55]

For Margaret Dewey, it was important that her son move forward on his own terms. Jack, for example, wanted to hear more about autistic people and was "less enthusiastic about reports which give a lot of credit to the parents, especially if they fail to mention the effort the autistic one has made."[56] In fact, after reading a letter from Clara about Jessy, Margaret Dewey wrote to Clara: "One thing Jack especially liked about your letter was that it expressed a lot of appreciation for what Jessy can do for *you*."

Indeed, learning is so often reciprocal. In their journey living with autism, parents had learned much from their autistic children as well.

CHAPTER 8

WATERCOLORS ON WET PAPER

O VER THE YEARS, Clara received numerous letters from readers who wanted to know how Jessy was doing. People wrote from different parts of the country and around the world, including Austria, South Africa, Russia, and Mexico. Parents, researchers, therapists, and autistic people thanked Clara for sharing with them Jessy's story. While in earlier years, the parents of autistic children had written that another parent had recommended her books, now many of them said that a psychologist or a psychiatrist had told them to read Clara's work. This reflected a sea change in a field that now valued a mother's perspective.

Continuing her advocacy work for education and services for autistic people, Clara gave talks to different audiences in the United States and also traveled internationally to discuss her work and offer advice based on her familiarity with many of the issues autistic people confronted, such as stigmatization and lack of resources. In 1980 she went to Spain to promote the recent translation of *The*

Siege into Spanish and gave talks and a TV interview. She also met
with the first group of parents of autistic children in the country. She
went to India several times, first to Rajasthan in northern India in
1985, then Delhi and Bombay in 1987 and again in 1992, where she
and David met with local autism activists. In 1990, they traveled to
Turkey. And in 1994, Clara delivered a speech at an autism conference in Denmark.[1]

Clara also received letters from autistic people. They too had
learned from her writings. Sometimes, they shared a problem they
were having and asked for advice. Clara told her experiences and offered them suggestions. Writing to one of her correspondents, Kathy,
in 1991, Clara recommended her to number the pages of her letters
because she had accidentally dropped one of them and then had
trouble putting the pages back in order. Clara added: "I numbered
them, 16!"[2]

In private correspondence and lectures, Clara talked about her
and her daughter's journey together. Jessy sometimes joined her.
Once given a medical diagnosis that painted a pessimistic outlook
for her future, Jessy's personal growth had been remarkable. By
1980, Jessy had graduated from high school after taking a combination of regular courses and classes with special education teachers. Having entered at thirteen basically unable to read and write,
she later passed the minimum competency test that required basic
skills in reading, writing, and arithmetic in order to graduate with a
high school diploma. She joined classes in cooking and typing. She
played sports. She learned to draw and paint under the guidance of
a gifted teacher and the twins, Anna and Diana. After graduating
at twenty-two, Jessy completed a job-training program. Her friend
Anna, working by then as a human resources specialist, found Jessy
a part-time position at Williams College sorting letters in the mail-
room and calculating telephone charges for each professor.

Jessy was most content when she was working, and performed
her tasks with incredible attention to detail. She typed the Spanish
translation of *The Siege* for her mother, with remarkably few er-
rors. She took care of some household chores in a reliable and thorough manner. Living with her parents, and during the summers with

housemates while her parents where in their Block Island house, Jessy was the household expert, a super-organized homemaker.

Some challenges remained. It was a long, hard fight to control her distress if her favorite seat was taken on her bus ride to high school. At work, she could barely control her anxiety if an object was out of place or her routine was changed in any way. The desire for sameness, which Kanner had identified as one of the main characteristics of autism, remained powerful.

In 1996, renowned neurologist and author Oliver Sacks featured Jessy in a television documentary, part of his series *The Mind Traveller*. The episode aired on the BBC in the UK and on PBS in the US. In the documentary, Sacks tried to make sense of Jessy's fascination with numbers, the weather, thermostats, stars, and the sun. Intrigued by the combination of specificity and complexity of Jessy's systems, he realized that Jessy wanted a world that was totally predictable. That was why other people were so difficult to understand for her, and why she preferred the invariability of numbers and the fixity of stars.

Two years after the documentary, in 1998, Clara reported on Jessy's life in an article, "Exiting Nirvana," published in the *American Scholar*. The piece received the 1999 National Magazine Award for Feature Writing, which encouraged her to expand it into a new book. In 2001, Clara published *Exiting Nirvana: A Daughter's Life with Autism*.[3] By this point, Clara and Jessy had moved into regular and quiet routines in their lives. When Clara was writing *Exiting Nirvana*, Jessy was forty. She was busy with her daily work and life. Her desire for order was an asset that helped her manage daily routines and other tasks. She was never late to work. She knew the opening times for the supermarket, ice cream shop, and post office. She carefully planned vacation schedules. Jessy balanced her checkbook meticulously and saved more money than her siblings. Clara was in her late seventies. *Exiting Nirvana* was a book about Jessy, not about her mother.

In *Exiting Nirvana*, Clara used the metaphor of a "journey." But this was no ordinary journey. It was, in fact, a most atypical journey, almost a journey in reverse. Travel is usually defined by its destination, but the voyage Clara recounted was not directed toward a specific place; instead, it was aimed at abandoning a state, the state of serene happiness of nirvana.

Clara chose the image of nirvana to convey what the symptoms of autism don't. She could give many depictions of Jessy's autism: Jessy, two years old, looking straight through her, as if she weren't there. Jessy, eight years old, filling a big box with three-quarter-inch squares of cut-up paper to sift endlessly between her fingers. Jessy, eleven years old, filling sheet after sheet with divisions by 3, by 7, 11, 13, 17, 19. . . . There are many images to convey autistic behavior. But Clara wanted an image to convey what the behavior could not show by itself: Jessy was *happy*. As Clara wrote: "Craving, the Buddha taught, is the source of all suffering, detachment the road to the serene equilibrium of Nirvana."[4] But every child needs to grow and, as Clara pointed out, "there is no growth in Nirvana."[5] Maybe craving wasn't so bad after all. Hence, Clara conceived the journey as a departure, rather than an arrival. *Exiting Nirvana* was the story of how Jessy abandoned her isolation.

Where their journey would lead could only be discovered in time, as there were no roadmaps to follow. Clara and Jessy needed to chart their path together. Clara's account revealed that Jessy had traveled a hard journey, since she had to make so many adjustments to a world that did not understand her perspective. But Clara also traveled her own journey from "bewilderment," from her inability to understand her child's world, toward understanding, acceptance, and celebration.[6]

Clara divided her book in three main sections on language, thought, and sociality, plus a short interlude on Jessy's painting. Her exploratory journey was interlaced with brief accounts of scientific research on autism during the 1980s and 1990s. But Clara's goal was not to review the science of autism, because, she noted, there were "many people better qualified to do that." She could write about "the experience of autism," her own journey from "initial bewilderment, and the slow growth of at least partial understanding."[7]

How does one describe experience? Many scientific descriptions are systematic and seek comprehensiveness, but the description of experience can only ever be anecdotal. As Clara put it: "Without anecdotes there are words but not experience. . . . Reality escapes between the lines. Anecdotes must recapture it." But how does one organize those anecdotes in order to figure out their significance?

Clara started by explaining her own system for documenting and cataloguing some events in their lives: "In our kitchen—where we eat, talk, work, watch TV, where so many things happen—there is a folder filled with envelopes and a pen kept handy. Inside the envelopes are bits of paper, slips I grab when Jessy does something, says something, that shows progress toward our world, . . . or (the other side of the coin) that reveals how different her experience remains." The envelopes had different titles: Obsessions, Social, Correlations/ Analogies, Strangeness/Secret Life. Interdependent, the categories multiplied, overlapped, and embodied different perspectives. Experience, Clara knew, can only be the foundation of expertise if it is properly organized so as to render it analyzable.[8] But she could not use categories that she had only learned along her journey to impose upon her account an order that would distort the complexity of the lived experience and the historical nature of learning. For example, one day Clara would see many of Jessy's "obsessions" as "enthusiasms," as Jessy herself saw them. It was a different category, and it involved a shift in perspective. But shifting one's perspective takes some learning.

Early in the book, Clara described some episodes depicting Jessy's own ways of organizing her experiences. For instance, on the morning of October 7, 1973, fifteen-year-old Jessy was cooking herself eight pieces of bacon. Clara asked her why eight pieces. Jessy answered: "Because of good. . . . And silence is eight. . . . Only politeness is sound." Jessy, her mother explained, did not want to hear phrases such as "please" and "thank you." These polite words created sound that bothered her. They were just noise. She enjoyed silence. She awarded silence her favorite number at the time: 8. Since Jessy loved bacon, it was thus logical for her to eat 8 pieces. She followed a logical process of decision-making. Still, Clara wondered how to describe Jessy's behavior toward polite phrases: Hypersensitive? Strange? "The categories bleed into each other, like watercolor on wet paper."[9] As

Clara saw it, it was difficult to categorize those experiences with the standard criteria. Or, we could say that the categories proved to be too simplistic and inadequate to describe Jessy's world.

SILENCE IS 8

In describing their joint journey, Clara focused first on language. Spoken language is not the only way to communicate, but it is one common way "to a shared world," one that had played a central role in Clara's own life.[10] In her childhood, Clara had learned the value of words, their capacity to hurt and their ability to soothe. Her grandmother taught her this lesson that she put to good use throughout her life. But could she teach it to her own daughter?

Jessy's own experience of sound and words and her own use of language reflected the working of her unique mind. As a child, she loved complicated terms and repeated some over and over. She could form sentences. "Hello, Mama," she greeted her mother on an occasion. Yet Jessy seemed happiest in silence. Would she ever use language more often to communicate, her mother wondered? If not, how could others understand her needs and wishes? When Jessy was a child, there were no technologies that could be used to communicate with others without language. Thus, in order to learn Jessy's own desires and needs, her family worked to understand Jessy's own ways to express herself and to teach her their own.

Her parents, siblings, and friends tried different ways to encourage Jessy. At first, only her family could decipher some of her sounds, but later her speech became clearer. She also gave a unique meaning to some words: "I looked at the clock by mistake." Doing this would cause her deep distress. Yet as her logical mother noted, one cannot *look at* something by mistake. What Clara eventually realized is that one can see something unexpectedly, and Jessy was very distressed by the unexpected. Over time Jessy learned to use words as others did. She began to be able to tell them about her experiences and her feelings. She would say: "I saw a star unexpectedly, I'm so sad."[11]

Clara came to appreciate Jessy's desire for silence when she herself felt what Jessy's experience of living among people who talk all the time might be like. It happened when they were living in France. For the 1969–70 academic year, David had a research sabbatical, and the Parks, Paul, and Jessy moved to France. Katy and Rachel were already in college. The family stayed in Saint-Cloud, a town in the western suburbs of Paris. As Clara wrote about her realization: "I found out what Jessy was up against when we spent a season in France. I had thought I knew—Jessy was eleven and we had been working on language since she was two. But *I had to become a foreigner to feel it.* I had far more French than Jessy had English. Yet I was awash in a sea of sound."[12]

Awash in a sea of sound. Having to process an overabundance of sounds leads to the feeling of drowning in an unintelligible cacophony. It leads to exhaustion and to tuning out. We experience this in the early stages of learning a new language whenever we find ourselves among native speakers. And the effects get amplified because the alien sounds are also accompanied by gestures, postures, and facial expressions that are peculiar to each culture. Clara realized that this must have been Jessy's experience with all language. That was what "Jessy was up against."

Body language plays a key part in understanding others. Oral communication does not simply involve using the right words with the established meaning. Even the silences convey meaning. Silences need to be interpreted. And they require a response as well—further silence, gestures, or words. In the 1930s, Austrian researcher Georg Frankl had already emphasized that autistic children had difficulty understanding the "emotional tone" of language. Emotional tone is conveyed not only through words but also through gestures. Clara understood Jessy's predicament: "Unable to read the silent indicators with which human beings communicate as surely and significantly as they do in words, Jessy was adrift in a far deeper sea."[13]

When adrift, one looks for directions and patterns. Jessy creatively developed her own way of grasping meaning and feelings and conveying them to others through what we could call "patterns of words." Clara described how Jessy, when she started to use language more often to communicate during her teenage years, resorted to verbal clichés and conventional phrases. Clara taught Jessy many of those, as her own grandmother had taught them to her. Jessy hung onto this "prefabricated" language because it helped her "pattern the inevitable fluidity of being in the world." When a kitchen knife was missing, Jessy would say: "Things come and go." Her mother understood: using this generic phrase did "not erase the anxiety," but it could "assuage it."[14] We all need to make sense of that "fluidity of being in the world," and we all do it a little differently. Jessy's method shared in a family tradition. Her great-grandma would have understood as well.

The same way Jessy used routines to organize her days, she also used this prefabricated language to manage her reactions to unexpected events. Clichés, as Clara put it, helped her "give structure to chaos." Once Jessy left the peacefulness of nirvana, she needed tools to make the world intelligible. Clichés were one of those tools. "Like maps, like charts, like calendars, like schedules," they enabled Jessy "to lay hold of her experience, bring it under the mind's control."[15] Jessy then went beyond clichés, and learned proverbs. "A stitch in time saves nine" moved Jessy's purposeful actions from mending a sweater to maintaining household appliances. Her mother had taught her: "Don't cross the bridge until you come to it." After worrying all day about their cat not coming home, Jessy said, upon his return: "Unnecessary sadness, and there wasn't any bridge!"[16]

In this way, Jessy uses language not only to communicate with others, but also to contain the messiness of what happens around her. She knows she often cannot predict how others behave. But she can use language to fit people's actions into some patterns and structure her own responses to an uncontrollable and unpredictable world: "No big deal" or "Nobody is perfect." We all do this—we repeat such mantras to help us accept what we find difficult to accept, to carry us through situations beyond our control. Jessy does it more than most of us because she needs it more. She sees more chaos than we do, and she needs more order.

Clara noted how Kanner's experience with his original sample of autistic children limited his understanding of their communication issues. Kanner's children had difficulties with pronouns—the famous pronominal reversal: "*You* want milk," they said, when they really meant: "*I* want milk." But most of them had few problems with other elements of language, such as plurals and verbal conjugations. Clara reasoned that because most children in Kanner's group had fewer language difficulties than Jessy (though three of them had no spoken language), he thought pronominal reversal was an "isolated—and temporary—grammatical oddity," rather than an indicator of more fundamental issues.[17] Clara did not see it that way. In her twenties, for example, Jessy would say something like: "I better remind Daddy about my dental appointment." The sentence was grammatically correct. Except the appointment was for her father, not for her. As Clara noted, "Pronouns shift. Nouns stay still."[18] Clara reasoned that pronominal reversal could reflect a difficulty in "perspective-taking."

Clara believed this interpretation was supported by research from the 1980s about children's ability to shift their point of view. British autism researchers Simon Baron-Cohen, Adam M. Leslie, and Uta Frith had argued that autistic people cannot shift perspective because they don't have a "theory of mind"—the ability to impute mental states to oneself and to others. Baron-Cohen, Leslie, and Frith used this concept to investigate the absence of pretend play among autistic children. They developed the "Sally–Anne task" test to evaluate this hypothesis. In this test, a child is shown a scenario depicting the actions of two dolls: Sally and Anne. Sally has a basket. Anne has a box. Sally has a marble and puts it in her basket. Then, she leaves the scene. While Sally is gone, Anne takes the marble out of the basket and places it inside her box. Then, Sally comes back. The child has been observing these events. Then, the researcher asks the child: Where will Sally look for her marble? Most children consistently answer correctly that Sally will look in the basket. However, most autistic children answer that Sally will look in the box.[19] That is, autistic children answer the questions based on their own knowledge of the location of the marble rather than on the basis of Sally's knowledge. To explain these results, Baron-Cohen and his colleagues hypothesized that autistic children do not form "second-order representations," i.e., they do not "impute beliefs to others," and that makes it very difficult for them to predict the behavior of other people.[20]

Reflecting on that research, Clara now suggested that what early autism researchers had perceived as emotional issues (obsession for sameness, intense relationships with objects, ignoring other people) could be due to underlying cognitive difficulties in understanding shifting relations. This was reflected in language too. "Insincerity and irony are beyond Jessy's powers," Clara wrote. "For her, language means only what it says."[21]

Language and thought: Should these be two different folders in Clara's kitchen cabinet? Two different sections in her book? How did they relate to social behavior as well? Were these three related aspects of Jessy's disability? Or could one disentangle them? How, Clara asked herself, could she support Jessy in one area without affecting the others? We go back to the usefulness and uselessness of rigid categories to capture the complexity of multifarious experiences.

To reach her daughter, and to appreciate her unique mind, Clara believed she needed to understand how Jessy thought.

Understanding Jessy's way of thinking required reaching the deeper recesses of Jessy's mind. Clara worked like an archaeologist, searching beneath the surface, trying to uncover the rules that structured Jessy's thinking. Clara's notes on Jessy's thinking—recorded over the years on scraps of paper kept in folders—filled a large, old-fashioned suitcase. Sifting through the suitcase full of these fragmentary records when she was writing her book, Clara wondered about the enormity of the challenge: "To write the past is to discover it. I am overwhelmed by the expenditure of mental energy it represents, by the sheer *activity* of a mind that in its inaccessibility could seem so empty."[22]

But Jessy's mind was never empty. And Jessy was always trying to fill it up, mainly with rules.

"Imagine finding this on a piece of paper," wrote Clara:

NO
KNOW
YES
KYESW

It's logical, isn't it? It figures. It is no weak or torpid mind that spontaneously processes KNOW into KYESW. It is a mind that has searched for a rule and found it.

That was Jessy at eleven, displaying her passion for logic. Logic is ruled by principles. And with principles one begins to order the world and one's experiences. Clara realized that Jessy's sense of patterns was so strong that it induced logic where there was none to be found: *Know* is to *no* as *kyesw* is to *yes*. *Men* is the plural of *man*; therefore, *meme* has to be the plural of *mama*.[23] Jessy's powerful inferential skills to find patterns revealed "the systematic quality of Jessy's mind." In Clara's view, Jessy enjoyed systems "for their formal qualities, not their use."[24]

Yet, in a sense those systems have been useful to Jessy. Clara was right that they were not useful for communicating with or relating to others. But Jessy built them for other purposes. Jessy used logic to systematize and organize the world's objects, the relations among them and between them, and her experiences of them. For many years, Jessy focused on numbers. Numbers are clear and their relations are logical.

In this area, Jessy's logical mind and her ability to detect patterns was an asset. Like many autistic people, Jessy had always been at home with numbers because mathematics, as Clara reminded us, "is predictable, logical, rule-governed" and, most importantly, "blessedly abstracted from shifting social contexts."[25] Galileo said that the book of nature is written in the language of mathematics. Without knowing its characters one pointlessly wanders around as if in a dark labyrinth. To Jessy, the world is, in its abundant irregularity and constant mutation, a dark labyrinth; numbers, on the other hand, are reliable.

When twelve-year-old Jessy kept reproducing a grid with fifty numbers, in no apparent order, it took the Parks' friend Freeman Dyson, a leading mathematician and theoretical physicist, to figure out the rationale. It turned out the grid contained the squares of the numbers 51–100, with the first twenty-five being the even numbers (arranged in terms of the number of powers of 2 they contained) and the last twenty-five being the odd numbers (this time arranged in ascending order).[26]

During this period, numbers became Jessy's "primary expressive instrument." She could use them better than words to apprehend and communicate about the world. They were an expressive instrument not only in the sense of representing things in the world, but also in the sense of making it possible for Jessy to be emphatic, passionate, and emotional. Many numbers tended to be "emotionally charged." For her, some numbers were "too good" and others were "HATE" numbers.[27] As Jessy grew older, Clara wrote, numbers lost their emotional charge for Jessy. It is worth noting, however, that her emotional relation to numbers belied the common view that autistic children had bare emotional lives. Jessy just had a different and complex emotional world.

In her book, Clara described Jessy's deep awareness of pattern, her fondness for system, and her intimate familiarity with numbers. For many years, Jessy also wrote many short books—still kept in her mother's old suitcase. These books reveal Jessy's complex interests as well as her deep emotional world. As a child, she wrote "Book About the Number with Three in It" and "Book About the Number *of* Three in It," the difference being the presence of the 3 as a digit in the former and divisibility by 3 in the latter. Then, as an adolescent, her books became records of her passions. Her emotional intensity was visible in the expressivity of the shapes of numbers and figures she included.[28]

As her language and her social experiences in adolescence grew, Jessy used her growing linguistic abilities, including reading and writing, to order the world in as logical a way as she could. She looked for patterns and systems beyond the world of numbers.

Philosophers refer to the things that exist in the world as its ontology. Ontology is the furniture of the world. The way we get to know these things is called epistemology. One could say that Jessy's mind has its own way of organizing the ontology of the world; it has its own epistemology. Eggs, bacon, toast, clouds, numbers, silences: these all are parts of her world. She connects them by following her own rules, always in a logical manner.

Jessy also has the ability to transfer the rules of system-making from one area to another. For example, when Jessy picked up a chart of weather conditions at a ski resort, she went on to apply the system to degrees of goodness. Since the weather chart had levels of "Cold, Very Cold, Extreme Cold, Bitter Cold," Jessy's goodness chart read: "Good, Very Good, Extreme Good, Bitter Good."[29] She enjoyed constructing the system, and who's to say that it was not useful in helping her understand the complex world of goodness? Was it the formal quality of the system that Jessy craved? Or did she find, in her formalism about goodness, a meaning that she could not find in the complex—and often illogical—ways the rest of us organize our world? For her mother it was difficult to say at the time, and it is difficult for us to say now.

Clara asked: Should we be surprised that Jessy scored above the 95th percentile among graduate students in technical and medical fields on tests that measure the ability to identify patterns and complete elements in a series? Maybe, as Clara suggested, it is the rest of us, with our penchant for irregularity and exception, who might be said to suffer from a cognitive impairment: the inability to be fully logical.[30] Clara described Jessy's thinking as a "unique amalgam of simplicity and complex logic." Compared to it, other ways of thinking might appear flatter and more uniform. Her mind was "free of conventional perceptions."[31] As Clara got to understand Jessy's mind better, she was able to see how Jessy's way of thinking could be interpreted in terms of difference and not just disability. It revealed the neurodiversity of the human mind, as we would put it today. Recognizing the diversity of minds, Clara also pointed out that Jessy's logical thinking becomes a disability for her because many of us are not logical. In that sense, Clara became aware of the role the social environment plays in constructing Jessy's difference as a disability.

There is always more than one way to look at things. Where others may see "obsessions," Jessy had a beautiful name for her special interests: she called them "enthusiasms." These were often emotionally charged discoveries of pattern, such as her delight at all words that end in -*nus* (*Venus, Janus, bonus*) because this is how you spell *sun* backwards.[32]

On one occasion, after delivering a speech, a member of the audience asked Clara how she had dealt with her daughter's obsessions. "Obsessions," Clara repeated while contemplating the question. And she answered: "Hmm. We've always thought of them as *enthusiasms*." Sitting in the audience, Barry M. Prizant, who had invited Clara to give her talk, reflected: "Sometimes a single word can change your perspective forever."[33]

IN HER OWN COLORS

Many of Jessy's enthusiasms became reflected in one of her main and most creative vehicles for expressing herself: painting.

Clara's account of Jessy's paintings served as an interlude before the last part of the book, "Living." Clara devoted only twenty pages to them, but her exposition showed their importance in Jessy's life. She wrote more about Jessy's paintings in other publications.[34]

Jessy had always enjoyed drawing and coloring as a child. At age five, she had come up with the terms "blue green" and "pink red" as soon as her mother taught her the name for some basic colors. She had more training in high school. When Jessy joined an art class in 1973, she met the twins Anna and Diana, who took it upon themselves to teach her to draw. Later, drawing and painting became a regular part of her life.

Jessy's least favorite artistic subject was humans. Only during a short time did Jessy paint portraits. She made them in 1973, on assignment from Anna and Diana. A representation of her dad while reading in his wicker chair depicts a foot in the foreground. As Clara noted, it is not intended as a disruption of mimetic representation or as whimsical addition. It is Jessy's own foot. It is in the drawing because it is part of what Jessy saw while seated on the bed opposite her father when she was drawing him. Her paintings reflect reality exactly as she sees it.[35] As part of what she saw when looking at her dad, her foot had to be included.

Jessy says that she does not paint human figures because they are too difficult. But it is also the case that humans have never been one of her enthusiasms.

*Jessica Park,
Portrait of David
Park (1973).*

Initially, Jessy's paintings were exact renditions of her enthusiasms: mechanical controls, quartz space heaters, stars, and buildings.
Jessy painted different versions of houses, banks, and bridges. These
"sources of delight," as her mother put it, were central in Jessy's art.
"What in psychiatry would be termed an obsession," Clara wrote,
"becomes in art the exploration of a theme."[36] In describing Jessy's
paintings, Clara highlighted that while some of the themes are ordinary, "her buildings are extraordinary. The incandescence of their
colors escapes the finest reproduction."

In her choice of colors, Jessy's creativity reaches its highest expression. Jessy also writes short descriptions of her paintings. She
described a small, high window in one of her paintings as "pur-
plish ultramarine." In her painting of the Flatiron Building in New
York City, the sky behind is "two different shades of salmon" because "clouds disrupt the blending of stratification." One side of

the building is "pale mint," and the other is "pale pink." She put lavender, lime, and peach on the medallions on the façade. Jessy's renditions of the building, all in different colors, reveal a beauty not appreciated before. Jessy's night skies are true to astronomical science and to the poetry of colors.

Furthermore, Clara emphasized how Jessy's paintings allow us to see "the colors of her secret world." They are like windows that "open into her private universe" and let us appreciate "the emotional intensity of her secret life," an emotional life "more thrilling than our own."[37] Once again, Jessy's artwork conveys the rich affective texture of her life.

For Clara, the extraordinary qualities of Jessy's art resulted both from her autism and her personality. "Individuals are individuals as well as autistic," she wrote. In Clara's view, in her paintings, one can see that Jessy's "own style" has to do with her "family" and "genetics" as much as with her "autism." Jessy's art conveys her individuality.[38] In her combination of science and art, Jessy also follows her family's tradition.

Over the years, Jessy's interest in painting came and went, until a clear incentive turned her into a professional artist. When she was twenty-one, her mother was participating in an autism meeting and suggested Jessy could draw as a way to keep herself busy. A man offered her five dollars for the drawing. Jessy did not care about the money, but she did care about numbers. So she was happy to see the number in her bank account grow each time she sold a painting.

An artist was born—from a love of numbers.

Numbers encouraged not only productivity, but also creativity. Jessy's renderings of objects are literal as if taken by a camera. But in the choice and combination of colors, Jessy's creativity is astonishing. Her eyes may record reality in its literalness. But her imagination transforms the buildings and bridges and night skies into stunningly colorful paintings. Jessy's inventiveness and playfulness with color make magical portrayals of accurate representations of the stars and constellations in the night sky.

Making art, and being involved in the various aspects that make her a successful artist—accepting commissions, having exhibitions, attending her openings, making paintings as presents for loved ones—provided structure to Jessy's time alone. It improved her social skills too. As Clara told her: One cannot snap or shout at one's admiring customers at an opening; and one has to engage in certain acts of politeness, even when one does not feel like it.

But Clara's own artistry in telling a good story does not tempt her into a simple happy ending. There is no ending, she will tell us later. But it is more than that. She does not want us to see Jessy's story, even the part of her being a successful artist, as one of unmitigated success. Jessy's journey out of nirvana is a fact. Her speech improvements, her bewitching paintings, her impressive ability to work, all of these things undoubtedly represent success and are a testament to her family's love and hard work, to the other people who helped her, and, most of all, to Jessy's own efforts. But her mother reminds the reader that such gains are never to be taken as a sign that Jessy can always function well in our social world.

LIVING

In her description of Jessy's life as an adult, Clara offered a portrayal of Jessy's days, which now included work, some reading, some movies, some times together with friends, some painting. Like other adults, she did some cleaning, cooking, and shopping.

Jessy's emotional world was incredibly complex: numbers, patterns, clouds, and skies were all emotionally charged. Grasping the emotions of other people and expressing her own in a neurotypical way in her society had been more challenging, but Jessy found her own ways to navigate those too. For a long time, Clara and Jessy worked together to comprehend what feelings mattered to her, and which emotions were important to other people as well. Together, they figured out what was important and what was trivial for each of them.

What does it mean to be discouraged, disappointed, or dismayed? How does it feel? Jessy, Clara told us, had to be taught all those things.[39] Her parents, siblings, other family members and friends all contributed to teaching her big and small lessons about how they experienced emotions and what emotions are expected in our society.

In the process, Jessy also taught them about her preferred ways to convey her own feelings.

Since reading the gestures of others to understand their feelings was not easy, Jessy applied her intelligence to uncover a pattern she could see and then interpret through one of her systems. She used her sophisticated system of clouds to understand the emotions of others: "Sometimes can tell when people are happy even if not smiling because can tell by the face. When people are happy eyes always glow and face. And if people are sad face always looks gloomy like clouds. And between happy and sad like partly cloudy."[40]

When our world is partly cloudy, empathy can help. And empathy, too, could be practiced. When Jessy was almost twenty years old, Joann, one of her house companions, set a new goal for Jessy: thinking of others. Like any general or abstract concept, this had to be broken down into specific actions. She got the hang of it through examples. Clara recounted Jessy saying: "I put nutmeg instead of cinnamon in the pudding because I know you don't like that."[41] A deceptively small, mundane step that revealed Jessy's ability to take the perspective of others and take their preferences into account in her decisions.

Over the years, Jessy developed her own strategies for learning the emotions of others and caring about them. She did so by using her powerful analytical mind and her passion for logic. Clara combined intelligence and love in her efforts to understand Jessy's perspective. Jessy found her own way of combining intelligence and love to navigate her social world and relate to her family. She learned to read their feelings and love them differently from the way they had learned to read her feelings and love her. And that enriched all of their lives.

Was Jessy aware of her progress and abilities? And was she aware of her history? Her mother's answer: yes. But Clara also noted: "Jessy is aware of herself, but there is a gap in her awareness. She is far more conscious of herself cognitively than emotionally." In addition, Clara believed that Jessy did not think of herself as different from others because to "feel your own difference you have to form a concept of what other people are like, how they live, what's expected of them."[42]

Most importantly, Clara asked, "What does autism . . . mean to her?" The way Clara saw it: "For Jessy autism was not a difficult social condition but a collection of specifics—mumbling, crying, staring at things that go round and round."[43] She uses the word in plural: those behaviors are her "autisms." She knows she shares some of them with other individuals.

When the movie *Rain Man* came out in 1988, David and Clara took Jessy to see it. In the movie Dustin Hoffman plays a middle-aged man with a variety of "autisms." Ruth Sullivan's son, Joe, and Bernard Rimland's son, Mark, were models for Hoffman's role. Jessy saw the movie twice. She recognized the main character's abilities, obsessions, and peculiarities. She noticed his "enthusiasms." She said she shared some of them.

Being aware of her "autisms" has helped Jessy. Focusing on one behavior at a time, the Park family developed strategies to negotiate adjustment, to create flexibility, even to use some of Jessy's assets, such as her reliability, to establish a reassuring daily order. As we would put it now, Jessy's family learned to play to her strengths. Jessy has also learned to appreciate her accomplishments: "Well, I haven't cried for a whole month," she may say proudly.[44]

At the end of the journey, Clara offers her final reflection. Jessy is now an accomplished painter. But for Clara "her real achievements are in the realm of the practical, the necessary, the unromanticizable—the things that make her employable in the community and useful and welcome at home." That is, Jessy's *social* accomplishments. Yet the process of social growth is "uneven" at best.[45] Clara noted that, as countless others who have experienced this condition know, "to present autism as all charm and interesting strangeness [is] to romanticize it past recognition."[46]

Exiting Nirvana was published in March of 2001. The date of publication was timed to coincide with an exhibition of Jessy's artwork at the Margaret Bodell Gallery in New York City. Both mother and daughter shared the success of their journey together. Oliver

Sacks introduced Jessy at the exhibit's opening. Jessy answered some questions from the audience in her usual straightforward way. When asked what she liked to look at most in an art museum, other painters or her own art, she answered: "my own, and the alarm system."

The reviews of *Exiting Nirvana* were enthusiastic. Seeing the book as a "sequel" to *The Siege*, they tended to emphasize the same elements characteristic of Clara's first book: the combination of a detailed, thoroughly documented, objective description of autism with a warm, loving account of the family's journey. Kathleen Quill, director of the Autism Institute in Essex, Massachusetts, noted: "There are insights into autism that can only be gained through the time-honored words of a mother's love." "Park has told Jessy's story," Donna Marchetti wrote in the Cleveland *Plain Dealer*, "with a clear objectivity but also with a mother's warmth."[47] Maternal love was no longer perceived as an obstacle to gaining knowledge. Indeed, for many reviewers, Clara's affection and dedication to Jessy were her main assets in understanding a disability that remained perplexing at many levels.

Oliver Sacks also highlighted the combination of insight and love, both in his Foreword to the book and in a review for the *New York Review of Books*. For him, *Exiting Nirvana* had been "written with an intelligence, a clear-sightedness, an insight, and a love that brought out to the full the absolute strangeness, the 'otherness' of the autistic mind." Freeman Dyson, Clara's longtime friend, called it a masterpiece, and added his own variation on the voyage metaphor: "Clara has navigated through the storms and come safe to shore."[48]

Perhaps the best description of the book appeared in an anonymous one-paragraph blurb in a mail-order book catalogue that captured its profundity: "Chronicling Jessy's progression from the serenity of isolation to the struggle of connection to others and the world about her, Park eloquently explores the limits of language and *the labors of affection*, the lessons of experience and the intractable truths of affliction, the mysteries of mind and self that autism poses."[49]

Praise was welcome, but, as with her previous books, it was the letters from other parents that meant the most to Clara. The mother of an autistic son wrote that she was thrilled about Jessy's progress and thanked Clara: "All parents, siblings, and others, who love *their* autistic person, will be forever grateful to you for this endeavor." Another mother wrote: "You've heard all the praise already, for the balance of science and story, for the depiction of individual and family character, for the clarity, for the respect, you name it." But she added: "May I tell you how it will affect one reader personally?" She explained how it would help her to be a better mother. But it would also help her be more understanding of adults who might be "doing their social best" like her engineer husband. When he was asked by the Lamaze teacher some years earlier: "And what was the birth experience like for you?" her husband had answered: "There were lots of cars in the parking lot."[50] Many mothers wrote not only about how interesting and encouraging her books had been, but also about how "useful" they were.[51] Nothing could have pleased Clara more.

Her readers transcended the autism community as well. An eighteen-year-old high school student who described herself as an avid reader recently diagnosed with major depressive disorder wrote about how touched she was by her book: "I don't know how I could justly express my feelings on *Exiting Nirvana*. We don't seem to have strong enough words for such depth! The best way I can describe my feelings are those of gratitude and enlightenment. . . . I know that, as a former teacher, you can probably appreciate the fact that you are still furthering the learning of young people."[52]

Over the years, the letters kept coming. As technology changed, some people emailed her. In 2007, the mother of an autistic boy wrote: "I have wanted to write to you for 27 years and I am finally doing it! When my son was 3, I read your book THE SIEGE. It made a huge difference in his life and the life of my family." Recounting an all-too-familiar story, the mother noted how the "strain of caring for a wild, tantrum tossing, up all night—literally, 3 year old, plus the guilt, was a terrible burden." After the usual rounds of psychologists, therapists, and counselors, this mother had found

Clara's book. It gave her the strength to initiate her own exploratory expedition with her son.[53]

Back in the mid-1960s, when an editor asked her whether she could write a book about her early experiences with her daughter, Clara's first thought was to suggest that she could have a book ready in "about ten years." Reminiscing about that in an interview with her Spanish translator some fifteen years later, Clara said she now realized "that in my mind I had the idea of waiting for the end of the story before starting to write it. After all we've been through, it seems inconceivable that at that point I could think that this never ending story could have an end."[54]

Discovering oneself and the selves of others is a lifelong journey.

CONCLUSION

J ESSY NOW LIKES TO BE CALLED JESSICA. She stills works as a mail clerk at Williams College and is a successful painter. She lives in her family's home in Williamstown and sees her sisters, Rachel and Katy, her brother, Paul, and their families regularly. Once a week, she sees Anna, one of the twins, who lives nearby, and with whom she has been friends for over thirty years. Jessica enjoys cooking, walking, and eating ice cream and chocolate. Like most of us, Jessica continues to work on developing her awareness of herself and others.

Social interaction is important to Jessica, but it needs to be purposeful and logical. Jessica is happy to see you, sometimes have dinner with you. She especially enjoys having a pizza together, and is always game for an outing to Lickety Split, a popular ice cream shop in town. Most of the time, she asks questions to obtain information, and she is happy to provide information if other people need it. Additional talk would be "politeness." She still does not want to be asked any "W" questions (why, what, where). She also does not like being "reassured," or being told that something will be okay.

The world has not changed, but Jessica has found her own ways of dealing with its unpredictability. She organizes her life into strict routines: a morning walk before heading to work at the same time every day; dinner at Anna's house on Tuesdays; pizza with Paul on

Wednesdays; grocery shopping with Rachel on Fridays. On Saturdays, she cleans her room and does the laundry. After the wash, she folds her clothing neatly. To turn on the dryer she wears her headphones, as she still finds the noise excruciating. Jessica always dresses in coordinated pastel-colored pants and shirts. She carefully chooses her outfit every evening so it is ready for the next morning.

To make sense of the world, and to assuage the pain that its disorder brings her, Jessica has always focused on organizing it.[1] She "loves to categorize the world," her mother told us.[2] As we saw at the start of this book, by age twelve Jessica had invented a system: sun with clear sky, four doors; sun with three clouds, one door. Depending on the kind of day, she adjusted the amount of juice in her green cup, as well as her expectations. The sky is full of surprises: sometimes clear, other times cloudy. Every day Jessica looked up to figure out how to adjust her hopes and fears for the day ahead.

Although idiosyncratic, Jessica's systems, neurologist Oliver Sacks reminds us, "bring to mind the elaborate, pseudoscientific systems of numerology and astrology."[3] Indeed, we too have looked to the skies for guidance and sought meaning in the stars.

In the 1970s, Jessica's father David and Philip Youderian, a mathematician, analyzed her system and pointed out an interesting gap that separates her "from the rest of us."[4] They discovered that Jessica's "obsession" for systems brings her not only clarity but also excitement: "One need not go beyond her wide swings of emotion as the sun came and went, or the trembling excitement with which she filled her glass in the evening, to see that Elly [Jessica] found her own ways to live a life as rich in excitement and happiness as any of us have found."[5]

Jessica's system is interesting also in the way that it dispenses with one of the basic goals of scientific systematizers: to fix referents in order to enable communication with others, and thus agreement, or debate. In its uniqueness, Jessica's system reminds us of the great variety of human experiences and the intricate ways of the human mind.

It also reveals that Jessica's intentions are similar to those guiding scientists: "to discover order in apparent chaos."[6] Thus, Jessica's system teaches us that containing unpredictability is not only a goal for apothecaries, cosmologists, archivists, and naturalists. Most of us search for principles to order our universes, to tame the terror of chaotic realities. Like Jessica, we too get up every morning and look through the window, wondering how many clouds the day may bring. It is exciting, and terrifying, to live in a world full of surprises.

In the late 1930s, as child psychiatrists encountered some behaviors that did not fit well into existing categories used to identify particular conditions, they decided to introduce a new category: autism. But the criteria used to separate autism as an independent category were never stable, and they have continued to change over the years. The story of scientific and clinical research on autism includes a continuous back and forth between splitting the category of autism into different subgroups and lumping different autistic behaviors together under a single category. The tension between lumping and splitting is common to attempts at classification in science because the world can be divided up in many different ways, as Jessica's systems remind us. In the case of autism, this tension also resulted from various more specific factors: there is no biological marker for autism, there is no pattern of behavior that is unique to all autistic people or that is present in all of them, and autistic behaviors occur in many individuals who also have mood and anxiety disorders or an intellectual disability.

The introduction of the notion of an autism spectrum starting in the 1980s helped to highlight the diversity of autistic experiences. But it also raised difficult questions: Does a successful musician with social anxiety and some stereotypical behaviors belong in the same category as a person who engages in self-stimulation constantly and injures himself? What is gained and what is lost by referring to both of them as "autistic"? When Lorna Wing introduced the idea of a continuum, she noted that many characteristics of autism were present in all humans. That is, we are all on the spectrum. But then, what criteria do we use to establish subcategories on this continuum?

More recently, ideas about neurodiversity have brought important advances while also raising difficult questions.[7] The recognition, acceptance, and celebration of people with diverse neurological makeups are undoubtedly crucial scientific and social advancements. Yet the concepts of neurotypical and neurodivergent also establish a new dichotomy that raises some issues. What counts as typical in neurotypicals? What is typical in defining neurodivergence? Does this division itself conflict with the idea of neurodiversity as existing along many different axes and a wide range of gradations?

Furthermore, by postulating that autistic people have "characteristically autistic styles of relating to others," are we not assuming that sociality is determined by our neurological wiring?[8] Historical and anthropological works have shown that the way we relate to others has changed over time and varies profoundly between different cultures. Dividing people into neurotypicals and neurodivergents seems to obscure the profound ways in which epigenetic, environmental, social, and cultural factors interact in particular historical contexts to shape the ways in which different people relate to one another.

These are all complex matters awaiting further research and debate. To make headway, we will need to better understand how autism has been conceptualized and experienced in different cultures. Much of what we know about autism, through scientific research and through autistic people, still relies on the contributions of what are now called "WEIRD" subjects—people in Western, educated, industrialized, rich, and democratic countries. As in other areas of psychological research, generalizations about the "human mind" and "human behavior" based on studies of such limited groups of people are highly problematic.[9]

Today, unlike a century or even fifty years ago, most autistic people, their families, researchers, and therapists agree on the nature of autism. For example, Lydia X. Z. Brown, an autistic activist and lawyer, provides a definition of autism that would be acceptable to all those groups. Brown presents autism as "a neurological, pervasive developmental condition. It is a disability. It is usually considered a disorder. It is not a disease. It is a lifelong condition that spans from infancy to adulthood. Autistic people usually share a variety of characteristics, including significant differences in information processing, sensory processing, communication abilities or styles, social skills, and learning styles." They would also agree that autistic people often have other conditions. As Brown puts it: "Some Autistic people also have co-occurring conditions of mental illness (such as bipolar disorder), behavioral or mood disorder (such as clinical depression or Tourette's Syndrome), learning disability (such as dyscalcula), or intellectual disability (formerly called mental retardation). Many Autistic people also have conditions like Executive Function Disorder, Sensory Processing Disorder (formerly called Sensory Integration Disorder), prosopagnosia (face blindness), dyspraxia, synesthesia, anxiety disorders, and learning disabilities."[10]

The scientific community, the autistic community, and the community of families of autistic people are not monolithic, but the points on which their members most often disagree with each other concern what to do about autism. Some participants in contemporary debates on this issue support work that aims to develop treatments to cure or at least ameliorate certain aspects of autism. Adopting a strong version of the social disability model, others argue that autism is fully socially constructed as a disability; in a world with adequate supports and without discrimination, an autistic person would not be disabled. Therefore, it would follow that it is not necessary to carry out research into the causes of autism or treatments; funding should go toward developing and providing supports that enhance quality of life for autistic people.

For autistic advocates who support this stance, the legacy of parental activism covered in this book is very problematic because they see those parents as largely trying to eradicate their children's autism through their search for a cure and their use of certain treatments. For instance, many autistic people believe that the use of applied behavioral analysis or ABA with autistic children is problematic, when not downright unethical. In general, the role of many parents in autism advocacy is considered harmful because parents are often seen as supporting the medical model of autism that disability justice advocates reject. In addition, some parents, especially mothers, have written about their key role in helping their children. Many autistic adults see these memoirs as encouraging a narrative that presents the parent as savior of the autistic child, who is a silent victim.

Situating the views and actions of parents between the 1960s and the 1980s in their historical context gives us a more nuanced picture. By raising their children at home, rather than putting them in custodial institutions as it was commonly done in the 1950s and 1960s, most parents provided a better environment for their children. The parents also fought against social stigma both for the children and the rest of their families. They also played an instrumental role in rejecting the psychoanalytic view that autism was a willful retreat, and, with proper therapy, the autistic child would "recover" and become "normal." Gathering into local and national organizations, the parents became activists who demanded their children's inclusion in all areas of society: school, summer camps, sports, and employment. They demanded that society make accommodations and provide supports for autistic children and adults.

Though it is true that the parents searched for and used therapies, they were often focused not on eradicating autistic behaviors such as rocking or eliminating their children's particular interests, but on teaching their children coping skills.

The fact that some parents, including Clara Park, supported the use of behavioral therapy or ABA has been another topic of debate. Many autistic advocates rejected ABA's use of aversives. Today, there is overwhelming consensus that the use of strong aversives such as electroshock is dehumanizing. These have been finally banned. But many advocates have also objected to what they see as the very goal of ABA: eliminating or ameliorating some autistic behaviors. Other autistic people, their families, and researchers believed using behavioral therapy in some cases was acceptable and some have argued that it remains so now.

Clara's approach to behavioral therapy does not fit the critics' vision of ABA as a form of authoritarian control, because she transformed ABA into a tool that gave equal agency to Jessy. Clara and Jessy agreed on specific rewards to alter behaviors that Jessy herself wanted to change or improve.

This revealing case suggests a more general point: to pass judgment about any therapy, we need to look not only at its theoretical grounding but also at its reality as practice. Several sociological and ethnographic studies have reported that mothers in many places, from the US to Morocco, also have adapted ABA in pragmatic ways that helped their children in specific contexts. Like Clara Park, these mothers translated scientific ideas into specific tools that they used to care for their children.[11]

In translating and adapting received scientific knowledge, these mothers also created new knowledge about the nature of autism and developed valuable new tools, such as Clara's contracts with Jessy. Thus, in order to appreciate the role of parents and advocates in the history of autism, it is important to go beyond the printed texts. Leading historians such as Katherine Park have shown that looking at medicine as a system of practice reveals a broad and heterogeneous world that is often not captured in printed sources.[12] The maternal practices and the parental advocacy work explored here left a small footprint in the published record. But non-textual knowledge can travel fast and influence practices. In that way, those activities shaped the story of autism in profound ways.

To assess the contributions of parents, we also need to consider that many of them were on the autism spectrum, a fact discussed in the scientific literature quite early. Asperger had defended the hereditary basis of autism. In a 1957 paper, after noting that many parents were "serious-minded and rather literal-minded," Kanner and Eisenberg remarked that many of them could be considered "successful, autistic adults."[13] Thus, in assessing the parents' actions, we must keep in mind that many of them were also being stigmatized for behaviors that today we see as being part of the autism spectrum. This was especially hard for mothers. In keeping their children at home and working with them, they were going against established norms for femininity and motherhood, as well as against more general normative assumptions about human affect and social relations.

Though categories in autism and psychological and medical science have changed over time, in the United States the vision of what counts as a "good mother" has hardly changed since Clara Park challenged the restrictive views of her time. Yes, nowadays there are more women writers. There are more women scientists. There are more women politicians. But in many communities in the West, childrearing is still mostly a mother's job, and it is still greatly undervalued. The normative view of mothers as responsible for their children's psychological development adds an enormous emotional burden to the hard work of raising children. And the standards for being a good parent are still deeply gendered. As Margaret Atwood has recently put it: "Bad mother is a much more devastating label than bad father."[14] Moreover, blaming mothers for whatever Western society perceives as "wrong" with children remains rampant.[15]

Clara Park herself was catalogued as a bad mother because she had an autistic child. But she fought that judgment with her heart and her mind. In doing so, Clara called into question many deeply entrenched dichotomies, including the opposition between the emotional and the cognitive in mothering and in autism, and the opposition between scientific expertise and personal experience in understanding autism. Challenging those divides suggested new ways of thinking about motherhood and autism, as well as new forms of knowledge that recognized the experience of autistic individuals and their families. Today, her example could inspire us to improve the ways we think about parental care, about autism, and about the kind of medical science we want practiced.

Autism is a dimension of human diversity. But is it a disability only because of social discrimination? Or is it, at least sometimes, associated with impairments that should be researched and treated? This is the most divisive question in the autism community today. But, following Clara's rejection of dichotomies, could we find a way of looking at autism that would help us both to appreciate the differences of all and alleviate suffering for some?

In her tenacious fight to have parents' voices recognized, Clara Park argued that knowledge of the lived experience is essential to understanding a condition. Today, more than ever, the experiences of autistic people are needed in conversation with the views of scientific researchers, families, and therapists. In her books about Jessy, Clara helped her readers understand how Jessy perceived the world.

Clara encouraged the collaboration of researchers, therapists, parents, and autistic people in order to improve the lives of both autistic people and other disabled people. In everything she pursued, she looked for the common needs of human beings that underlie and transcend our differences in abilities, training, and our lots in life.

Even long after Clara published her books, she continued to reply to letters from mothers of children with special needs, students, teachers, therapists, autistic people, and many others who read her books. Describing their own troubles with the medical establishment and their difficulties living in a society with rigid views about normality, they praised Clara's fortitude and compassion and thanked her. Clara always answered them, with gratitude, advice, and encouragement.

Clara Park died on July 3, 2010.

Beginning in early adulthood, Clara lamented that being a woman had kept her out of the big events of the world. She could not be on the front lines of wars or revolutions. She could not be among world leaders discussing peace, religion, or economic affairs. Without participating in those events, she felt she could not write valuable literature either.

Clara wrote that a mother's work was "unrecognized in the world of Things That Count," but her life and work showed that helping an infant grow and find her place in the world belongs in the category of Things That Count. And because raising a child should count, it also deserved to be a subject matter for great literature. Previously, few works of art had told the story of a disabled child and her mother. In her two books about raising Jessy, Clara Park provided "raw data" for scientists along with soothing prose of the highest literary quality. She thought literature could have many uses. While raising her children, she engaged in a lifelong search for words that could be beautiful and truthful. She knew how necessary such words are for the hard task of living.

In her youth, Clara could find no bildungsroman for women. But in her life and work she constructed one. Challenging the dichotomy between emotions and intellect that supported a very restrictive vision of motherhood, Clara and other activist mothers proved that mothers could be caretakers *and* intellectuals *and* social activists. They rejected a family model in which mothers were exclusively responsible for their children's emotional well-being and expected to devote themselves wholly to loving them instinctually in order to be good mothers.

Intelligence and love are not natural enemies, but it is still up to us to build a society in which they are not perceived and experienced as such. One could do worse than look to Clara Park for insights useful in navigating the troubled waters of life—with logic and love, with science and literature, without sentimentalism, but with lyricism. No dichotomies.

ACKNOWLEDGMENTS

I AM DEEPLY GRATEFUL TO THE PARK FAMILY. I interviewed Clara and David Park many years ago. They were generous and friendly. Katy Park, Rachel Park, Paul Park, and Jessica Park have also generously shared their views and recollections with me and patiently answered many queries. They also made the family archives available for my research. I thank them for their trust and their kindness.

I thank my late father, José Vicedo, my mother, Margarita Castelló, my brothers Josep and Chimo, my sisters Raquel and Silvia, and my nieces and nephews for loving and supporting me. HAT and company also brought fun into our lives.

The support of several teachers, mentors, and friends has been crucial. I hope Peter Galison, Ellen Herman, Evelyn Fox Keller, and Katy Park know how much their steadfast belief in this project has meant to me. I am grateful to colleagues at the University of Toronto who have provided encouragement over many years: Craig Fraser, Nikolai Krementsov, and Denis Walsh. For their help with this project, Juan Ilerbaig and Mark Solovey deserve special mention.

History could not be written without the work of dedicated archivists and librarians who conserve the materials that are essential to understand the past. I gratefully acknowledge the help I received from Marjorie Kehoe and Phoebe Evans Letocha at the Alan Mason Chesney Medical Archives of the Johns Hopkins Medical Institutions;

Deena Gorland and Gary McMillan at the Melvin Sabshin, MD, Library and Archives, American Psychiatric Association, Washington, DC; Lizette Royer Barton at the Archives of the History of American Psychology in the Cummings Center for the History of Psychology, Akron, Ohio; Martin Akeret at the archives of the University of Zurich; Caitlin Angelone at the Historical Medical Library of the College of Physicians of Philadelphia; Elizabeth Shepard at the Medical Center Archives of New York-Presbyterian/Weill Cornell; Sandra E. Yates at the McGovern Historical Center at the Texas Medical Center Library, Houston, Texas; and the librarians at the Special Collections of the Maryland Historical Society in Baltimore.

It is a pleasure to thank some people who kindly allowed me to use materials in private collections: Freeman Dyson, for access to his personal papers; Julie Sullivan, Ruth Christ Sullivan's daughter, for some letters from her mother's personal archive; Stephen M. Edelson and Gloria Rimland, for access to the papers of Bernard Rimland at the Autism Research Institute, San Diego, California; Jane Rhodes, historian and Marie Singer's niece, for providing copies of some materials in the Marie Singer personal archive; and Margaret Miller, for the NSAC newsletters at the Autism Society of America offices in Bethesda, Maryland.

For interviews that provide useful information not available in written materials, I also thank the following people: Stephen M. Edelson, Mark Rimland, Gloria Rimland, and Anna Saldo-Burke.

For reading earlier versions of this book and providing useful feedback, I am most grateful to Stephen M. Edelson, Gil Eyal, Peter Galison, Esmond Harmsworth, Ellen Herman, Juan Ilerbaig, Evelyn Fox Keller, Paul Park, Mical Raz, and Mark Solovey.

I was privileged to receive ample institutional support and funding for this project. I thank the Institute for Advanced Studies, Princeton, New Jersey, for a fellowship in 2015–16 at the School of Historical Studies. I am also grateful for support received at the University of Toronto from the Jackman Humanities Center, Victoria College, and the Institute for the History and Philosophy of Science and Technology. I am thankful for a History of Medicine Project Grant from the Canadian Associated Medical Services (AMS) and the Nova Scotia Health Research Foundation, and for an Insight Grant from the Social Sciences and Humanities Research Council of Canada.

When all the research, thinking, and writing are almost done, there are still people who play a crucial role in shaping the project and turning it into a published book. For his wisdom and support during this process, I am most grateful to my agent, Esmond Harmsworth. I am honored to be publishing this book with Beacon Press, and I thank its director Helene Atwan and my editor, Joanna Green, for believing in this project from the start. I thank Joanna Green and Catherine Tung for their valuable editorial suggestions. For copyediting, I am grateful to Will Morningstar. I thank Susan Lumenello for her careful copyediting too and for her encouragement and patience. For their good work and support, I am grateful to other members of the team at Beacon who participated in this project: Perpetua Charles, Carol Chu, Christian Coleman, Beth Collins, and Alison Rodriguez.

NOTES

INTRODUCTION

1. Clara Claiborne Park, *Exiting Nirvana: A Daughter's Life with Autism* (Boston: Little, Brown, 2001), 82.

2. Clara Claiborne Park, *The Siege: A Family's Journey into the World of an Autistic Child*, orig. 1967 (Boston: Little, Brown, 1982), 3. The 1967 original had the subtitle *The First Eight Years of an Autistic Child*. I use the 1982 edition since it is more widely available and contains an epilogue: "Fifteen Years After."

3. The literature on disability is vast. For some recent general historical studies and edited collections, and studies with a focus on the United States, see Susan Burch and Michael Rembis, eds., *Disability Histories* (Urbana: University of Illinois Press, 2014); Lennard Davis, ed., *The Disability Studies Reader*, 5th ed. (New York: Routledge, 2017); Michael Rembis, Catherine Kudlick, and Kim E. Nielsen, eds., *The Oxford Handbook of Disability History* (Oxford, UK: Oxford University Press, 2018); Philip L. Safford and Elizabeth J. Safford, eds., *Children with Disabilities in America: A Historical Handbook and Guide* (Westport, CT: Greenwood Press, 2006); Susan M. Schweik, *The Ugly Laws: Disability in Public* (New York: New York University Press, 2009); Sharon L. Snyder and David T. Mitchell, *Cultural Locations of Disability* (Chicago: University of Chicago Press, 2006); Paul K. Longmore and Lauri Umansky, eds., *The New Disability History: American Perspectives* (New York: New York University Press, 2001); Kim E. Nielsen, *A Disability History of the United States* (Boston: Beacon Press, 2012).

4. Eli Clare, *Brilliant Imperfection: Grappling with Cure* (Durham, NC: Duke University Press, 2017); Michael Oliver, *The Politics of Disablement: A Sociological Approach* (London: Macmillan Education, 1990); Michael Oliver and Colin Barnes, *The New Politics of Disablement* (New York: Palgrave Macmillan, 2012).

5. On the social model of disability, see Michael Oliver, *Understanding Disability: From Theory to Practice* (orig. 1996; London: Palgrave Macmillan,

2009); Tom Shakespeare, *Disability Rights and Wrongs Revisited,* 2nd ed. (New York: Routledge, 2014).

6. Influential studies on the construction of the "normal" include Georges Canguilhem, *On the Normal and the Pathological* (Dordrecht, Netherlands: Reidel Publishing, 1978), and Rosemarie Garland-Thomson, *Extraordinary Bodies: Figuring Physical Disability in American Culture and Literature* (New York: Columbia University Press, 1997).

7. On the history of the disability rights movement, see Joseph P. Shapiro, *No Pity: People with Disabilities Forging a New Civil Rights Movement* (New York: Times Books, 1994); James I. Charlton, *Nothing About Us Without Us: Disability Oppression and Empowerment* (Berkeley: University of California Press, 1998). On the history of legislation about disability in the United States, see Lennard J. Davis, *Enabling Acts: The Hidden Story of How the Americans with Disabilities Act Gave the Largest US Minority Its Rights* (Boston: Beacon Press, 2015).

8. On the history of the self-advocacy in autism and the neurodiversity movement, see Judy Singer, "Why Can't You Be Normal for Once in Your Life? From a 'Problem with No Name' to the Emergence of a New Category of Difference," in *Disability Discourse,* eds. Mairian Corker and Sally French (Buckingham: Open University Press, 1999), 59–67; Nancy Bagatell, "From Cure to Community: Transforming Notions of Autism," *Ethos: Journal of the Society for Psychological Anthropology* 38, no. 1 (2010): 33–55; Judy Singer, *NeuroDiversity: The Birth of an Idea* (Kindle Publishing, 2016); Steve Silberman, *Neurotribes: The Legacy of Autism and the Future of Neurodiversity* (New York: Avery, 2015); Anne McGuire, *War on Autism: On the Cultural Logic of Normative Violence* (Ann Arbor: University of Michigan Press, 2016); Jennifer S. Singh, *Multiple Autisms: Spectrums of Advocacy and Genomic Science* (Minneapolis: University of Minnesota Press, 2016).

9. Andrew J. Hogan, "Moving Away from the 'Medical Model': The Development and Revision of the World Health Organization's Classification of Disability," *Bulletin of the History of Medicine* 93 (2019): 241–69, 246.

10. On the discussion about impairment and disability, see Carol Thomas, "Disability and Impairment," in *Disabling Barriers, Enabling Environments,* eds. John Swain, Sally French, Colin Barnes, and Carol Thomas (London: Sage, 2004), 21–27; Tom Shakespeare and Nicholas Watson, "The Social Model of Disability: An Outdated Ideology?," in *Exploring Theories and Expanding Methodologies: Where We Are and Where We Need to Go,* vol. 2, *Research in Social Science and Disability,* ed. Sharon N. Barnarrt and Barbara M. Altman (Amsterdam: Emerald Publishing, 2001), 9–28; Bill Hughes and Kevin Paterson, "The Social Model of Disability and the Disappearing Body: Towards a Sociology of Impairment," *Disability and Society* 12, no. 3 (1997): 325–40.

11. On the history of autism, see Majia Holmer Nadesan, *Constructing Autism: Unravelling the "Truth" and Understanding the Social* (New York: Routledge, 2005); Roy Richard Grinker, *Unstrange Minds: Remapping the World of Autism* (New York: Basic Books, 2007); Gil Eyal, Brendan Hart, Emine Oncular, Neta Oren, and Natasha Rossi, *The Autism Matrix: The*

Social Origins of the Autism Epidemic (Cambridge, UK: Polity, 2010); Adam Feinstein, *A History of Autism: Conversations with the Pioneers* (London: Wiley-Blackwell, 2010); Chloe Silverman, *Understanding Autism: Parents, Doctors, and the History of a Disorder* (Princeton, NJ: Princeton University Press, 2012); Mitzi Waltz, *Autism: A Social and Medical History* (London: Palgrave Macmillan, 2013); Silberman, *Neurotribes*; John Donvan and Caren Zucker, *In a Different Key: The Story of Autism* (New York: Crown, 2016); Bonnie Evans, *The Metamorphosis of Autism: A History of Child Development in Britain* (Manchester: University of Manchester Press, 2017).

12. Charles E. Rosenberg, "Framing Disease: Illness, Society, and History," in *Framing Disease: Studies in Cultural History*, ed. Charles E. Rosenberg and Janet Golden (New Brunswick, NJ: Rutgers University Press, 1992), xiii. See also Arthur M. Kleinman, *The Illness Narratives: Suffering, Healing, and the Human Condition* (New York: Basic Books, 1998).

CHAPTER 1: BECOMING CLARA PARK

1. Clara Park personal archive, Williamstown, MA. These papers will be deposited at the Arthur and Elizabeth Schlesinger Library on the History of Women in America, Radcliffe Institute for Advanced Study, Harvard University, Cambridge, MA.

2. Biographical information in *A Guide to the Papers of Robert Watson Claiborne 1934–1966*, University of Virginia Library, https://ead.lib.virginia .edu/vivaxtf/view?docId=uva-sc/viu03360.xml.

3. "Median Age at First Marriage," *Infoplease*, https://www.infoplease .com/us/marital-status/median-age-first-marriage-1890-2010, accessed July 28, 2019.

4. See Paul Park, "Ghosts Doing the Orange Dance: The Parke Family Scrapbook Number IV," *Magazine of Fantasy & Science Fiction*, January/ February 2010.

5. Robert W. Claiborne, *The Way Man Learned Music* (Camden, NJ: Haddon Craftsmen, 1927).

6. Clara Park, interview with the author, May 26 and 27, 2003, Williamstown, MA.

7. Clara Park, "On Putting One Foot in Front of the Other," *Berkshire Eagle*, July 9, 1972, 2.

8. Clara Park, "Grandma Was a Cannibal, Poetically Speaking," *Berkshire Eagle*, April 21, 1961.

9. Clara Park, interview.

10. Rye Country Day School, report on Clara Claiborne, signed by Morton Snyder and dated February 1932, Clara Park personal archive.

11. Paul Park, *Ghosts Doing the Orange Dance* (Hornsea, UK: PS Publishing, 2013), 65.

12. Clara Park, interview.

13. Clara Park, "Remembering Jill," notes read at Jill Hellendale memorial, April 2002, Clara Park personal archive.

14. Clara Park, "Remembering Jill."

15. Clara Park, "Remembering Jill."

16. Dalton annual, 1940. Clara Park's copy, with handwritten annotations by her friends, Clara Park personal archive.

17. Ruth Hubbard, "Memories of Life at Radcliffe," in *Yards and Gates: Gender in Harvard and Radcliffe History*, ed. Laurel Ulrich (New York: Palgrave Macmillan, 2004), 229–32, available at http://nrs.harvard.edu/urn -3:HUL.InstRepos:4677602.

18. Janet Thompson Keep, "The Remarkable Clara Park," letter to the editor, *Berkshire Eagle*, July 11, 2010.

19. Clara Park to her mother, Bal, November 17, 1943, Clara Park personal archive.

20. Clara Park to David Park, May 3, 1943, Clara Park personal archive.

21. Clara Park to David Park, September 5, 1943, Clara Park personal archive.

22. Clara Park, "Foibles of Fickle Fashion," *Berkshire Eagle*, November 10, 1961.

23. David Park, "Looking Around" (typewritten autobiographical sketch), David Park personal archive, Park family, Williamstown, MA.

24. Clara Park to Parjo (her father), January 2, 1949, Clara Park personal archive.

25. Clara Park to Parjo (her father), January 2, 1949, Clara Park personal archive.

26. Freeman Dyson to his mother, July 22, 1948, Freeman Dyson personal archive, Institute for Advanced Study, Princeton, NJ.

27. Clara Park to Bal, June 1948, Clara Park personal archive.

28. Clara Park to Bal, August 18, 1948, Clara Park personal archive.

29. Clara Park to Bal, August 18, 1948, Clara Park personal archive.

30. Clara Park, interview.

31. Clara Park to Bal, November 27, 1948, Clara Park personal archive.

32. Clara Park to Bal, December 1, 1948, Clara Park personal archive.

33. Clara Park to Bal, April 9, 1950, Clara Park personal archive.

34. David Park, "Looking Around," David Park personal archive.

35. Clara Park to Bal, May 18, 1951, Clara Park personal archive.

36. Clara Park to Parjo (her father), November 17, 1951, Clara Park personal archive.

37. Clara to Bal, undated, Clara Park personal archive.

38. Katharine Park, interview with the author, July 2, 2015, Cambridge, MA.

39. Clara Park, "The High Cost of Human Machines in Ceylon," *Berkshire Eagle*, April 10, 1959.

40. Clara described her experiences in an article: Clara Claiborne Park, "Bringing College to Students," *New Englander*, April 1965, 43–44.

41. Clara Park, interview; Paul Park, interview with the author, North Adams, June 2015.

42. Clara Park, "The Home and Mother Boom," *Berkshire Eagle*, May 8, 1959; Park, "Mother of Four Says Eating Babies Isn't Nice," *Berkshire Eagle*, May 6, 1960.

43. Clara Park, "Negro Voting Rights Admit No Compromise," *Berkshire Eagle*, March 23, 1960.

44. Clara Park, "The Easter Idea Reborn in Southern Jails," *Berkshire Eagle*, April 1, 1961.

45. Clara Park, "Mrs. Ramsay—Mother Supreme," *Berkshire Eagle*, August 11, 1961.

46. Arnold Gesell, *The Mental Growth of the Pre-School Child: A Psychological Outline of Normal Development from Birth to the Sixth Year, Including a System of Developmental Diagnosis* (New York: Macmillan, 1926); Arnold Gesell, *Infancy and Human Growth* (New York: Macmillan, 1928); Ellen Herman, "Families Made by Science: Arnold Gesell and the Technologies of Modern Child Adoption," *Isis* 92 (2001): 684–715. On how American mothers were increasingly influenced by scientific advice in the twentieth century, see Julia Grant, *Raising Baby by the Book: The Education of American Mothers* (New Haven, CT: Yale University Press, 1998); Rima Apple, *Perfect Motherhood: Science and Childrearing in America* (Rutgers, NJ: Rutgers University Press, 2006).

47. Clara Park, first notebook, Clara Park personal archive.

48. Sydney Gellis to Edmund Larkin, May 15, 1961, Clara Park personal archive.

49. Sydney Gellis to Clara Park, May 18, 1961, Clara Park personal archive.

50. Sydney Gellis to David Park, June 19, 1961, Clara Park personal archive.

CHAPTER 2: AUTISTIC CHILDREN . . . AND THEIR MOTHERS

1. Leo Kanner, "Childhood Psychosis: A Historical Overview," *Journal of Autism and Childhood Schizophrenia* 1 (1971): 14–19, 15.

2. Wilhelm T. Preyer, *Die Seele des Kindes* (Leipzig: T. Grieben, 1882); G. Stanley Hall, *The Contents of Children's Minds on Entering School* (New York: E. L. Kellogg, 1893); Henry Maudsley, *The Physiology and Pathology of Mind* (London: Macmillan, 1867); J. Langdon Down, *On Some of the Mental Affections of Childhood and Youth* (London: J & A Churchill, 1887); Marcel Manheimer, *Les Troubles Mentaux de L'Enfance: Précis de Psychiátrie Infantile* (Paris: Société d'Éditions Scientifiques, 1899).

3. On the history of cognitive disability, especially in the United States, see James W. Trent, *Inventing the Feeble Mind: A History of Intellectual Disability in the United States* (Oxford, UK: Oxford University Press, 1995/2017); David Wright and Anne Digby, eds., *From Idiocy to Mental Deficiency: Historical Perspectives on People with Learning Disabilities* (London: Routledge, 1996); Steven Noll, *Feeble-Minded in Our Midst: Institutions for the Mentally Retarded in the South, 1900–1940* (Chapel Hill: University of North Carolina Press, 1995); Steven Noll and James W. Trent, eds., *Mental Retardation in America: A Historical Reader* (New York: New York University Press, 2004).

4. Eugen Bleuler, *Dementia praecox oder Gruppe der Schizophrenien* (Leipzig: Franz Deuticke, 1911), 10, 52.

5. See Jeffrey P. Baker and Birgit Lang, "Eugenics and the Origins of Autism," *Pediatrics* 140 (2017): e20171419.

6. For a general overview of eugenics, see Diane Paul, *Controlling Human Heredity: 1865 to the Present* (Atlantic Highlands, NJ: Humanities Press, 1985); Sharon L. Snyder and David T. Mitchell, *Cultural Locations of Disability* (Chicago: University of Chicago Press, 2006), trace how disabled people came to be viewed as biologically deviant. On the search for the hereditary basis of mental disorders, see Theodore M. Porter, *Genetics in the Madhouse: The Unknown History of Human Heredity* (Princeton, NJ: Princeton University Press, 2020).

7. Eugen Bleuler, *Textbook of Psychiatry* (New York: Macmillan, 1924), 214.

8. G. E. Ssucharewa (Sukhareva), "Die schizoiden Psychopathien im Kindesalter," *Monatsschrift für Psychiatrie und Neurologie* 60 (1926): 235–61; Ssucharewa, "Über den Verlauf der Schizophrenien im Kindesalter," *Zeitschrift für die Gesamte Neurologie und Psychiatrie* 142 (1932): 309–21, 310, 312, 313.

9. E. Grebelskaja-Albatz, "Zur Klinik der Schizophrenie des frühen Kindesalters," *Schweizer Archiv für Neurologie und Psychiatrie* 34 (part 1, 1934): 244–53, and 35 (part 2, 1935): 30–40; Jakob Lutz, "Über die Schizophrenie im Kindesalter," *Schweizer Archiv für Neurologie und Psychiatrie* 39 (part 1, 1937): 335–72, and 40 (part 2, 1937): 141–63; Howard W. Potter, "Schizophrenia in Children," *American Journal of Psychiatry* 89 (1933): 1253–70, 1254; J. Louise Despert, "Schizophrenia in Children," *Psychiatric Quarterly* 12 (1938): 366–71.

10. Georg Frankl, "Befehlen und Gehorchen," *Zeitschrift für Kinderforschung* 42 (part 1, 1934): 463–79, and 43 (part 2, 1934): 1–21, 469, 470.

11. Georg Frankl, "Über postenzephalitischen Parkinsonismus und verwandte Störungen im Kindelsalter," *Zeitschrift für Kinderforschung* 46 (1937): 199–249, 211; Georg Frankl, "Triebhandlungen bei Dissozialität nach Enzephalitis epidemica und anderen psychopathischen Störungen des Kindesalters," *Zeitschrifft für Kinderforschung* 46 (1937): 401–48, 423.

12. Anni Weiss, "Qualitative Intelligence Testing as a Means of Diagnosis in the Examination of Psychopathic Children," *American Journal of Orthopsychiatry* 5 (1935): 154–79, 154, 160, 173.

13. Hans Asperger, "Das psychisch abnorme Kind," *Wien Klinische Wochenschrift* 49 (1938): 1314–17, 1314. An English translation by Dean Falk is available, published online only as appendix 1 to his article "Non-Complicit: Revisiting Hans Asperger's Career in Nazi-Era Vienna," *Journal of Autism and Developmental Disorders* 50 (2020): 2573–84, https://doi.org/10.1007/s10803-019-03981-7.

14. Asperger, "Das psychisch abnorme Kind," 1316.

15. Asperger, "Das psychisch abnorme Kind," 1316, 1317.

16. Hans Asperger, "Die 'Autistischen Psychopathen' im Kindesalter," *Archiv für Psychiatrie und Nervenkrankheiten* 117 (1944): 76–136, 132.

17. Authors who argue for strong connections between Asperger and the Nazis are Edith Sheffer, *Asperger's Children: The Origins of Autism in Nazi Vienna*

(New York: W. W. Norton, 2018); Herwig Czech, "Hans Asperger, National Socialism, and 'Race Hygiene' in Nazi-Era Vienna," *Molecular Autism* 9 (2018), https://doi.org/10.1186/s13229-018-0208-6. Falk, "Non-Complicit: Revisiting Hans Asperger's Career in Nazi-Era Vienna," 2573–84, challenges their views.

18. Kanner, unpublished autobiography, "Freedom from Within," Box 100695, Leo Kanner (1894–1981) Papers, Melvin Sabsin Library and Archives, American Psychiatric Association, Washington, DC; Victor D. Sanua, "Leo Kanner (1894–1981): The Man and the Scientist," *Child Psychiatry & Human Development* 21 (1990): 3–23.

19. On Meyer, see Susan Lamb, *Pathologist of the Mind: Adolf Meyer and the Origins of American Psychiatry* (Baltimore: Johns Hopkins University Press, 2014).

20. Leo Kanner, *Child Psychiatry* (Springfield, IL: Charles C. Thomas, 1935); Marga Vicedo and J. Ilerbaig, "Leo Kanner's Call for a Pediatric–Psychiatric Alliance," *Pediatrics* 145 (2020): e20194047.

21. "Henry Phipps Psychiatric Clinic Staff Conference, October 27, 1938," Unit XII/23, Folder 592, Adolf Meyer Collection, Alan Mason Chesney Medical Archives, Johns Hopkins Medical Institutions, Baltimore.

22. Lutz's presentation in "Henry Phipps Psychiatric Clinic Staff Conference, April 1, 1938," Unit XII/23, Folder 549, Adolf Meyer Collection. On Donald, see John Donvan and Caren Zucker, *In a Different Key: The Story of Autism* (New York: Crown, 2016).

23. Leo Kanner, "Exoneration of the Feebleminded Persons and Their Consequences," *American Journal of Psychiatry* 99 (1942): 17–22, 20.

24. Kanner, "Freedom from Within," 381.

25. Marga Vicedo and Juan Ilerbaig, "Autism in Baltimore, 1938–1943," *Journal of Autism and Developmental Disorders* (2020), https://doi.org/10.1007/s10803-020-04602-4. My account thus differs from Steve Silberman's in *Neurotribes*, and from others who have also argued that Kanner stole his ideas from Frankl or Asperger. See Vicedo and Ilerbaig, "Autism in Baltimore," for references to this discussion. See also John E. Robison, "Kanner, Asperger, and Frankl: A Third Man at the Genesis of the Autism Diagnosis," *Autism* 21 (2016): 862–71.

26. Vicedo and Ilerbaig, "Autism in Baltimore."

27. C. Sterwald and J. Baker, "Frosted Individuals: How Dr. Leo Kanner Constructed the Autistic Family," *Perspectives in Biology and Medicine* 62 (2019): 690–709, 694.

28. "Henry Phipps Psychiatric Clinic Staff Conference, April 23, 1941," Unit XII/23, Folder 827, Adolf Meyer Collection.

29. Leo Kanner, "Autistic Disturbances of Affective Contact," *Nervous Child* 2 (1943): 217–50, 242, 245, 242.

30. Kanner, "Autistic Disturbances," 248, 249.

31. Kanner, "Autistic Disturbances," 250.

32. "Henry Phipps Psychiatric Clinic Staff Conference, April 6, 1943," pp. 15, 21, 22, 24, 26. In Series III, Folder 35 (Infantile Autism), Papers of Hilde Bruch, Manuscript Collection no. 7, Harris County Medical Archive, Texas Medical Center Library.

33. George Frankl, "Language and Affective Contact," *Nervous Child* 2 (1943): 251–62, 261.

34. Kanner, "Early Infantile Autism," *Journal of Pediatrics* 25 (1944): 211–17.

35. Kanner, *Child Psychiatry*, 93.

36. Leo Kanner, *In Defense of Mothers: How to Bring Up Children in Spite of the More Zealous Psychologists* (New York: Dodd, Mead, 1941), 4, 27.

37. "Review of *In Defense of Mothers*, by Leo Kanner," *Journal of Pediatrics* 19 (1941): 873–74, 874.

38. Kanner, "Autistic Disturbances."

39. Kanner, "Autistic Disturbances," 248, 250, 225.

40. Leo Kanner, "Convenience and Convention in Rearing Children," *Scientific Monthly* 59 (October 1944): 301–6, 301–2. Leo Kanner, "Child-Rearing by the Book," *American Mercury* 60 (January 1945): 23–28, 25.

41. Ellen Herman, *The Romance of American Psychology: Political Culture in the Age of Experts* (Berkeley: University of California Press, 1995), 88–99; Marga Vicedo, *The Nature and Nurture of Love: From Imprinting to Attachment in Cold War America* (Chicago: University of Chicago Press, 2013).

42. Edward A. Strecker, "Presidential Address," *American Journal of Psychiatry* 101 (1944): 1–8, 3.

43. Gordon W. Allport, "Scientific Models and Human Morals," *Psychological Review* 54 (1947): 182–92, 189.

44. Sigmund Freud, "On Narcissism: An Introduction" [1914], in vol. 14 of *The Complete Standard Edition of the Complete Psychological Works of Sigmund Freud* (London: Hogarth, 1971), 78.

45. Karl Menninger and Jeanetta Lyle Menninger, *Love Against Hate* (New York: Harcourt, Brace, 1942), 32.

46. David M. Levy, *Maternal Overprotection* (New York: Columbia University Press, 1943).

47. Edward A. Strecker, *Their Mothers' Sons: The Psychiatrist Examines an American Problem* (Philadelphia: Lippincott, 1946); Amram Scheinfeld, "Are American Moms a Menace?," *Ladies Home Journal*, November 1945, 36; "Mama's Boys," *Time*, November 25, 1946; "Momism," *Washington Post*, February 11, 1951.

48. See Ruth Feldstein, *Motherhood in Black and White: Race and Sex in American Liberalism, 1930–1965* (Ithaca, NY: Cornell University Press, 2000); Michael Daryl Scott, *Contempt and Pity: Social Policy and the Image of the Damaged Black Psyche, 1880–1996* (Chapel Hill: University of North Carolina Press, 1997).

49. William M. Tuttle Jr., *"Daddy's Gone to War": The Second World War in the Lives of America's Children* (New York: Oxford University Press, 1993), 71; L. M. Stolz, "Effects of Maternal Employment on Children: Evidence from Research," *Child Development* 31 (1960): 749–82, 751.

50. David M. Levy, "Primary Affect Hunger," *American Journal of Psychiatry* 94 (1937): 643–52, 643–44.

51. Margaret Ribble, *The Rights of Infants: Early Psychological Needs and Their Satisfaction* (New York: Columbia University Press, 1943), 8, 13.

52. René A. Spitz, "Hospitalism: An Inquiry into the Genesis of Psychiatric Conditions in Early Childhood," *Psychoanalytic Study of the Child* 1 (1945): 53–74; René A. Spitz, "Anaclitic Depression: An Inquiry into the Genesis of Psychiatric Conditions in Early Childhood, II," *Psychoanalytic Study of the Child* 2 (1946): 313–42; René A. Spitz, "The Importance of Mother-Child Relationship During the First Year of Life," *Mental Health Today* 7 (1948): 7–13.

53. Leo Kanner, *Child Psychiatry*, 2nd ed. (Springfield, IL: Charles C. Thomas, 1948), 117.

54. Kanner, *Child Psychiatry* (2nd ed.), 129.

55. Kanner, *Child Psychiatry* (2nd ed.), 131.

56. J. Louise Despert to Leo Kanner, July 12, 1943, Box 100696, Folder 43, Leo Kanner (1894–1981) Papers, American Psychiatric Association Foundation, Melvin Sabshin, MD, Library and Archives, Washington, DC.

57. Kanner to Despert, July 15, 1943, Box 100696, Folder 43, Leo Kanner Papers.

58. Despert to Kanner, April 30, 1946, Box 100696, Folder 43, Leo Kanner Papers.

59. Frieda Fromm-Reichmann, "Notes on the Development of Treatment of Schizophrenics by Psychoanalytic Psychotherapy," *Psychiatry* 11 (1948): 263–73, 265. On mother blame in psychiatry and psychoanalysis, see Edward Dolnick, *Madness on the Couch: Blaming the Victim in the Heyday of Psychoanalysis* (New York: Simon and Schuster, 1998); Deborah Weinstein, *The Pathological Family: Postwar America and the Rise of Family Therapy* (Ithaca, NY: Cornell University Press, 2013); Anne Harrington, "Mother Love and Mental Illness: An Emotional Story," *Osiris* 31 (2016): 94–115. On psychiatry and gender, see Elizabeth Lunbeck, *The Psychiatric Persuasion: Knowledge, Gender, and Power in Modern America* (Princeton, NJ: Princeton University Press, 1994).

60. Trude Tietze, "A Study of Mothers of Schizophrenic Patients," *Psychiatry* 12 (1949): 55–65, 57, 61.

61. Kanner, *Child Psychiatry* (2nd ed.), 722.

62. Leo Kanner, "Problems of Nosology and Psychodynamics of Early Infantile Autism," *American Journal of Orthopsychiatry* 19 (1949): 416–26, 420.

63. Kanner, "Problems of Nosology," 419.

64. Kanner, *Child Psychiatry* (2nd ed.), 720, see also 728.

65. Kanner, "Problems of Nosology," 422, 425.

66. Kanner, "Problems of Nosology," 426.

67. "Frosted Children," *Time*, April 26, 1948, p. 81. See Christopher Sterwald and Jeffrey Baker, "Frosted Intellectuals: How Dr. Leo Kanner Constructed the Autistic Family," *Perspectives in Biology and Medicine* 62 (2019): 690–709.

68. Leo Kanner, "The Specificity of Early Infantile Autism," *Zeitschrift für Kinderpsychiatrie* 25 (1958): 108–13, 109, 110.

69. Erik H. Erikson, *Childhood and Society* (New York: W. W. Norton, 1950).

70. Erikson, *Childhood and Society*, 249.

71. John Bowlby, "Maternal Care and Mental Health," *Bulletin of the World Health Organization* 3 (1951): 355–534, reissued as John Bowlby, *Maternal Care and Mental Health*, 2nd ed. (World Health Organization, 1952).

72. Bowlby, *Maternal Care*, 53.

73. On maternal deprivation and its effects on children, see Eduardo Duniec and Mical Raz, "Vitamins for the Soul: John Bowlby's Thesis of Maternal Deprivation, Biomedical Metaphors and the Deficiency Model of Disease," *History of Psychiatry* 22, no. 1 (2011): 93–107; Marga Vicedo, "The Social Nature of the Mother's Tie to Her Child: John Bowlby's Theory of Attachment in Post-War America," *British Journal of the History of Science* 44, no. 3 (2011): 401–26. On the multiple theories of deprivation and how they shaped American social policy in the 1960s, see Mical Raz, *What's Wrong with the Poor? Psychiatry, Race, and the War on Poverty* (Chapel Hill: University of North Carolina Press, 2013).

74. J. Louise Despert, "Some Considerations Relating to the Genesis of Autistic Behavior in Children," *American Journal of Orthopsychiatry* 21 (1951): 335–50, 343.

75. Margaret Ribble, "Discussion of Louise Despert's Paper," *American Journal of Orthopsychiatry* 21 (1951): 347–50, 348.

76. Margaret S. Mahler, "On Child Psychosis and Schizophrenia: Autistic and Symbiotic Infantile Psychoses," in *The Psychoanalytic Study of the Child*, 7 (1952): 286–305, 294, 297.

77. Leo Kanner, "To What Extent Is Early Infantile Autism Determined by Constitutional Inadequacies?," in *Genetics and the Inheritance of Integrated Neurological and Psychiatric Patterns*, ed. D. Hooker and C. C. Hare (Baltimore: Williams and Wilkins, 1954), 378–85, 382, 383.

78. Leon Eisenberg and Leo Kanner, "Early Infantile Autism, 1943–55," *American Journal of Orthopsychiatry* 26 (1956): 556–66.

79. Eisenberg and Kanner, "Early Infantile Autism, 1943–55," 564.

80. Mical Raz, "Deprived of Touch: How Maternal and Sensory Deprivation Theory Converged in Shaping Early Debates over Autism," *History of the Human Sciences* 27 (2014): 75–96.

81. Kurt Glaser and Leon Eisenberg, "Maternal Deprivation," *Pediatrics* 18 (1956): 626–42, 627.

82. Richard Pollak, *The Creation of Dr. B: A Biography of Bruno Bettelheim* (New York: Simon and Schuster, 1997). See also Dolnick, *Madness on the Couch*.

83. Bruno Bettelheim, "Individual and Mass Behavior in Extreme Situations," *Journal of Abnormal and Social Psychology* 38 (1943): 417–52.

84. For an appreciative biography of Bettelheim, see Theron Raines, *Rising to the Light: A Portrait of Bruno Bettelheim* (New York: Knopf, 2002).

85. Bruno Bettelheim, *Love Is Not Enough: The Treatment of Emotionally Disturbed Children* (Glencoe, IL: Free Press, 1950), 14, 16. See also Bruno Bettelheim, *Truants from Life: The Rehabilitation of Emotionally Disturbed Children* (Glencoe, IL: Free Press, 1955).

86. Bruno Bettelheim, "Schizophrenia as a Reaction to Extreme Situations," *American Journal of Orthopsychiatry* 26 (1956): 507–18, 507, 508.

87. Bettelheim, "Schizophrenia as a Reaction to Extreme Situations," 511.

88. Bettelheim, "Schizophrenia as a Reaction to Extreme Situations," 511, 512, 513.

89. Bettelheim, "Schizophrenia as a Reaction to Extreme Situations," 513; Bruno Bettelheim, "Joey: A 'Mechanical Boy,'" *Scientific American* 200 (March 1959): 116–27.

90. Bettelheim, "Joey," 118, 117, 118, 122.

91. Bettelheim, "Joey," 126.

92. Bettelheim, "Joey," 117.

93. Bettelheim, "Joey," 127.

94. Susan Sontag, *Illness as Metaphor* (New York: Random House, 1977), 57. On Sontag and metaphor in autism, see Zoe Gross, "Metaphor Stole My Autism: The Social Construction of Autism as Separable from Personhood, and Its Effect on Policy, Funding, and Perception," in *Loud Hands. Autistic People, Speaking*, ed. Autistic Self Advocacy Network (Washington, DC: Autistic Press, 2012), 258–69. For analysis of how autism figures in cultural narratives, see Mark Osteen, ed., *Autism and Representation* (New York, NY: Routledge, 2008); Stuart Murray, *Representing Autism* (Liverpool: Liverpool University Press, 2008).

CHAPTER 3: ON TRIAL

1. Sydney Gellis to Clara Park, November 30, 1961, Clara Park personal archive.

2. Marian Cabot Putnam Papers, Francis A. Countway Library of Medicine, Harvard University, Boston, MA.

3. Paul Roazen, *Freud and His Followers* (New York: Knopf, 1975), chap. 8; Paul Roazen, "Tola Rank," *Journal of the American Academy of Psychoanalysis* 18 (1990): 247–59.

4. Beata Rank, "Adaptation of the Psychoanalytic Technique for the Treatment of Young Children with Atypical Development," *American Journal of Orthopsychiatry* 19 (1949): 130–39.

5. Marian C. Putnam, "Case Study of an Atypical Two-and-a-Half-Year-Old," *American Journal of Orthopsychiatry* 18 (1948): 1–30, 27; Beata Rank, Marian C. Putnam, and Gregory Rochlin, "The Significance of the 'Emotional Climate' in Early Feeding Difficulties," *Psychosomatic Medicine* 10 (1948): 279–83, 279.

6. Rank, "Adaptation of the Psychoanalytic Technique," 131.

7. Rank, "Adaptation of the Psychoanalytic Technique," 131, 132.

8. Rank, "Adaptation of the Psychoanalytic Technique," 131, 134.

9. David E. Reiser, "Psychosis of Infancy and Early Childhood, as Manifested by Children with Atypical Development," *New England Journal of Medicine* 269 (1963): 790–98, 790, 791.

10. Reiser, "Psychosis of Infancy," 793.

11. Phillip H. Gates, "Etiology and Treatment of Atypical Development in Children (Childhood Psychosis)," in *Mental Retardation: Proceedings of the First International Medical Conference at Portland, Maine*, ed. Peter W. Bowman and Hans V. Mauner (New York: Grune and Stratton, 1960), 493–504.

12. Reiser, "Psychosis of Infancy," 791–92.

13. Clara Park, untitled handwritten report on the visit to the Putnam. This four-page report has the dates "Feb. 62" and "3/25/62" written at the top. Clara Park personal archive.

14. Clara Claiborne Park, *The Siege: A Family's Journey into the World of an Autistic Child*, orig. 1967 (Boston: Little, Brown, 1982), 136.

15. Clara Park, untitled report on visit to the Putnam, Clara Park personal archive; Park, *The Siege*, 135–36.

16. Clara Park, untitled report on visit to the Putnam.

17. Clara Park, untitled report on visit to the Putnam; Reiser, "Psychosis of Infancy," 792.

18. Rank, "Adaptation of the Psychoanalytic Technique," 136.

19. Clara Park notebooks, Clara Park personal archive.

20. Park, untitled report on visit to the Putnam.

21. Sidney S. Gellis to Clara Park, April 24, 1962, Clara Park personal archive.

22. Clara Park, Notebook 2, on Jessy, entry from February 2, 1962, Clara Park personal archive.

23. Park, Notebook 2, on Jessy, entry from February 11, 1962, Clara Park personal archive.

24. Clara Park to Bal, April 23, 1962, Clara Park personal archive.

25. Document titled "JESSICA PARK June 1962 Three years ten months," Clara Park personal archive.

26. Sydney Gellis to Anna Freud, June 15, 1962; Gellis to Phillip Gates, June 15, 1962, Clara Park personal archive.

27. Report on "Park, Jessica," dated July 10, 1962, and signed by Dr. Phillip H. Gates, Clara Park personal archive.

28. Clara Park notebook, undated, noting two articles by Kanner and Eisenberg "suggested by Dr. Gellis in May 1961," Clara Park personal archive.

29. Notebook entries on books and articles read on autism, Clara Park personal archive. Rosalind Oppenheim, "They Said Our Child Was Hopeless," *Saturday Evening Post*, June 17, 1961.

30. Clara Park, "Modern Inconveniences." Unpublished short paper. Undated, but written in 1962, Clara Park personal archive.

31. Clara Park to her mother Bal, April 23, 1962, Clara Park personal archive.

32. Paul Park, interview with the author, June 2015, North Adams, MA.

33. Katharine Park, interview with the author, July 2, 2015, Cambridge, MA.

34. Miss [Sylvia] Ini, "Interview with Parents. Jessica Park, September 12, 1962," Marie Battle Singer personal archive, in possession of Jane Rhodes.

35. Notebook, Clara Park personal archive; Park, *The Siege*, 149–50.

36. Paul Park, interview with the author, June 2015.

37. Lisa Appignanesi and John Forrester, *Freud's Women* (London: Phoenix, 1992), 273.

38. James Robertson, "Anna Freud and the Robertsons," memorial tribute to Anna Freud, delivered January 28, 1983. Available at http://www.robertson films.info/anna&robertsons.htm.

39. Anna Freud and Dorothy Burlingham, *Infants Without Families: Reports on the Hampstead Nurseries, 1939–1945*, in *The Writings of Anna Freud*, vol. III (New York: International Universities Press, 1973), 399–402, 400, 401, 402.

40. See Marga Vicedo, *The Nature and Nurture of Love: From Imprinting to Attachment in Cold War America* (Chicago: University of Chicago Press, 2013).

41. Anna Freud, "The Concept of the Rejecting Mother" (1955), in *The Writings of Anna Freud*, vol. IV (New York: International Universities Press, 1968), 586–602, 602.

42. Anna Freud, *Normality and Pathology in Childhood: Assessments and Development*, in *The Writings of Anna Freud*, vol. VI (New York: International Universities Press, 1965), 46.

43. Doris Wills, "Fifty Years of Child Guidance," *Journal of Child Psychotherapy* 4 (1958): 97–102; "Doris Wills: 1908–1993," *Bulletin of the Anna Freud Centre* 17 (1994): 57–65.

44. John Bolland, "Interview. Jessica Park," Ini, "Interview," September 12, 1962, and September 19, 1962; copies in Marie Battle Singer personal archive.

45. Ann Bolton, "In Memoriam: Marie Battle Singer," *Journal of Child Psychotherapy* 11 (1985): 3; Pauline Cohen, "Marie Battle Singer," *Bulletin of the Anna Freud Centre* 8 (1985): 213–15.

46. Marie Battle Singer, "Fantasies of a Borderline Patient," *Psychoanalytical Study of the Child* 15 (1960): 310–56, 311 n. 2.

47. John Forrester and Laura Cameron, *Freud in Cambridge* (Cambridge, UK: Cambridge University Press, 2017), 558.

48. Cohen, "Marie Battle Singer," 213.

49. David Astor, quoted in Cohen, "Marie Battle Singer," 214.

50. Clara Park to Emily Kirby, December 27, 1962. Clara Park personal archive.

51. Park, *The Siege*, 164; Bolton, "In Memoriam"; Cohen, "Marie Battle Singer."

52. Park, *The Siege*, 143.

53. Park, *The Siege*, 163.

54. Clara Park to Emily Kirby, December 27, 1962, Clara Park personal archive.

55. Clara Park to Emily Kirby, December 27, 1962, Clara Park personal archive.

56. Park, *The Siege*, 169.

57. Clara Park to Emily Kirby, December 27, 1962.

58. Park, *The Siege*, 163.

59. Singer, "Fantasies," 311; Clara Park, Notebook 3, Clara Park personal archive.

60. Clara Park to Marie Singer, April 8, 1963, Clara Park personal archive.

CHAPTER 4: IGNITING A REVOLT

1. David Park to Bal, November 18, 1963, Clara Park personal archive.

2. Clara Park to Emily Kirby, October 8, 1963, Clara Park personal archive.

3. Bernard Rimland, *Infantile Autism: The Syndrome and Its Implications for a Neural Theory of Behavior* (New York: Appleton-Century-Crofts, 1964).

4. Clara Park to Bernard Rimland, April 18, 1964, Bernard Rimland personal archive. Autism Research Institute, San Diego, CA.

5. Gloria Rimland, interview with the author, September 26, 2014, San Diego, CA.

6. Gloria Rimland, interview.

7. Rimland to Kanner, July 30, 1959; Rimland to Kanner, n.d. (probably October 1959), Bernard Rimland personal archive.

8. Rimland to Kanner, July 29, 1960; Rimland to Kanner, October 6, 1961, Bernard Rimland personal archive.

9. Rimland to Kanner, July 23, 1962; Rimland to Kanner, December 3, 1962, Bernard Rimland personal archive.

10. Rimland, *Infantile Autism*, vii.

11. Rimland, *Infantile Autism*.

12. Leo Kanner, "Preface," in Rimland, *Infantile Autism*, v, vi.

13. Kanner, "Preface," in Rimland, *Infantile Autism*, v.

14. Rimland, *Infantile Autism*, viii.

15. Gloria Rimland, interview with the author.

16. Lorraine Daston and Peter Galison, *Objectivity* (New York: Zone Books, 2017), 29, 19; Ellen Herman, *The Romance of American Psychology: Political Culture in the Age of Experts* (Berkeley: University of California Press, 1995); Mark Solovey, *Social Science for What? Battles over Public Funding for the 'Other Sciences' at the National Science Foundation* (Cambridge, MA: MIT Press, 2020).

17. C. G. Polan and Betty L. Spencer, "A Check List of Symptoms of Autism of Early Life," *West Virginia Medical Journal* 55 (1959): 198–204, 202, 203.

18. "Diagnostic Check List for Behavior-Disturbed Children (Form E-1)," Bernard Rimland personal archive. The second printing contained Form E-2.

19. Arne van Krevelen to Rimland, January 7, 1963, Bernard Rimland personal archive.

20. Rimland to van Krevelen, June 28, 1963, Bernard Rimland personal archive.

21. Rimland, *Infantile Autism*, 40.

22. Rimland, *Infantile Autism*, 45. For an analysis of these criticisms, see Marga Vicedo, *The Nature and Nurture of Love: From Imprinting to Attachment in Cold War America* (Chicago: University of Chicago Press, 2013).

23. Rimland, *Infantile Autism*, 64.

24. Rimland, *Infantile Autism*, 79.

25. Rimland, *Infantile Autism*, chapter 6.

26. Rimland, *Infantile Autism*, 119–20, 25.

27. Rimland, *Infantile Autism*, 27.

28. Rimland, *Infantile Autism*, 38, 30.

29. Peter Mittler, "Review of Rimland: *Infantile Autism*," *British Journal of Social and Clinical Psychology* 4 (1965): 157–59, 158; Valerie Cowie, "Review of Rimland: *Infantile Autism*," *British Journal of Psychology* 111

(1965): 455–56; Mark Rutter, "Review of Rimland: *Infantile Autism*," *Journal of Child Psychology and Psychiatry* 6 (1965): 132–33.

30. D. W. Winnicott, "Review of Rimland: *Infantile Autism*," *British Medical Journal* 2 (1966): 634.

31. D. W. Winnicott, "Psychoses and Child Care," in Winnicott, *Through Pediatrics to Psycho-Analysis* (New York: Basic Books, 1958), 219–28, 219.

32. Mildred Creak, "Schizophrenic Syndrome in Childhood: Progress Report (April, 1961) of a Working Party," *British Medical Journal* 2 (1961): 889–90, 889. On the history of autism in Britain, see Bonnie Evans, *The Metamorphosis of Autism: A History of Child Development in Britain* (Manchester, UK: University of Manchester Press, 2017).

33. Rimland, "On the Objective Diagnosis of Infantile Autism," 17. The manuscript, dated June 25, 1965, was aimed for distribution among the members of the working group and subsequent discussion during the group's meeting on July 10. The discussion was postponed to the November 27 meeting, according to the minutes of the group. E. M. Creak, "9 Points Group–Minutes of a meeting held at the Hospital for Sick Children . . . on Saturday July 10th, 1965," Bernard Rimland personal archive.

34. Clara Park to Bernard Rimland, April 18, 1964, Bernard Rimland personal archive. Rimland, "The Differentiation of Childhood Psychoses: An Analysis of Checklists for 2,218 Psychotic Children," *Journal of Autism and Childhood Schizophrenia* 1 (1971), 161–74.

35. Clara Park to Rimland, April 18, 1964.

36. Clara Park to Rimland, April 18, 1964.

37. William Blanchard to Bernard Rimland, October 21, 1964; Frances Eberhardy to Bernard Rimland, October 29, 1964; Patricia [mother of Terry] to Bernard Rimland, October 26, 1964; [mother of Danny] to Bernard Rimland, undated (week of October 25–31, 1964): all in Bernard Rimland personal archive.

38. [Parent of Becky] to Bernard Rimland, January 13, 1965, Bernard Rimland personal archive.

39. Bernard Rimland to parent, October 14, 1964, Bernard Rimland personal archive.

40. Rimland's letter, December 29, 1964, Bernard Rimland personal archive; Rimland to "Dear parents," undated (probably summer 1965), Ruth Sullivan personal archive.

41. Rimland to Clara Park, August 16, 1965; Park to Rimland, undated (July or August 1965), Bernard Rimland personal archive; Rimland to Patricia Caruthers, October 22, 1965, Ruth Sullivan personal archive.

42. Rosalind Oppenheim, "They Said Our Son Was Hopeless," *Saturday Evening Post*, June 17, 1961, 23, 56–58, 56.

43. Oppenheim, "They Said Our Son Was Hopeless," 58.

44. Patricia Caruthers to Bernard Rimland, date illegible (replied on February 9, 1965); Rimland to Peter Mittler, February 9, 1965, Bernard Rimland personal archive.

45. Oppenheim, "They Said Our Son Was Hopeless"; D. Moser and A. Grant, "Screams, Slaps, and Love: A Surprising, Shocking Treatment Helps

Far-Gone Mental Cripples," *Life*, May 7, 1965, pp. 90–96; Louisa Bates Ames to Bernard Rimland, April 16, 1964, Bernard Rimland personal archive.

46. Rimland to Ruth Sullivan, October 29, 1965, Bernard Rimland personal archive.

47. Ruth Sullivan, "A Brief History of NSAC," January 1968, in Bernard Rimland personal archive (the typescript provides no authorship information, but a memo from Sullivan dated March 11, 1968, says "I wrote this checking its validity with Joan Rusten of Albany, who was at the Teaneck meeting, and Bernard Rimland"); "Where We've Been and Where We're Going: The Autism Society's Proud History," *Autism Advocate* 61, no. 3 (Fall/Winter 2011).

48. Sullivan, "A Brief History of NSAC." See also Frank Warren, "The Role of the National Society in Working with Families," in *The Effects of Autism on the Family*, ed. E. Schopler and G. Mesibov (New York: Plenum, 1984), 99–115, 102 (Sullivan quotation), 105.

49. Rimland to Kanner, March 23, 1966; Kanner to Rimland, March 26, 1966; Rimland, newsletter, February 11, 1966, all in Bernard Rimland personal archive. *NSAC Newsletter* 1, no. 1 (Autumn 1966).

50. Mooza V. P. Grant, "Message to Members," *NSAC Newsletter* (Autumn 1966).

51. Rimland, "History of Infantile Autism," *NSAC Chal'lenge* 1, no. 2 (1967): 1–2. Only this issue of the newsletter appears to have had its title changed from *NSAC Newsletter* to *NSAC Chal'lenge*.

52. Rimland to William Kemmel, December 31, 1968, Bernard Rimland personal archive.

53. *NSAC Newsletter* (Fall 1968).

54. Ruth Sullivan, "President's Message," *NSAC Newsletter* (December 1968).

55. Ruth Sullivan to Rimland, December 31, 1965, Ruth Sullivan personal archive.

56. Warren, "Role of the National Society," 108.

57. "Joint Conference on Childhood Mental Illness" and "Report Written by Clara Claiborne Park for the Capital District Chapter and Other Chapters of the National Society for Autistic Children," New York City, 1968, in Bernard Rimland personal archive.

58. Gil Eyal, Brendan Hart, Emine Oncular, Neta Oren, and Natasha Rossi, *The Autism Matrix: The Social Origins of the Autism Epidemic* (Cambridge, UK: Polity, 2010), 170, 171.

59. *The Invisible Wall*, dir. Barnet Addis, Behavioral Sciences Audiovisual Laboratory, University of Oklahoma Medical Center, 1968, 16mm film; Stephen M. Edelson, "The Invisible Wall," in Bernard Rimland, *Infantile Autism: The Syndrome and Its Implications for a Neural Theory of Behavior*, fiftieth-anniversary updated ed., ed. Stephen M. Edelson (London: Jessica Kingsley, 2015), 296–98.

CHAPTER 5: A MOTHER'S PLEA FOR INTELLIGENT LOVE

1. Clara Park to Bernard Rimland, April 18, 1964, Bernard Rimland personal archive.

2. Clara Park to Bernard Rimland, April 18, 1964, Bernard Rimland personal archive.

3. Bernard Rimland to Clara Park, May 18, 1964, Clara Park personal archive.

4. All quotations in this and previous paragraphs from Clara Park to Bernard Rimland, July 4, 1964, Bernard Rimland personal archive.

5. Clara Park to Bernard Rimland, March 13, 1965, Bernard Rimland personal archive.

6. Clara's notebooks on Jessy, entry for March 1965, Clara Park personal archive.

7. Clara's notebooks on Jessy, entry for December 1965; entry for March 1965, Clara Park personal archive.

8. Clara Park to Dr. Gellis, January 18, 1966, Clara Park personal archive.

9. Clara Park to Dr. Gellis, January 18, 1966.

10. On applications of Skinner's ideas, see Alexandra Rutherford, *Beyond the Box: B.F. Skinner's Technology of Behaviour from Laboratory to Life, 1950–1970s* (Toronto: University of Toronto Press, 2009).

11. Clara Park to Bernard Rimland, April 6, 1965, Clara Park personal archive.

12. All quotations in this and previous paragraphs from Clara Park to Bernard Rimland, April 6, 1965, Clara Park personal archive.

13. On the other hand, some autistic people say that they did not want to be alone. See, for example, John Elder Robison, *Look Me in the Eye* (New York: Broadway Books, 2007), 211.

14. All quotations in this and previous paragraphs from Clara Park to Bernard Rimland, March 13, 1965.

15. Clara Park to Bernard Rimland, March 13, 1965.

16. Clara Park to Bal, March 5, 1967, Clara Park personal archive.

17. Clara Claiborne Park, *The Siege: A Family's Journey into the World of an Autistic Child*, orig. 1967 (Boston: Little, Brown, 1982), 14.

18. On motherhood in America after WWII, see Stephanie Coontz, *The Way We Never Were: American Families and the Nostalgia Trap* (New York: Basic Books, 1992); Elaine Tyler May, *Homeward Bound: American Families in the Cold War Era* (New York: Basic Books, 1988); Arlene S. Skolnick, *Embattled Paradise: The American Family in an Age of Uncertainty* (New York: Basic Books, 1991); Ruth Feldstein, *Motherhood in Black and White* (Ithaca, NY: Cornell University Press, 2000); Rebecca Jo Plant, *Mom: The Transformation of Motherhood in Modern America* (Chicago: University of Chicago Press, 2010).

19. Clara Park to Freeman Dyson, July 8, 1994, Freeman Dyson personal archive.

20. Betty Friedan, *The Feminine Mystique* (New York: W. W. Norton, 1963)

21. Park, *The Siege*, 15.

22. Park, *The Siege*, 23.

23. Park, *The Siege*, 46, 45.

24. Park, *The Siege*, 12.

25. Park, *The Siege*, 188.

26. Stephen Shore, *Beyond the Wall: Personal Experiences with Autism and Asperger Syndrome* (Shawnee Mission, KS: AAPC Publishing, 2003). He also remarks how his mother was not allowed to provide any input about his development when he attended the Putnam's nursery school. Clara's experience of having her views rejected was not an isolated incident.

27. Ido Kedar, *Ido in Autismland: Climbing Out of Autism's Silent Prison* (self pub., 2012). The first memoir by a child labeled autistic is Temple Grandin and Margaret M. Scariano, *Emergence: Labeled Autistic* (Novato, CA: Arena Press, 1986).

28. For studies of *The Siege*, see Jane Taylor McDonell, "Mothering an Autistic Child: Reclaiming the Voice of the Mother," 58–75, in *Narrating Mothers: Theorizing Maternal Subjectivities*, ed. Brenda O. Daly and Maureen T. Reddy (Knoxville: University of Tennessee Press, 1991); Debra L. Cumberland, "Crossing Over: Writing the Autistic Memoir," 183–96, and Sheryl Stevenson, "(M)Othering and Autism: Maternal Rhetorics of Self-Revision," 197–211, both in *Autism and Representation*, ed. Mark Osteen (New York: Routledge, 2008). Mitzi Waltz, *Autism: A Social and Medical History* (London: Palgrave Macmillan, 2013), 113, also points out that *The Siege* is a narrative with no miracle cure at the end.

29. Park, *The Siege*, 125–26.

30. Park, *The Siege*, 130.

31. Park, *The Siege*, 160.

32. Park, *The Siege*, 14.

33. On the history of views about maternal instincts, see Elisabeth Badinter, *Mother Love: Myth and Reality* (New York: Macmillan, 1981); Cynthia Eagle Russett, *Sexual Science: The Victorian Construction of Womanhood* (Cambridge, MA: Harvard University Press, 1989); Stephanie A. Shields, "To Pet, Coddle, and 'Do For': Caretaking and the Concept of Maternal Instinct," in *In the Shadow of the Past: Psychology Portrays the Sexes*, ed. Miriam Lewin (New York: Columbia University Press, 1984), 256–73; Marga Vicedo, "Mother Love and Human Nature: A History of the Maternal Instinct" (PhD diss., Harvard University, 2005).

34. Park, *The Siege*, 130–31.

35. Peggy Brooks to Clara Park, June 3, 1965, Clara Park personal archive.

36. Charles Darwin to Thomas Henry Huxley, January 30, 1868, in Darwin Correspondence Project, "Letter No. 5817," http://www.darwinproject.ac.uk/DCP-LETT-5817, accessed December 19, 2017.

37. Charles Darwin, "A Biographical Sketch of an Infant," *Mind* 2 (1877): 285–94.

38. William T. Preyer, *Die Seele des Kindes: Beobachtungen über die geistige Entwicklung des Menschen in den ersten Lebensjahren* (Grieben: Leipzig, 1882).

39. See Doris B. Wallace, Margery B. Franklin, and Robert T. Keegan, "The Observing Eye: A Century of Baby Diaries," *Human Development* 37 (1994): 1–29.

40. See Christine Oertzen, "Science in the Cradle: Milicent Shinn and Her Home-Based Network of Baby Observers, 1890–1910," *Centaurus* 52 (2013): 175–95. See also David Hoogland Noon, "Situating Gender and Professional

Identity in American Child Study, 1880–1910," *History of Psychology* 7 (2004): 107–29. On the value of observation in science, see Lorraine Daston and Elizabeth Lunbeck, eds., *Histories of Scientific Observation* (Chicago: University of Chicago Press, 2011); on the relation of observation to experience, see Katharine Park, "Observations in the Margins, 500–1500," 15–44 in that volume.

41. Noon, "Situating Gender and Professional Identity in American Child Study."

42. Ellen Herman, "Families Made by Science: Arnold Gesell and the Technologies of Modern Child Adoption," *Isis* 92 (2001): 684–715.

43. Marian Radke Yarrow, "Problems of Methods in Parent–Child Research," *Child Development* 34 (1963): 215–26, 225.

44. Park, *The Siege*, 195.

45. Park, *The Siege*, 181, 182.

46. Park, *The Siege*, 183, 182, 180.

47. Park, *The Siege*, 186.

48. Park, *The Siege*, 196.

49. Jaimie Ann Blue to Clara Park, May 22, 1994, Clara Park personal archive.

50. Peggy Randolph, "Mother Discusses Care of Retarded," *Tulsa World*, January 14, 1968, copy in Clara Park personal archive.

51. *Falcon's Nest*, book review (no author), March 1968, copy in Clara Park personal archive.

52. Elizabeth P. Nichols, review of *The Siege*, in *Library Journal*, November 1, 1967, copy in Clara Park personal archive.

53. Colin Smythe, "The Siege," *Christchurch Press* (New Zealand), May 3, 1969, copy in Clara Park personal archive.

54. W. B. Trafford to Clara Park, May 14, 1968, Clara Park personal archive.

55. Frances Eberhardy to Clara Park, April 7, 1968, Clara Park personal archive.

56. Chris Griffith to Clara Park, January 8, 1968, Clara Park personal archive.

57. Karl Meninger, "Reading Note" on *The Siege*, attached to his letter to Amy Meeker (Atlantic Monthly Press), July 8, 1982, copy in Clara Park personal archive.

58. Evelyn Fox Keller, *Reflections on Gender and Science* (New Haven, CT: Yale University Press, 1985).

59. Park, *The Siege*, 306.

CHAPTER 6: FROM CULPRITS TO COLLABORATORS

1. Bruno Bettelheim, *The Empty Fortress: Infantile Autism and the Birth of the Self* (New York: Free Press, 1967).

2. Bettelheim, *Empty Fortress*, 25.

3. Bettelheim, *Empty Fortress*, 32–33.

4. See Marga Vicedo, "'The Father of Ethology and the Foster Mother of Ducks': Konrad Lorenz as an Expert on Motherhood," *Isis* 100 (2009): 263–91; Marga Vicedo, "Mothers, Machines, and Morals: Harry Harlow's

Work on Primate Love from Lab to Legend," *Journal of the History of the Behavioral Sciences* 45 (2009): 193–218. On the importance of animal studies during this period, see Erika L. Milam, *Creatures of Cain: The Hunt for Human Nature in Cold War America* (Princeton, NJ: Princeton University Press, 2019).

5. Bettelheim, *Empty Fortress*, 125.

6. Bettelheim, *Empty Fortress*, 405.

7. Richard Pollak, *The Creation of Dr. B: A Biography of Bruno Bettelheim* (New York: Simon and Schuster, 1997), 270–75. On Bettelheim, see also Silverman, *Understanding Autism*; Katherine DeMaria Severson, James Arnt Aune, and Denise Jodlowski, "Bruno Bettelheim, Autism, and the Rhetoric of Scientific Authority," in *Autism and Representation*, ed. Mark Osteen (New York: Routledge, 2008), 65–77.

8. Clara Park to Bal, March 5, 1967, Clara Park personal archive.

9. Pollak, *The Creation of Dr. B*, 267–68.

10. Bruno Bettelheim to Bernard Rimland, April 29, 1966; this was in response to Rimland to Bettelheim, April 25, 1966; copies in Clara Park personal archive.

11. Clara Park to Bernard Rimland, December 2, 1966; Clara Park to Bal, March 5, 1967, Clara Park personal archive.

12. Frances Eberhardy, "The View from 'the Couch,'" *Journal of Child Psychology and Psychiatry* 8 (1967): 257–63, 257, 258.

13. Eberhardy, "The View from 'the Couch,'" 259, 260.

14. Eberhardy, "The View from 'the Couch,'" 261.

15. Eberhardy, "The View from 'the Couch,'" 263.

16. John K. Wing, "Review of *The Empty Fortress* by B. Bettelheim," *British Journal of Psychology* 114 (1968): 788–91; Harry Harlow, "A Brief Look at Autistic Children," *Psychiatry & Social Science Review* 3 (1969): 27–29, 27; Leo Kanner to Arn van Krevelen, February 25, 1967, Box 100697, Folder 98, Leo Kanner Papers.

17. Clara Park and Leon Shapiro, *You Are Not Alone: Understanding and Dealing with Mental Illness* (Boston: Atlantic Monthly Press, 1976), xiii, 124.

18. Lawrence Casler, "Maternal Deprivation: A Critical Review of the Literature," *Society for Research in Child Development* 26 (1961): 1–63.

19. On Harlow, see Vicedo, "Mother, Machines, and Morals."

20. Bettelheim, "Joey," 116–27; Bettelheim, *Empty Fortress*, 239.

21. Bettelheim, *Empty Fortress*, 247–50.

22. Bettelheim, *Empty Fortress*, 246.

23. Bettelheim, *Empty Fortress*, 234–38.

24. John Bowlby, *Separation: Anxiety and Anger* (New York: Basic Books, 1973), 190. See Marga Vicedo, "Etho-Pathology and Civilization Diseases: Niko and Elisabeth Tinbergen on Autism," *Canadian Bulletin of Medical History* 35 (2018): 1–31.

25. Elizabeth Irvine to Clara Park, August 8, 1973; Albert Solnit to Clara Park, April 30, 1974; "Child Psychiatrists to Meet in Philadelphia," *Psychiatric News*, April 17, 1974, announcing the conference that took place July 29–August 2. All in Clara Park personal archive.

26. Elizabeth Irvine to Clara Park, May 12, 1974, Clara Park personal archive.

27. Clara Park to Margaret Dewey, August 8, 1974, Clara Park personal archive.

28. Clara Park, "The Positive Value of Parents," 8th International Congress of the International Association for Child Psychiatry and Allied Professions, Philadelphia, July 28–August 2, 1974; typescript in Clara Park personal archive.

29. Eric Schopler and Julie Loftin, "Thought Disorders in Parents of Psychotic Children: A Function of Test Anxiety," *Archives of General Psychiatry* 20 (1969): 174–81, 180.

30. Eric Schopler, "Parents of Psychotic Children as Scapegoats," *Journal of Contemporary Psychotherapy* 4 (1971): 17–22.

31. Eric Schopler and Robert Reichler, "Parents as Cotherapists in the Treatment of Psychotic Children," *Journal of Autism and Childhood Schizophrenia* 1 (1971): 87–102, 88.

32. Clara Park to Eric Schopler, May 28, 1969, Clara Park personal archive.

33. Leo Kanner to Sen. Charles Larkins, April 1, 1971; S. Clarence Griffith Jr. to Sen. Charles Larkins, April 1, 1971, copies in Clara Park personal archive.

34. Silverman, *Understanding Autism*, 115–16.

35. Mary S. Akerley, "Parents Speak: Introduction," *Journal of Autism and Childhood Schizophrenia* 4 (1974): 347.

36. Eric Schopler, "New Publisher, New Editor, Expanded Editorial Policy—Goal: An Improved Journal," editorial, *Journal of Autism and Childhood Schizophrenia* 4 (1974): 91–92; E. James Anthony, "Editorial Query," *Journal of Autism and Childhood Schizophrenia* 4 (1974): 93; Schopler's response, 94.

37. For example, Clara published "Growing Out of Autism," in *Autism in Adolescents and Adults*, ed. E. Schopler and G. B. Mesibov (New York: Plenum Press, 1983), 279–95; "Social Growth in Autism," in *Social Behavior in Autism*, ed. E. Schopler and G. B. Mesibov (New York: Plenum Press, 1986), 81–99.

38. O. Ivar Lovaas, Gilbert Freitag, Vivian J. Gold, and Irene C. Kassorla, "Experimental Studies in Childhood Schizophrenia: Analysis of Self-Destructive Behavior," *Journal of Experimental Child Psychology* 2 (1965): 67–84.

39. Don Moser and Allan Grant, "Screams, Slaps, and Love: Surprising, Shocking Treatment Helps Far-Gone Mental Cripples," *Life*, May 7, 1965, 90–101, 90, 92.

40. Moser and Grant, "Screams, Slaps, and Love," 93.

41. Moser and Grant, "Screams, Slaps, and Love," 96, 97.

42. James Q. Simmons and O. Ivar Lovaas, "Use of Pain and Punishment as Treatment Techniques with Childhood Schizophrenics," *Journal of Psychotherapy* 23 (1969): 23–36.

43. Paul Chance, "'After You Hit a Child, You Can't Just Get Up and Leave Him; You Are Hooked to That Kid': A Conversation with Ivar Lovaas

About Self-Mutilating Children and How Their Parents Make It Worse," *Psychology Today* (January 1974): 76–84.

44. Robert Claiborne, "Ideas and Trends: Education, Psychology, Archeology," *New York Times*, April 28, 1974.

45. O. Ivar Lovaas, Robert Koegel, James Q. Simmons, and Judith Stevens Long, "Some Generalization and Follow-Up Measures on Autistic Children in Behavior Therapy," *Journal of Applied Behavior Analysis* 6 (1973): 131–66.

46. O. Ivar Lovaas, Laura Schreibman, and Robert L. Koegel, "A Behavior Modification Approach to the Treatment of Autistic Children," *Journal of Autism and Childhood Schizophrenia* 4 (1974): 111–29, 127.

47. Lovaas et al., "Some Generalization and Follow-Up Measures on Autistic Children in Behavior Therapy," 163.

48. O. Ivar Lovaas, with Andrea Ackerman, Dean Alexander, Paula Firestone, Marlyn Perkins, and Douglas B. Young, *Teaching Developmentally Disabled Children: The Me Book* (Baltimore: University Park Press, 1981), ix.

49. Lovaas et al., *The Me Book*, xi.

50. Lovaas et al., *The Me Book*, x.

51. O. Ivar Lovaas, "The Development of a Treatment-Research Project for Developmentally Disabled and Autistic Children," *Applied Behavior Analysis* 26 (1993): 617–30, 627. On the key role of parents in the success of ABA, see Silverman, *Understanding Autism*.

52. Gloria Rimland, interview.

53. Josh Greenfeld, *A Child Called Noah: A Family Journey* (San Diego: Harcourt Brace Jovanovich, 1972); Greenfeld, *A Place for Noah* (New York: Holt, Rinehart and Winston, 1978). For Noah's brother's perspective, see Taro Greenfeld, *Boy Alone: A Brother's Memoir* (New York: HarperCollins, 2009).

54. For supportive assessments of ABA, see Catherine Maurice, *Let Me Hear Your Voice: A Family's Triumph Over Autism* (New York: Fawcett Columbine, 1993); Carol Johnson and Julia Crowder, *Autism: From Tragedy to Triumph*, 2nd ed. (Boston: Branden Books, 2014). For a negative assessment, see Kedar, *Ido in Autismland*.

55. Gil Eyal, Brendan Hart, Emine Oncular, Neta Oren, and Natasha Rossi, *The Autism Matrix* (Cambridge, MA: Polity, 2010).

CHAPTER 7: FROM CUSTODIAL CARE TO EDUCATION FOR AUTISTIC CHILDREN

1. Lawrence J. Friedman, *Identity's Architect: A Biography of Erik H. Erikson* (New York: Scribner, 1999), 210.

2. Clare, *Brilliant Imperfection*, 39, 40. On psychiatry and children, see Kathleen Jones, *Taming the Troublesome Child: American Families, Child Guidance, and the Limits of Psychiatric Authority* (Cambridge, MA: Harvard University Press, 1999); Blythe Doroshow, *Emotionally Disturbed: A History of Caring for America's Troubled Children* (Chicago: University of Chicago Press, 2019). Gil Eyal et al., *The Autism Matrix: The Social Origins of the Autism Epidemic* (Cambridge, MA: Polity, 2010), argues that deinstitutionalization had a great impact on the rise of autism diagnosis in the United States.

3. Clara Park to Eric Schopler, May 28, 1969, Clara Park personal archive.

4. *Autism's Lonely Children*, NET Film Service, New York, 1965, dir. Philip Burton Jr. and Jack Willis, prod. David Prowitt.

5. Clara Park to Eric Schopler, May 28, 1969, Clara Park personal archive.

6. Clara Park to Bernard Rimland, April 6, 1965, Clara Park personal archive.

7. Interview with Anna Saldo, July 2019. See also Anna Saldo-Burke, *Green Mittens Covered Her Ears: A Look at Autism; My Story with Jessica Park*, ill. Diana M. Saldo (self pub., 2010).

8. David Park, "Operant Conditioning of a Speaking Autistic Child," *Journal of Autism and Childhood Schizophrenia* 4 (1974): 189–91.

9. David Park, "Operant Conditioning," 190; Clara Claiborne Park, *Exiting Nirvana: A Daughter's Life with Autism* (Boston: Little, Brown, 2001), 158.

10. Park, *Exiting Nirvana*, 159.

11. David Park, "Operant Conditioning," 190.

12. Park, *Exiting Nirvana*, 168–69.

13. Park, *Exiting Nirvana*, 161–62.

14. David Park, "Operant Conditioning," 191.

15. See Brendan Hart, "Autism Parents and Neurodiversity: Radical Translation, Joint Embodiment and the Prosthetic Environment," *BioSocieties* 9 (2014): 284–303, who also shows how parents in this period and now radically transform techniques to adapt them to their children.

16. Elizabeth M. Flagler to Dr. and Mrs. Park, August 27, 1974, Clara Park personal archive.

17. Silverman, *Understanding Autism*, notes that one of NSAC's major goals was convincing society and legislators that autistic children were educable.

18. See Task Force on Children Out of School, *The Way We Go to School: The Exclusion of Children in Boston* (Boston: Beacon Press, 1971).

19. See "Pennsylvania Association for Retarded Citizens (PARC) v. Commonwealth of Pennsylvania," https://www.pubintlaw.org/cases-and-projects/pennsylvania-association-for-retarded-citizens-parc-v-commonwealth-of-pennsylvania.

20. Clara C. Park, "Elly and the Right to Education," *Phi Theta Kappan* 55 (1974): 535–37, 536. This short yet influential paper was reprinted several times.

21. Park, "Elly and the Right to Education," 537.

22. Park, "Elly and the Right to Education," 536.

23. Clara Park with Leon Shapiro, *You Are Not Alone: Understanding and Dealing with Mental Illness; A Guide for Patients, Families, Doctors and Other Professionals* (Boston: Atlantic Monthly Press, 1976), 364.

24. Victor Lotter, "Epidemiology of Autistic Conditions in Young Children: I. Prevalence," *Social Psychiatry* 1 (1966): 124–37, 124.

25. Mildred Creak, "Schizophrenic Syndrome in Childhood: Progress Report (April 1961) of a Working Party," *British Medical Journal* 2 (1961): 889–90, 889.

26. Lotter, "Epidemiology," 125.

27. Lotter, "Epidemiology," 126–27, 130.

28. Victor Lotter, "Epidemiology of Autistic Conditions in Young Children: II. Some Characteristics of the Parents and Children," *Social Psychiatry* 1 (1967): 163–73, 172.

29. Michael Rutter, "Concepts of Autism: A Review of Research," *Journal of Child Psychology and Psychiatry* 9 (1968): 1–25, 4.

30. Rutter, "Concepts of Autism," 6.

31. Carolyn Betts, *Label Me Jeff: A Special Kind of Normal* (Living and Existing Publishers, 1979; CBYC Publications, 2010); Clara Park, interview; Edward R. Ritvo et al., "Social Class Factors in Autism," *Journal of Autism and Childhood Schizophrenia* 1 (1971): 297–310. On gender and autism, see Jordynn Jack, *Autism and Gender: From Refrigerator Mothers to Computer Geeks* (Urbana: University of Illinois Press, 2014). On race and autism, see Lydia X. Z. Brown, E. Ashkenazy, and Morénike Giwa Onaiwu, eds., *All the Weight of Our Dreams: On Living Racialized Autism* (Lincoln, NE: DragonBee Press, 2017). See also M. S. Durkin et al., "Autism Spectrum Disorder Among US Children (2002–2010): Socioeconomic, Racial, and Ethnic Disparities," *American Journal of Public Health* 107 (2017): 1818–26.

32. Committee on Nomenclature and Statistics of the American Psychiatric Association, *DSM-II: Diagnostic and Statistical Manual of Mental Disorders (Second Edition)* (Washington, DC: American Psychiatric Association, 1968).

33. D. Arn van Krevelen, "Autismus Infantum: Introduction," *Acta Paedopsychiatrica* 35 (1968), 97–98, 97.

34. Hans Asperger, "Zur Differentialdiagnose des kindlichen Autismus," *Acta Paedopsychiatrica* 35 (1968): 136–45, 145, 142.

35. Rutter, "Concepts of Autism," 5.

36. Kanner, "Autistic Disturbances," 247.

37. Clemens E. Benda, Malcolm J. Farrell, and Catherine E. Chipman, "The Inadequacy of Present-Day Concepts of Mental Deficiency and Mental Illness in Child Psychiatry," *The American Journal of Psychiatry* 107 (1951): 721–29, 723.

38. Leo Kanner, "Follow-Up Study of Eleven Autistic Children Originally Reported in 1943," *Journal of Autism and Childhood Schizophrenia* 1 (1971): 119–45, 143, 144.

39. Kanner, "Follow-up Study," 145.

40. D. Arn van Krevelen, "Early Infantile Autism and Autistic Psychopathy," *Journal of Autism and Childhood Schizophrenia* 1 (1971): 82–86, 83, 84.

41. Margaret Dewey to Clara Park, undated (but late 1971 or 1972), Clara Park personal archive.

42. Margaret Dewey to Clara Park, May 14, 1968, Clara Park personal archive.

43. Margaret Dewey to Clara Park, undated (but late 1971 or 1972), Clara Park personal archive.

44. Dewey to Clara, undated (1971 or 1972), Clara Park personal archive.

45. Lorna Wing, "Asperger's Syndrome: A Clinical Account," *Psychological Medicine* 11 (1981): 115–29, 120, 123.

46. Michael Rutter, "Autistic Children: Infancy to Adulthood," *Seminars in Psychiatry* 2 (1970): 435–50; Kanner, "Follow-Up Study."

47. Gil Eyal et al., *The Autism Matrix: The Social Origins of the Autism Epidemic* (Cambridge, MA: Polity 2010), 224.

48. *NSAC Newsletter*, 4, no. 1 (1972): 7.

49. Ruth Sullivan to Clara Park, August 4, 1979, Clara Park personal archive.

50. Clara Park to Margaret Dewey, March 5, 1972, Clara Park personal archive.

51. James Flagler, "How I Feel," *Advocate* (July/August 1986), 10.

52. Clara Park to John Wing, October 24, 1974, Clara Park personal archive.

53. Eyal et al., *The Autism Matrix*, also note that the parents were the first to bring the children and adolescents who would become the self-advocates to public forums.

54. Ruth Christ Sullivan, "Foreword," in Temple Grandin, *The Way I See It: A Personal Look at Autism and Asperger's* (Arlington, TX: Future Horizons, 2008). When she became a public speaker, Grandin sometimes asked her mother to join her in lecturing. See Eustacia Cutler, *A Thorn in My Pocket: Temple Grandin's Mother Tells Her Family Story* (Arlington, TX: Future Horizons, 2004).

55. Margaret Dewey to Clara and David Park, December 23, 1974, Clara Park personal archive.

56. Margaret Dewey to Clara Park, December 29, 1986, Clara Park personal archive.

CHAPTER 8: WATERCOLORS ON WET PAPER

1. Clara Park to Freeman Dyson, May 21, 1980, December 15, 1984; Park to Dyson, December 21, 1987; Park to Dyson, February 5, 1992, Clara Park personal archive.

2. Clara Park to Kathy Park, January 1, 1991, Clara Park personal archive.

3. Clara Claiborne Park, "Exiting Nirvana," *American Scholar* 67, 2 (1998): 29–43; Clara Claiborne Park, *Exiting Nirvana: A Daughter's Life with Autism* (Boston: Little, Brown, 2001).

4. Park, *Exiting Nirvana*, 7.

5. Park, *Exiting Nirvana*, 10.

6. Park, *Exiting Nirvana*, 3.

7. Park, *Exiting Nirvana*, 24.

8. Park, *Exiting Nirvana*, 24–25, 25.

9. Park, *Exiting Nirvana*, 26.

10. Park, *Exiting Nirvana*, 29.

11. Park, *Exiting Nirvana*, 29, 30.

12. Park, *Exiting Nirvana*, 31, emphasis added.

13. Park, *Exiting Nirvana*, 33.

14. Park, *Exiting Nirvana*, 35.

15. Park, *Exiting Nirvana*, 37.

16. Park, *Exiting Nirvana*, 37–39.

17. Park, *Exiting Nirvana*, 43.

18. Park, *Exiting Nirvana*, 43–44, 45.

19. Simon Baron-Cohen, Alan M. Leslie, and Uta Frith, "Does the Autistic Child Have a 'Theory of Mind'?" *Cognition* 21 (1985): 37–47.

20. Baron-Cohen et al., "Does the Autistic Child Have a 'Theory of Mind'?," 43.

21. Park, *Exiting Nirvana*, 56.

22. Park, *Exiting Nirvana*, 66.

23. Park, *Exiting Nirvana*, 66.

24. Park, *Exiting Nirvana*, 67, 71.

25. Park, *Exiting Nirvana*, 88.

26. Park, *Exiting Nirvana*, 93–94.

27. Park, *Exiting Nirvana*, 89, 94–95.

28. Park, *Exiting Nirvana*, 97, 102.

29. Park, *Exiting Nirvana*, 71–72.

30. Park, *Exiting Nirvana*, 70.

31. Park, *Exiting Nirvana*, 28, 4.

32. Park, *Exiting Nirvana*, 116.

33. Barry M. Prizant with Tom Fields-Meyer, *Uniquely Human: A Different Way of Seeing Autism* (New York: Simon and Schuster, 2015), 53. For a psychiatrist who focuses on the unique strengths of autistic children, see Peter Szatmari, *A Mind Apart: Understanding Children with Autism and Asperger Syndrome* (New York: Guildford Press, 2004).

34. Clara Park, "Autism into Art: A Handicap Transfigured," in *High-Functioning Individuals with Autism*, ed. Eric Schopler and Gary B. Mesibov (New York: Plenum Press, 1991), 250–59. See also Tony Gengarelly and Adria A. Weatherbee, eds. *Exploring Nirvana: The Art of Jessica Park* (North Adams, MA: Massachusetts College of Liberal Arts, 2008); Tony Gengarelly, ed. *A World Transformed: The Art of Jessica Park* (North Adams, MA: Jessica Park Project, Massachusetts College of Liberal Arts, 2014).

35. Park, *Exiting Nirvana*, 123; portrait, 124.

36. Park, "Exiting Nirvana" (1998), 35.

37. Park, *Exiting Nirvana*, 200, 201.

38. Park, *Exiting Nirvana*, 131.

39. Park, *Exiting Nirvana*, 140–41.

40. Quoted in Clara Park, "Social Growth in Autism: A Parent's Perspective," in *Social Behavior in Autism*, ed. Eric Schopler and Gary B. Mesibov (New York: Plenum Press, 1986), 81–99, 94.

41. Park, *Exiting Nirvana*, 147.

42. Park, *Exiting Nirvana*, 182, 183.

43. Park, *Exiting Nirvana*, 183, 185.

44. Park, *Exiting Nirvana*, 185.

45. Park, *Exiting Nirvana*, 202, 192.

46. Park, *Exiting Nirvana*, 187.

47. Kathleen Quill, author of *Teaching Children with Autism*, book blurb for *Exiting Nirvana*; Donna Marchetti, "Tale Makes Autism Less of a Mystery," *Plain Dealer*, April 15, 2001.

48. Oliver Sacks, Foreword, in Park, *Exiting Nirvana*, ix; Sacks, "Leaving Nirvana," *New York Review of Books*, March 29, 2001; Freeman Dyson to Mary Tondorf-Dick, September 22, 2000, Freemon Dyson personal archive.

49. A Common Reader, printout of discontinued online book catalog dated April 2, 2001, Clara Park personal archive.

50. Judy Dodge to Clara Park, April 5, 2001; Lauretta C. Clough to Clara Park, December 5, 2001, Clara Park personal archive.

51. Christine Barton to Susan, January 12, 2002; Charlotte Moore to Clara Park, November 27, 2002, Clara Park personal archive.

52. Aimee White to Clara Park, September 3, 2004, Clara Park personal archive.

53. Barbara Roy to David Park, October 25, 2007, David Park personal archive.

54. Clara Park, interview with Benigno Sánchez, 1980, Clara Park personal archive.

CONCLUSION

1. This feature of Jessica's mind led Temple Grandin to realize that autistic people are "pattern thinkers." See Temple Grandin and Richard Panek, *The Autistic Brain: Thinking Across the Spectrum* (Boston: Houghton Mifflin, 2013), 141.

2. Park, *Exiting Nirvana*, 67.

3. Sacks, "Foreword," xi.

4. David Park and Philip Youderian, "Light and Number: Ordering Principles in the World of an Autistic Child," *Journal of Autism and Childhood Schizophrenia* 4 (1974): 313–23, 321.

5. Park and Youderian, "Light and Number," 322.

6. Lorraine Daston, "Cloud Physiognomy," *Representations* 135 (2016): 45–71, 48.

7. For critical analysis of certain aspects of the neurodiversity movement, see Michael Orsini, "Contesting the Autistic Subject: Biological Citizenship and the Autism/Autistic Movement," in *Critical Interventions in the Ethics of Healthcare: Challenging the Principle of Autonomy in Bioethics*, ed. Stuart Murray and Dave Holmes (Farnham: Ashgate, 2009), 115–30; Francisco Ortega, "The Cerebral Subject and the Challenge of Neurodiversity," *BioSocieties* 4, no. 4 (2009): 425–45.

8. "Introducing ANI (Autism Network International)," http://www.autreat .com/intro.html, accessed June 3, 2020.

9. Joseph Henrich, Steven J. Heine, and Ara Norenzayan, "The Weirdest People in the World," *Behavioral and Brain Sciences* 33 (2010): 61–135. On the assumption that some mothering practices are or should be universal, see Heidi Keller et al., "The Myth of Universal Sensitive Responsiveness: Comment on Mesman et al. (2017)," *Child Development* 89 (2018): 1921–28. One of the few studies that goes beyond autism in Europe and North America is Roy Richard Grinker, *Unstrange Minds: Remapping the World of Autism* (New York: Basic Books, 2007).

10. Autism FAQ, https://www.autistichoya.com/p/introduction-to-autism -faqs-of-autism.html, accessed May 24, 2020.

11. Gail Heidi Landsman, *Reconstructing Motherhood and Disability in the Age of "Perfect" Babies* (New York: Routledge, 2009); Brendan Hart,

"Autism Parents and Neurodiversity: Radical Translation, Joint Embodiment and the Prosthetic Environment," *Biosocieties* 9 (2014): 284–303. On mothers, maternal care, and advocacy for disabled children, see also Gail Heidi Landsman, "Mothers and Models of Disability," *Journal of Medical Humanities* 26, nos. 2/3 (2005): 121–39; Eva Feder Kittay, *Love's Labor: Essays on Women, Equality, and Dependency* (New York: Routledge, 1999); Valerie Leiter, "Parental Activism, Professional Dominance, and Early Childhood Disability," *Disability Studies Quarterly* 24, no. 2 (2004), http://www.dsq-sds .org/article/view/483/660; Sara Ryan and Katherine Runswick Cole, "From Advocate to Activist? Mapping the Experiences of Mothers of Children on the Autism Spectrum," *Journal of Applied Research on Intellectual Disabilities* 22, no. 1 (2009): 43–53; Priya Lalvani, ed. *Constructing the (M)other: Narratives of Disability, Motherhood, and the Politics of Normal* (New York: Peter Lang, 2019).

12. Katharine Park, "Medicine and Society in Medieval Europe, 500–1500," in *Medicine in Society: Historical Essays*, ed. Andrew Wear (Cambridge, UK: Cambridge University Press, 1992), 59–90, 67. For another case in which the focus on practices reveals a rich world beyond the textual knowledge of the medical profession, see Katharine Park, "Managing Childbirth and Fertility in Medieval Europe," in *Reproduction*, ed. Nick Hopwood, Rebecca Flemming, and Lauren Kassell (Cambridge, UK: Cambridge University Press, 2018), 153–66.

13. Leo Kanner and Leon Eisenberg, "Childhood Problems in Relation to the Family," *Pediatrics* 20 (1957): 155–64, 163. See also Gerhard Bosch, *Infantile Autism*, originally published 1962 in German (Berlin: Springer, 1970).

14. Margaret Atwood, review of Maggie Doherty, *The Equivalents: A Story of Art, Female Friendship, and Liberation in the 1960s*, *Globe and Mail*, May 22, 2020.

15. On blaming mothers, see Stella Chess, "The 'Blame the Mother' Ideology," *International Journal of Mental Health* 11 (1982): 95–107; Molly Ladd-Taylor and Lauri Umansky, eds., *"Bad" Mothers: The Politics of Blame in Twentieth-Century America* (New York: New York University Press, 1998); Diane E. Eyer, *Motherguilt: How Our Culture Blames Mothers for What's Wrong with Society* (New York: Random House, 1996); Linda C. Fentiman, *Blaming Mothers: American Law and the Risks to Children's Health* (New York: New York University Press, 2019). See also *Refrigerator Mothers*, dir. David E. Simpson, Kartemquin Films, 2002; DVD, 2003.

INDEX

ableism, 4–5

affective contact, disturbances of, 39, 41, 47–50, 55, 64, 69–70

Akerley, Mary S., 153

Anthony, James, 175

Applied Behavior Analysis (ABA) methods, 154–57, 163, 170, 213, 214–15

Asperger, Hans: early work on autistic psychopathy, 4, 35, 42–44, 45, 47, 98, 215; Nazi ideology and politics, 42, 43–44; views contrasted with Kanner's, 98, 177–78, 180–82; views on innate character of autistic psychopathy, 43, 215; views on mothers of children he diagnosed as autistic psychopaths, 43

Asperger's syndrome, 116, 177–78, 180–81

attachment, 59, 140–41

atypical development. *See* Rank, Beata

autism: as stand-alone diagnosis, 6, 40, 44, 48; as symptom of schizophrenia, 35, 37, 39–40; conceptualized as condition of the emotions in the 1950s, 65–66; diagnostic criteria,

175–76; dichotomy between intellectual/cognitive and emotional/affective in, 99, 115–19, 129, 138, 196, 216–17; different meanings of, 8, 39, 212–13; discovery of, 4, 39; diversity of terms employed to refer to, 37, 62, 82–83, 96, 174–75, 177; innateness of, 43, 49–50; medical model of, 6–7, 39, 65, 113, 125, 170, 213; rarity of, 49, 50, 51, 57, 109, 113; as stand-alone diagnosis, 6, 40, 44, 48; as symptom of schizophrenia, 35, 37, 39–40; variations within, 179–182, 211–13. *See also* Asperger's syndrome; childhood schizophrenia; form E-1; form E-2; *Infantile Autism*; Kanner, Leo; neurodiversity; spectrum

Autism Research Institute. *See* Institute for Child Behavior Research (ICBR)

Autism's Lonely Children (film), 163–64

autistic persons: described in the psychiatric literature before Asperger and Kanner, 38–42; developing identity and sense of